Pronunciation Myths

Pronunciation Myths

Applying Second Language Research to Classroom Teaching

LINDA GRANT

with Donna M. Brinton
       Tracey Derwing and Murray J. Munro
       John Field
       Judy Gilbert
       John Murphy
       Ron Thomson
       Beth Zielinski and Lynda Yates

Ann Arbor
University of Michigan Press

∞ Printed on acid-free paper

ISBN: 978-0-472-03516-8

2017   2016   2015   2014   4   3   2   1

Contents

Acknowledgments

I owe a debt of gratitude to the authors for agreeing to contribute to this volume in the first place and then for their ongoing support throughout the development of the manuscript. Special thanks to Tracey Derwing and John Murphy in this regard. I would also like to recognize and thank Ee Ling Low for her early involvement in this book. Finally, I want to acknowledge the expert editorial guidance of Kelly Sippell, executive acquisitions editor at the University of Michigan Press. She also deserves special thanks for her genuine interest in a topic that needs a great deal more exposure in the ESL literature.

Introduction

How This Book Came to Be

About twenty years ago, I read an article called "Pronunciation Myths and Facts" (Wong, 1993). In the space of two pages, the author examined and effectively debunked four common myths about second language pronunciation. Ever since then, I have begun pronunciation workshops by asking participants to share their beliefs and preconceptions about pronunciation teaching. The answers help me gauge the level of the workshop participants, but most interesting are the myths I hear over and over:

> "My students are fossilized. They don't seem to make progress in pronunciation."

> "Pronunciation is mostly repetition and minimal pair drills. That isn't a very interesting way to teach."

> "Beginning students are too busy learning basic grammar and vocabulary to concentrate on pronunciation."

> "My students are from so many different language backgrounds. I can't possibly meet their pronunciation needs."

Given my penchant for pronunciation myths, it is no wonder that I was lured into the University of Michigan book exhibit at the international TESOL conference a few years ago by two titles, *Writing Myths* and *Vocabulary Myths*. Why not *Pronunciation Myths*, I thought? I must have been thinking out loud because soon after Kelly Sippell, ESL acquisitions editor, approached me and asked if I would consider writing this volume. Once she assured me that I could opt to edit the book as a collection of articles written by colleagues, we had an agreement. And that is the genesis of *Pronunciation Myths*.

Why Pronunciation Myths Persist

Myths do surround the teaching of pronunciation, and, even though they have little or no basis in empirical research, they are widespread. The prevalence of myths is not surprising, however. First of all, many ESL teachers lack the "basic confidence, skills, and knowledge" to teach pronunciation (Macdonald, 2002, p. 3). In a study of master's level teacher preparation programs in the United States, Murphy (1997) found that few MATESOL courses in phonology were taught from a practical language-teaching perspective. A later study in Canada (Breitkreutz, Derwing, & Rossiter, 2001) reported that well over half of the ESL instructors surveyed had no preparation in teaching pronunciation. And a follow-up to that Canadian study (Foote, Holtby, & Derwing, 2011) revealed that only 20 percent of the teachers surveyed had attended a university-level course expressly devoted to the teaching of pronunciation.

Another reason that myths persist is the relative shortage of information about pronunciation in the second language (L2) literature. Despite a recent increase in L2 pronunciation studies, research in this area lags far behind "other skills such as grammar and vocabulary" (Derwing & Munro, 2005, p. 380). A 2009 study analyzed the topics in 14 second language professional journals and found that the percentage of pronunciation-related articles published from 1999 to 2008 was similarly disproportionate (Deng, Holtby, Howden-Weaver, Nessim, Nicholas, Nickle, Pannekoek, Stephan, & Sun, 2009).

As we all know, nature abhors a vacuum, and these voids in reliable information open the door to misinformation and hearsay from a variety of sources. One is the popular media, which is sometimes accurate in its reporting of accented speech and often not. Another is accent reduction specialists with questionable training who promise quick, easy fixes for pronunciation issues that take time and effort to resolve. Unfortunately, conference sessions can also become sources of misinformation if the presenters have had only cursory training in applied phonology. At a recent state-sponsored TESOL conference, a speaker incorrectly claimed that learners could distinguish /b/ from /v/ by holding a tissue in front of the mouth and observing a puff of air (called aspiration) move the tissue for /b/ but not for /v/. The fact is that neither /b/ nor /v/ are produced with a puff of air. Because aspiration does, however, distinguish /p/ from /b/, the speaker was likely confounding the /b/–/v/ and /p/–/b/ distinctions.

Misconceptions about pronunciation also originate from ESL course books, specifically those that claim to integrate pronunciation but do so only nominally. When pronunciation is routinely relegated to token "listen and repeat" exercises at the ends of chapters, students and teachers are apt to develop a simplistic view of pronunciation teaching and learning or to perceive pronunciation as incidental to oral proficiency.

The most serious problem with myths is that they shape the way teachers teach and can lead to counterproductive teaching practices. For example, when teachers assume that pronunciation is mostly individual consonant and vowel sounds, they may spend limited class time teaching all of the sounds as opposed to prioritizing and teaching the features that most impact overall intelligibility. And when teachers believe that the majority of adult learners are fossilized, class time devoted to pronunciation is likely to be negligible.

How the Book Is Organized

To set up the chapters, the book begins with **Prologue to the Myths: What Teachers Need to Know**. This updated look at basic pronunciation principles and concepts is strongly recommended as background reading for the chapters that follow. The body of the book has seven chapters, each dedicated to an established myth about L2 pronunciation. We did not necessarily choose the most popular myths because we do not yet have the research necessary to refute some of the more pervasive or preposterous misconceptions. The book concludes with an **Epilogue** by Donna Brinton, which brings closure to the discussions in the chapters.

Each chapter has three sections. The first, **In the Real World**, introduces and illustrates the myth with a first-person, real-world anecdote.

The second section, **What the Research Says**, brings research to bear in dispelling the myth or the parts of the myth that are unfounded. The final section, **What We Can Do**, provides practical suggestions for classroom activities, methods, and materials informed by the research.

Seven pronunciation authorities from four countries contributed chapters to this volume. Some authors are primarily researchers; others are mainly teacher educators, methodologists, or materials designers. What they all have in common is the unique ability to bridge the gap between research and practice.

Who Should Read This Book

Any pre- or in-service teacher, program administrator, or researcher who desires information about recent L2 pronunciation research and its application to classroom practice will benefit from this book. We see this volume as a potential resource for personal professional development, as supplementary reading in a semester-long applied phonology course, or as a course book in a short-term ESL teacher-preparation course.

Because we are acutely aware of the overall need for accurate, accessible information about L2 pronunciation, we have tried to avoid terminology and descriptions that are overly technical. Consequently, we hope this book will appeal to pronunciation non-specialists as well to more informed and experienced teachers/teacher-educators who wish to be more current with relevant research and the rapidly changing contexts for pronunciation teaching. More than 20 years ago, Joan Morley (1991), a pioneer in re-shaping L2 pronunciation pedagogy, commented that pronunciation instruction was not a one-size-fits-all endeavor. She was commenting on groups of learners whose unique needs challenged traditional views of pronunciation instruction in the mid-to-late1980s. Nowadays, her statement has acquired new meaning as English has globalized and speaking and teaching contexts have diversified.

We hope *Pronunciation Myths* helps close the considerable divide between research and practice in pronunciation and inspires more collaboration between researchers and educators. Your feedback is welcome. Please direct comments and questions to the editors and authors through the University of Michigan Press at esladmin@umich.edu.

References

Breitkreutz, J., Derwing, T. M., & Rossiter, M. J. (2001). Pronunciation teaching Practices in Canada. *TESL Canada Journal*, 19, 51–61.

Brown, A. (1991). *Teaching English pronunciation: A book of readings.* London: Routledge.

Deng, J., Holtby, A., Howden-Weaver, L., Nessim, L., Nicholas, B., Nickle, K., Pannekoek, C., Stephan, S., & Sun, M. (2009). *English pronunciation research: The neglected orphan of second language acquisition studies?* (PMC Working paper WP O5-09). Edmonton, AB: Prairie Metropolis Centre.

Derwing, T. W., & Munro M. J. (2005). Second language accent and pronunciation teaching: A research-based approach. *TESOL Quarterly*, 39, 379–397.

Foote, J. A., Holtby, A. K., & Derwing, T. M. (2011). Survey of the teaching of pronunciation in adult ESL programs in Canada, 2010. *TESL Canada Journal*, 29, 1–22.

Macdonald, S. (2002). Pronunciation—views and practices of reluctant teachers. *Prospect*, 17, 3–18.

Murphy, J. (1997). Phonology courses offered by MATESOL programs in the U.S. *TESOL Quarterly*, 31, 741–764.

Morley, J. (1991). The pronunciation component in teaching English to speakers of other languages. *TESOL Quarterly*, 25, 481–520.

Wong, R. (1993). Pronunciation myths and facts. *English Teaching Forum* (October), 45–46.

Prologue to the Myths:
What Teachers Need to Know

Linda Grant

In this volume, pronunciation specialists discuss common myths about second language (L2) pronunciation. This introduction lays the groundwork for the chapters by covering concepts, terms, and issues central to pronunciation teaching and learning. This information is especially useful for the many teachers who lack a solid background in L2 speech research/linguistics and its application to pronunciation teaching. For informed practitioners, this overview provides an updated look at key pronunciation topics. The introduction is divided into four parts:

1. **The last four decades of pronunciation teaching:** If we know where we have been, we often have a better understanding of where we are and where we need to go.

2. **Accent vs. intelligibility:** Fundamental to discussing pronunciation research and practice is developing a common language related to the goals and realities of L2 pronunciation in the 21st century. What is the aim of teaching English pronunciation to adults? To reduce an accent? To improve intelligibility? And what is intelligibility exactly?

3. **Sound system rudiments:** Examining pronunciation research and practice also presupposes a working familiarity with the features of speech. What basic information do teachers need about **segmental** (i.e., consonants and vowels) and the less well-understood **suprasegmental** (i.e., stress, rhythm, and intonation) features?

4. **Levels of pronunciation teaching and learning**: Understandably, many of us assume that pronunciation is mostly about pronouncing, or articulating, sounds. Pronunciation change, however, occurs on multiple levels, not just the physical level. When we recognize the deeply rooted perceptual, psycho-social and cognitive aspects of pronunciation learning, we have a better understanding of why progress in adults is more gradual than many of us have been led to believe.

The Last Four Decades of Pronunciation Teaching

The first ESL pronunciation class I ever taught was almost four decades ago—and it was a pedagogical disaster. I was teaching in a large intensive English program at the Georgia Institute of Technology in Atlanta, and the **audiolingual method (ALM)**, though losing traction, was still dominant. Because this method placed a high priority on both grammatical and pronunciation accuracy, most pronunciation classes were devoted to intensive aural-oral drills designed to help students acquire a native-like accent. The required text for my intermediate class, a staple in the ALM tradition, marched students through listen-and-repeat exercises with every English consonant and vowel sound, primarily in a **minimal pair** format (i.e., *ship-sheep; Who found the ship?–Who found the sheep?*). Admittedly, aspects of the Audiolingual approach had merits, but I had serious reservations about subjecting my students to 50 minutes of highly controlled practice each day. On the other hand, as a novice ESL teacher in a department where instructors were expected to follow the prescribed syllabi, I was not eager to revamp the course plan at the zero hour.

By mid-semester, class attendance had declined by almost half. The remaining students showed little interest—or improvement—in their pronunciation. The only noticeable change was unrelated to speaking. After about 15 minutes of tedious drills, most students assumed the same fixed, glassy-eyed expression. In the manner of frogs whose transparent inner eyelids drop to protect their eyes underwater, it was as if transparent eyelids had become the students' means of adaptation for surviving the class.

My experience underscores some of the basic tenets of teaching pronunciation 40 years ago: an overriding concern for accuracy; a quest for native-like speech; an almost exclusive focus on consonant and vowel sounds; an emphasis on aural-oral drilling, often in minimal pair format; and, the centrality of the pronunciation course in the curriculum. Since that time, the position of pronunciation in the field of ESL has had its ups and downs. Dominant during the '60s and early to mid-'70s, and peripheral through the late '70s and early '80s, pronunciation teaching has been making a slow, but steady, comeback over the last 25 years.

Along with the changes in the status of pronunciation have been changes in methodology. By the late '70s, aspects of traditional pronunciation instruction, specifically the unattainable goals and the exclusive focus on decontextualized drills, had fallen into disfavor. In response, most ESL programs dropped pronunciation instruction altogether. At about the same time, as disenchantment with ALM opened the door to communicative language teaching, the focus in most ESL classrooms shifted to meaning and what you said in place of accuracy and how you said it (Morley, 1991). For the next decade or so, it was assumed that ESL students would pick up L2 pronunciation just by being exposed to it.

Without formal instruction, however, L2 speakers struggled to achieve intelligible speech. Serious oral proficiency needs of L2 speakers began to surface in specific occupational, professional, and academic populations (e.g., international teaching assistants in U.S. universities), prompting a return to pronunciation teaching in the late '80s (Morley, 1991). This renewed interest in ESL pronunciation has continued without interruption, but, as Keys (2000) points out, "The point of return is a different place from the point of departure" (p. 92).

CONTEMPORARY APPROACHES TO
L2 PRONUNCIATION TEACHING

The '80s and '90s saw the release of a handful of innovative classroom texts and teacher resource books such as *Clear Speech* (Gilbert, 1984, 1993, 2005, 2010) and *Teaching Pronunciation* (Celce-Murcia, Brinton, & Goodwin, 1996, 2010). These widely used books played a major role in shaping current methodology, but it was not until the start of the 21st century that later editions of these books and the work of other L2 pronunciation experts began to reflect evolving research in this area (Murphy & Baker, forthcoming). To provide a point of comparison, in 1991, Morley wrote a watershed piece on the state of the art of pronunciation practice for the 25th anniversary edition of the *TESOL Quarterly;* fewer than ten empirical studies were cited. Morley concluded that the challenge for the future was developing an "informed expertise" (p. 513). Almost 25 years later, another landmark article on L2 pronunciation appeared in the *TESOL Quarterly* (Derwing & Munro, 2005). In this article, the authors, leading researchers in the field, discussed the importance of applying research to pronunciation teaching and cited more than 80 empirical studies. With that frame of reference, what does pronunciation practice look like in today's classrooms?

Current approaches to pronunciation instruction combine the influences of communicative and audiolingual approaches. The minimal pair drill, a chief constituent in traditional approaches to instruction, is still used but more judiciously and often in pair-practice motifs that are more meaningful and interactive. Present-day instruction favors a broader instructional model with increased emphasis on suprasegmental features and the ultimate attainment of functional and communicative intelligibility (Celce-Mucia, Brinton, & Goodwin, 2010). Most important, perhaps, pronunciation goals are now more realistic and achievable. The majority of present-day teachers have abandoned the goal of perfect, native-like speech in favor of clear, fluent speech that is intelligible to the listener.

These updated goals of intelligibility also fit better with the aims of teaching English for global communication. More to the point, because most interactions in English occur exclusively between two or more non-native speakers and may not involve native English speakers at all, contemporary English models are represented by more than just native-speaker norms from countries like Britain, Australia, the United States, and Canada (Kannelou, 2009). These more recent models include varieties of English that are spoken locally as well as a global variety of English intelligible to non-native speakers interacting with each other in international contexts. Because native-speaker standards are not required for either context, some pronunciation experts have suggested that non–native speaking English teachers are equally, and in some cases potentially better, qualified to teach pronunciation than their native-speaking colleagues (Jenkins, 2000; Walker, 2010).

Along with an increase in pronunciation models has been an expansion in the contemporary definition of pronunciation. In addition to consonant and vowel sounds, it now includes stress, rhythm, and intonation, features of pronunciation that are more easily integrated into communicative, discourse-level language teaching. In view of pronunciation's expanded scope, teachers need guidance in trimming the pronunciation syllabus from all elements of speech to those that most affect intelligibility. Fortunately, in the last two decades, research has provided some definitive findings in terms of features that

---

ESL (English as a second language) is the study of English by non-native speakers in locations such as Australia and the United States, where English is spoken by the majority of residents. In these environments, teachers select pronunciation features for instruction based on what makes speech intelligible to native speakers.

EIL (English as an international language) or **ELF (English as a lingua franca)** has developed in response to the global spread of English. It refers to the pursuit and study of an international standard of pronunciation that is mutually intelligible to non-native speakers from different language backgrounds interacting with each other.

merit priority in instruction. Derwing and Munro, Myth 1, and Gilbert, Myth 4, examine the studies (e.g., Derwing, Munro, & Wiebe, 1998; Field, 2005; Hahn, 2004; Munro & Derwing, 2006; Zielinski, 2008) that point us to empirically based teaching priorities in ESL settings. For a tentative subset of pronunciation features that promote mutual intelligibility in English as an international language (EIL) settings, see also preliminary data from Jenkins (2000).

A look at present-day approaches to pronunciation instruction (see Table P.1) would not be complete without discussing **integration**. Because of the interrelatedness between pronunciation and skills like speaking and listening, experts agree that pronunciation can no longer be taught in a "vacuum" apart from other segments of the curriculum

TABLE P.1: Summary of Traditional vs. Contemporary Approaches to Pronunciation Instruction

	Traditional Approaches	**Current Approaches**
Learner goals	Perfect, native-like pronunciation	Comfortable intelligibility
Speech features	All segmentals (consonant and vowel sounds)	Selected segmentals and suprasegmentals (stress, rhythm, and intonation) based on need and context
Practice formats	Decontextualized drills	Controlled aural-oral drills as well as semi-communicative and communicative practice formats
Language background of teachers	Native-speaking teachers	Native-speaking and proficient non-native speaking teachers
Speaking models	Native-speaker models	Variety of models and standards depending on the listener, context, and purpose
Curriculum choices	Stand-alone courses isolated from the rest of the curriculum	Stand-alone courses or integrated into other content or skill areas, often listening and speaking

(Celce-Murcia, Brinton, & Goodwin, 2010, p. 365). If, as Dalton and Seidlhofer (1994) claim, the goal of pronunciation is "a means to negotiate meaning in discourse" (p. ix), then pronunciation awareness needs to be integrated into the rest of the ESL courses. In the last few years, the trend has been to weave pronunciation into speaking and listening coursework because of the strong reciprocal links, but effective integration, especially pertaining to pronunciation and listening, remains a work in progress (Celce-Murcia, Brinton, & Goodwin, 2010).

To support pronunciation instruction, most of us have long incorporated focused listening or listening discrimination exercises into our pronunciation classes. And, in fact, Celce-Murcia, Brinton, and Goodwin (2010) cite a growing body of research (e.g., Bradlow, Pisoni, Akahane-Yamamda, & Tohkura, 1997; Wang & Munro, 2004) that upholds the wisdom of **auditory training**—that is, training the ears to hear speech features and sound distinctions that do not exist in the L1. However, when we teach listening, we often overlook the flip-side—the role pronunciation plays in supporting listening instruction, specifically bottom-up listening (i.e., attending to sounds, words and other parts of the acoustic signal to process the message). When students are taught speech sounds, word stress, reductions, and connected speech, they are also learning how to decode the speech stream and segment it into recognizable words (Brown, 2011).

In a 2011 study (Foote, Holtby, & Derwing, 2011) investigating the teaching of pronunciation in Canada, the majority of teachers surveyed replied that they regularly integrated pronunciation into their classes, but, when asked how much class time was spent on pronunciation, the average was only 6 percent, and the most frequent response was 2 percent. Since 73 percent of the respondents also reported that they regularly corrected mispronounced words, the researchers speculated that the integrated instruction many students receive consists primarily of incidental correction, not systematic teaching.

If the major international pronunciation interest groups are any indication, it appears integration will remain a topic of discussion. Several years ago, the Pronunciation Special Interest Section associated with the **TESOL International Association** renamed itself the **Speech,**

Pronunciation, and Listening Interest Section (SPLIS), thereby offi-
cially linking pronunciation to speaking and listening. Similarly, the
Pronunciation Special Interest Group affiliated with the **International
Association of Teaching English as a Foreign Language (IATEFL)**
based in the U.K. is considering broadening its scope to include listening and speaking skills. See Zielinski and Yates, Myth 2, for suggestions
concerning systematic integration of pronunciation into a general
beginner all-skills ESL course.

There is little doubt that L2 pronunciation has gained ground over
the last few decades. Yet, compared with other skill areas, pronunciation remains the "orphan of ESL/EFL" (Gilbert, 2010, p. 3). It has yet to
occupy its fair share of course time in the ESL curriculum or in teacher
education programs (Derwing & Munro, 2005; Foote, Holtby, &
Derwing, 2011; Levis, 2005). And, though we have seen a growing body
of published pronunciation research, its influence in the classroom
and its presence in the professional literature is still relatively marginal.
During a recent nine-year period, Deng et al. (2009) found that only a
very small percentage of articles appearing in leading scholarly journals
were pronunciation-related.

Accent vs. Intelligibility

As mentioned earlier, struggling to master a native-like accent during
the Audiolingual period was futile for most adult learners. Nowadays,
the profession is more mindful of the **intelligibility principle,** which
maintains that the goal for most learners is to be easily understood
(Levis, 2005). The fact that the notion of comfortable intelligibility
dates back at least 65 years (Abercrombie, 1949) dismays me whenever
I see the yawning gaps between what we know about intelligibility and
what is happening in the real world. For instance, while I was writing
this introduction, a British phonologist on one listerv posted a strenu-
ous and legitimate objection to the title of Amazon's best-selling pronunciation text in the United Kingdom: *Get Rid of Your Accent.*

At about the same time, the Arizona Department of Education was being investigated for civil rights violations because of its policy regarding non-native school teachers who spoke accented English. According to an article in the *New York Times* (Lacey, 2011), the state of Arizona was requiring local school districts to remove teachers from classrooms containing English language learners if the teachers' spoken English was judged to be heavily accented. Additionally, some teachers had been written up by state monitors for mispronunciations like *da* for *the* and *leeves here* for *lives here*, whether or not these errors interfered with overall intelligibility.

Issues surrounding L2 accents have become more relevant now that the number of non-native English speakers world-wide has surpassed the number of native English speakers. Two of the more timely and controversial issues are the place of non-native speaking teachers in the L2 pronunciation classroom and the growth of the accent reduction/elimination industry. As far as the first issue, we had hoped to dispel in this book the myth that non-native speaking teachers cannot teach pronunciation, but after investigation, we concluded that we needed more impartial evidence to examine that topic in the manner suitable for this book. The second issue, accent reduction vs. pronunciation instruction, is treated in depth by Thomson in Myth 6. As a prelude to that discussion and because the concepts of accent, intelligibility, and comprehensibility recur throughout this volume, an overview of these terms is in order.

RELATIONSHIP AMONG ACCENT, INTELLIGIBILITY, AND COMPREHENSIBILITY

Dictionaries define **accent** as the manner or style of pronunciation that identifies the country, region, or background a person is from. Everyone has an accent, even though many native speakers of English consider their speech to be standard or accent-free (Lippi-Green, 2012). That point was impressed upon me in my early 20s when I was camping in Northern New York. A few hours after arriving at my site, an older gentleman wandered over and politely asked, in what I perceived to be a strong Southern accent, where I was from. I replied that I had been living in Atlanta for about six months but that I had grown up in Ohio. "Aha, Ohio!" he said. "That explains your strong accent." I was taken aback. Born and raised in the Midwest, I assumed my speech was neutral or accent-free. He was the one with the accent, I thought. We were both classic examples of those who think only other people have accents.

A foreign accent or **accentedness** refers to the extent to which an individual's L2 speech differs from a particular variety of English (Derwing & Munro, 2005). In this volume, you will see the terms accent and accentedness used interchangeably. Though it may be possible for a highly motivated adult English learner to speak English with a near native-like accent, such a goal is beyond reach of most adult learners. (See Grant, Myth 5, for what the research says about age and ultimate attainment in L2 pronunciation.) As Derwing and Munro (2011) have stated, "If we take a native-like accent as the goal, pronunciation is destined to fall short" (p. 4).

Much more feasible and desirable than the goal of a native-like accent are the goals of improved intelligibility and comprehensibility. **Intelligibility** is the extent to which a listener understands a speaker's message; **comprehensibility** is the amount of listener effort it takes to understand a message (Derwing & Munro, 2011).

A couple of points about intelligibility warrant mentioning. First, Derwing and Munro (1997) have established that accent and intelligibility are semi-independent dimensions. Practically speaking, that means that speech does not have to be native-like to be intelligible. Rather, an L2 speaker can have a strong foreign accent and still be readily understood. Second, evidence shows that intelligibility and comprehensibility can be improved through formal pronunciation instruction (Derwing, Munro, & Wiebe, 1998). These and other investigations by Derwing, Munro, and their colleagues have been instrumental in changing the direction of L2 pronunciation research away from measures of native-like accent toward measures of intelligibility.

THE ROLE OF THE LISTENER IN INTELLIGIBILITY/COMPREHENSIBILITY

When I taught international teaching assistants at Georgia Tech in the late '80s, doctoral engineering students, primarily from Korea and China, occasionally attended social get-togethers in my home. With more than ten years of exposure to non-native speakers, I understood more of what my students said with far less effort than my husband— that is, until the topic of conversation shifted to the students' research. Then I usually experienced a perceptible drop in intelligibility, whereas my husband, a professional engineer and former professor at Georgia Tech, experienced noticeable improvement!

If we do not understand a message, we tend to blame the person who is speaking. In other words, full responsibility for intelligibility usually falls to the speaker. But intelligibility is "a two-way process involving both listener and speaker" (Zielinski, 2008, p. 70) and can be influenced by familiarity with the topic of discussion or with the speaker's accent (Gass and Veronis, 1984).

Attitudes of listeners can also influence intelligibility. In an often cited and compelling study, Rubin (1992) investigated listener bias in perceived intelligibility among undergraduates at a U.S. university. Sixty-two students listened to one of two short introductory lectures in science or the humanities, both of which were pre-recorded by the same native-English speaker. During the lecture, each group of subjects saw a photograph of the presumed lecturer. Half of the students saw a Caucasian female; the other half saw an Asian female. Following the lecture, the two groups completed a lecture comprehension test. Even though both groups had heard the same native English speaker, the group that believed it had heard the Chinese speaker had lower test scores and markedly so in the science lecture test (i.e., presumed Caucasian lecturer—12.5/14 correct; presumed Asian lecturer—7.31/14 correct). This study revealed that the perceptions of intelligibility were subjective and influenced by the suggestion that one of the lecturers spoke accented English. A subsequent study by Lindeman (2011) similarly concluded that the attitudes and expectations of listeners toward

NNESs and their language backgrounds influenced how they judged intelligibility, even if the listeners harbored no negative biases. On a more promising note, research (e.g., Derwing, Rossiter, & Munro, 2002) indicates that with proper training, L1 listeners can improve their dispositions toward L2 speech with potentially positive effects on intelligibility.

THE ROLE OF CONTEXT IN INTELLIGIBILITY/COMPREHENSIBILITY

On a recent visit to Houston, Texas, the hotel receptionist informed me I was fortunate to have found a room since it was the first day of the Offshore Technology Conference, an event that had drawn 75,000 delegates from all over the world. As I made my way to the elevator, I passed numerous small groups from markedly dissimilar languages all speaking in English. To my surprise, though the conference was being held in an English-speaking country, there were few native speakers participating in these conversations.

With most interactions in English now occurring between two or more non-native speakers, Jenkins (2000) has cautioned that we can no longer view intelligibility only from the perspective of the native speaker/listener. In 2005, however, Levis observed that most pronunciation texts and syllabi continue to be defined by what makes speech intelligible to the native speaker/listener in ESL contexts. He urged teachers to take context into account when selecting features of speech for instruction. Just as intelligibility recognizes the dual roles of speaker and listener, a state-of-the-art pronunciation syllabus is based on both speaker and listener—what the speaker needs to do to be understood easily and what the potential listener needs to understand easily (see Table P.2).

TABLE P.2: Moving from Accent toward Intelligibility

Moving From	Moving Toward
Accent seen as inherently a problem	Accent accepted as part of normal variation
Accent reduction or eradication	Intelligibility enhancement
Native speaker emulation	Intelligibility-based goals
Scattergun pedagogy: when teaching pronunciation, give everything equal importance	Selective pedagogy: focus mainly on problems likely to interfere with intelligibility
100% responsibility for intelligibility on the L2 speaker	Listener awareness and listener training

Chart adapted and reprinted with the permission of Murray Munro and Tracey Derwing. From the 2012 Australia Pronunciation Symposium presentation *What should L2 learners be able to expect from their language classrooms: A research perspective.*

Sound System Rudiments

DEFINITION OF PRONUNICATION

When we consider what pronunciation entails, most of us think first of consonants and vowels. At one time, I did too. When I started teaching ESL, I was regularly assigned pronunciation classes because of my degrees in speech pathology and audiology. Unquestionably, my education prepared me well in the area of **articulatory phonetics** (i.e., the manner in which we produce each consonant and vowel sound). For several years, I took for granted that I knew what was needed to teach pronunciation effectively, and I conducted my classes without moving much beyond the pronunciation of sounds in words and isolated sentences.

Then in 1984, Judy Gilbert published a seminal text in ESL pronunciation, the aforementioned *Clear Speech*. This was one of the first classroom texts with a teaching paradigm that emphasized stress, rhythm, and intonation—suprasegmental features that direct the listener's attention to information that is relatively more important in the flow of speech. At the time, I wondered how I had used these critical features of speech all of my life and failed to notice them. Interestingly, however, native speakers use suprasegmental features unconsciously. Like their students, native-speaking teachers are seldom aware of speech features like English rhythm and intonation and how they impact meaning unless those concepts are explicitly pointed out.

Letters of the alphabet, on the other hand, are visible on the printed page, so native-speaking teachers tend to be more aware of and comfortable with segmentals (i.e., consonant and vowel sounds). Segmentals are also regarded by some pronunciation specialists as more teachable (Dalton & Seidlhofer, 1994). For example, instructing a learner to produce the consonant sounds /f/ in *fine* and /p/ in *pine* is more straightforward than teaching focus or prominence, a suprasegmental feature that is more bound to context. Consider these examples of focus:

X: What's wrong?   →   Y: Jim lost his <u>CELL</u> phone.

X: I heard you lost
   your cell phone.   →   Y: <u>JIM</u> lost his cell phone.

Before reading further, please take a moment to consider how you would define pronunciation. Because most authors in this book view pronunciation in the broadest sense, they would probably agree with this description (Fraser, 2001):

"... all those aspects of speech which make for an easily intelligible flow of speech, including segmental articulation, rhythm, intonation and phrasing, and more peripherally even gesture, body language and eye contact" (p. 6).

Fraser's definition consists of three categories:

- **peripheral features** (gesture, body language, and eye contact)
- **suprasegmentals** (stress, rhythm, intonation, and phrasing)
- **segmentals** (consonant and vowel sounds)

To these categories, following peripheral features, I would add **global features** (volume, rate of speech, and voice quality setting). I will break down these categories, beginning with the most general, and outline what teachers need to know.

PERIPHERAL FEATURES

Have you ever noticed how a proficient English speaker will nod or gesture when emphasizing an important word? This is an example of a peripheral feature, sometimes called a **paralinguistic** or non-verbal feature. Peripheral features are the broadest pronunciation components and often operate in synchrony with English stress, rhythm, and intonation. See Zielinski and Yates, Myth 2, and Gilbert, Myth 4, for ways to incorporate peripheral features into suprasegmental instruction.

GLOBAL FEATURES

Most of us are familiar with two global characteristics, volume and **speech rate,** and how they can affect understanding. As far as speed, most listeners typically want a speaker who is difficult to understand to slow down. Indeed, research by Munro and Derwing (1995) indicates that native listeners require a longer time to process non-native speaker speech that is hard to comprehend. Contrary to conventional wisdom, however, slowing down is not an effective blanket strategy. Non-native speakers typically speak English more slowly than native speakers, and, for some speakers, further slowing their speech might actually impede understanding. In fact, some students might need to increase their speed to improve comprehensibility (Munro & Derwing, 2001).

Less familiar to most ESL teachers is the global feature termed **voice quality setting** or **articulatory setting**. Articulatory setting refers to the characteristic long-term quality of the voice over continued stretches of speech. Much like the distinctive vocal qualities that enable us to identify individual speakers by their voices, languages have distinctive qualities arising from the long-term positions of **articulators** (i.e., vocal cords, mouth, tongue, lips, throat, and facial muscles). French, for example, is characterized by a tense, more rounded lip posture whereas the English spoken in the United States has a more spread lip posture and a more open jaw (Esling and Wong, 1983).

As a global dimension, articulatory setting or posture can affect the pronunciation of lower-level features like individual sounds. For that reason, articulatory setting has long been recommended as an effective jumping off point in pronunciation instruction (Esling & Wong, 1983; Jones & Evans, 1995) but has received little attention in research or in published teaching materials.

SUPRASEGMENTAL FEATURES

Suprasegmentals, also called **prosodics** or **prosody,** are features of pronunciation that stretch over more than one sound or segment. For example, primary stress in words extends over syllables; intonation contours stretch over phrases or short sentences. Research has established that suprasegmental features constitute a major part of making ourselves clearly understood (Derwing, Munro, & Wiebe, 1998; Field, 2005; Hahn, 2004; Zielinski, 2008), and, while most teachers recognize the importance of these features, many teachers also find them difficult to teach (Foote, Holtby, & Derwing, 2011). A brief review of these less well-known components of speech follows.

Word Stress

In words of two or more syllables, one syllable is stressed or stronger than the others. Though stressed syllables are louder and higher in pitch, the most salient aspects of stress are length and clarity. Stressed syllables are relatively longer in duration and have full, clear vowel sounds. Unstressed syllables, on the other hand, are shorter and spoken with the reduced, neutral vowel **schwa** /ə/ or a schwa-like vowel sound.

> Example: CA na da   /ˈkæ nə də/

Misplacing stress can lead to misunderstandings and not just within words, but across words boundaries. For example, the word *hisTOry* might sound like the phrase *his story*. Placing more or less equal stress on all syllables can also cause confusion. If a speaker gave equal emphasis to both syllables in the word *tumor*, it might be perceived as the phrase *two more* (Wong, 1993). Field (2005) points out another significant function of word stress. Because 90 percent of content words in running speech are either single-syllable or have stress on the first syllable, word stress is a tip-off as to where words begin and end in the stream of speech. Thus, faulty word stress can interfere with listening at the level of not just the word, but also at the level of connected speech. Accurate word stress, on the other hand, enables native listeners (as well as non-native listeners) to identify words and word boundaries within stretches of running speech.

Rhythm

English rhythm is the alternation of strong and weak words and sylla-bles. Native English speakers expect words with relatively more meaning (i.e., nouns, main verbs, adjectives, adverbs, *wh*-words, and negatives) to be stressed and words with less meaning (i.e., articles, prepositions, con-junctions, pronouns, and auxiliary verbs) to be weakened or reduced.

> Example: WHAT did ya DO with 'is KEYS? (or)
> WHAT dija DO with 'is KEYS?

Thought Groups and Pausing

Thought groups are groupings of words that go together semantically and grammatically. Fluent speakers divide long utterances into thought groups (or chunks) to help listeners process messages more easily. A thought group is often followed by a brief pause.

> Example: If you'd like to speak to an operator / press zero.

Connected Speech

Fluent speakers do not speak word by word. Instead, the final sound of one word is linked to the initial sound of the next word in each thought group.

> Example: *presszero* (sounds like one word)

Intonation

Intonation is the rise and fall in the pitch of the voice. Each thought group has its own intonation contour. The shape of that contour hinges, in large part, on two components of intonation:

- **Focus** or **Prominence** (also called **primary sentence stress**): The focus word or prominent word is the most important word in each thought group. Like stressed words and syllables, the focus word is louder and relatively longer in duration, but the most salient aspects of focus are clarity and pitch. Speakers signal the key information with a major pitch change on the focus word (or on the stressed syllable of the focus word). Often with the last content word, the focus can also shift to other words to highlight new information or contrasting information.

  Examples: He MAjored in lin<u>GUIS</u>tics . . . (last content word)

             ap<u>PLIED</u> linguistics.   (new information)

- **Final Intonation:** After the pitch change on the focus word, the pitch then falls or rises according to the speaker's intent.

  Examples:

  a. He MAjored in lin<u>GUIS</u>tics.   ↘   (certainty)

  b. He MAjored in lin<u>GUIS</u>tics?   ↗   (uncertainty)

  c. He MAjored in lin<u>GUIS</u>tics. . . .   →   (more to come)

Celce-Murcia, Brinton, and Goodwin (2010) point out that discrepancies involving suprasegmentals can lead to more serious misunderstandings than those involving segmentals. In Myth 4, Gilbert describes several conversations "gone awry" due to intonational miscues.

It is not enough to spend classroom time simply teaching the perception and production of each prosodic feature (i.e., the **form**). It is equally important that learners understand the role each feature plays in communicating meaning (i.e., the **function**). For example, word stress helps native and non-native speaker listeners identify words and locate them in the continuous flow of speech (Field, 2005); rhythm and focus call attention to what is relatively more important in utterances; and, final intonation alerts listeners to the speaker's intention

FIGURE P.1: Review of Suprasegmental Pronunciation Features

Word Stress:	e.g., HIS-to-ry vs. his-STO-ry
Rhythm (Sentence Stress):	e.g., WHAT did ya DO with 'is KEYS?
Thought Groups and Pausing:	e.g., If you'd like to speak to an operator /
	press zero.
Connected Speech:	e.g., presszero
Focus (Prominence or	e.g., I MAjored in linGUIStics . . .
Primary Sentence Stress):	apPLIED linguistics.
Final Intonation:	e.g., He MAjored in linGUIStics. ➘
	He MAjored in linGUIStics? ➚
	He MAjored in linGUIStics. . . . ➞

and also guides turn-taking. If the communicative value of suprasegmentals is not made clear, learners may decide learning suprasegmental features is not worth the effort (see Figure P.1).

SEGMENTAL (CONSONANT AND VOWEL) FEATURES

About fifteen years ago, I taught an oral communication course to international graduate nursing students. As part of the requirements, students prepared brief presentations on topics related to their nursing specialties. In one talk, a student from China announced her topic, which I perceived as *brain regions*. It was not until she displayed her first power point slide that I realized she would be discussing *brain lesions*. Part of the mix-up may have been her coloring of the /ʒ/ in *lesions*, but most of my misunderstanding was related to her pronunciation of /l/ for /r/. Granted, an example of a Chinese speaker replacing /l/ for /r/ is timeworn, but it illustrates how segment-level errors can also impair intelligibility.

Not all segmental problems are dependent on the mother tongue, but general patterns of difficulty tend to characterize speakers of particular languages (Swan & Smith, 2001). For example, some Arabic learners might confuse /p/ and /b/, Spanish-speaking learners may have difficulty distinguishing /s/ and /z/, and Korean learners might pronounce /f/ as /p/. In addition to substituting one sound for another, learners might omit sounds (e.g., *freeway* as *feeway*), insert or add sounds (e.g., *page six* as *page-ee six*), or alter sounds (e.g., drop the /n/ and nasalize the preceding vowel sound, as in a word like *ten*), depending on the influence from the first language.

In heterogeneous ESL classrooms, it is not unusual for teachers to be faced with an array of segmental needs. With more than 40 sounds in English that are potentially problematic, teachers frequently wonder how they can meet so many varied needs in one class. The good news is that preliminary research with the so-called **Functional Load chart** (see Myth 1, Derwing & Munro) shows promise in identifying the segmentals that merit more consideration in the classroom based on their contribution to intelligibility. Also, contrary to popular belief, not all segmental difficulties are language-specific. Patterns of difficulty can affect learners from many different language backgrounds. In the consonant domain, for example, speakers from numerous L1s **devoice** final consonant sounds like /b/, /d/, and /g/ such that *I'll tag it* sounds like *I'll tack it*. In addition, the L1s of many learners have a predominately **open syllable structure** consisting of consonant + vowel (CV)— that is, most syllables/words begin with one consonant sound and end in a vowel sound (as in *tea* and *o-ri-ga-mi*). These learners tend to omit final consonant sounds in general, like the final /k/in *black*, even when the same sounds present no problems in word initial positions. Even more challenging to these learners are sounds occurring in clusters or sequences of two or three consonants, like the /ks/ in *box*. As far as vowel sounds, students from various L1s struggle with the with **lax-tense vowel distinctions** (e.g., *hit* vs. *heat*, *full* vs. *fool*, and *let* vs. *late*) and with the most common vowel sound in English, the **schwa** (i.e., /ə/ as in *about*).

As mentioned earlier, English language teachers tend to be more familiar with the aspects of pronunciation that are based squarely in the segmental realm. Those teachers with a background in applied linguistics have no doubt encountered the **International Phonetic Alphabet (IPA)**, the special set of alphabet-like symbols representing the sounds, or phonemes, of a language. Throughout the book, we represent various English sounds and words with IPA symbols. Before introducing the symbols in Table P.3, I should mention that not all pronunciation experts transcribe words in the same way. Symbols deviate, especially with regard to vowels, depending on the purpose for transcription and the linguistic variety being represented. In this respect, the British, Australian, and North American authors in this book use different applications of the IPA to better represent their sound systems. (For an in-depth comparison of phonetic and phonemic alphabets, see Celce-Murcia, Brinton, & Goodwin, 2010, Appendix 3.) The information in Table P.3 is similar to versions that appear in several widely used pronunciation texts in North America and follows the precedent set by Celce-Murcia, Brinton, and Goodwin (2010). The consonant symbols are more or less standard and based on the version of the IPA adopted by the International Phonetic Association in 2005 with two exceptions: /r/ in *rain* and /y/ as in *yes* (in IPA, these two sounds are represented as /ɹ/ and /j/, respectively). In contrast, the vowel symbols were developed by linguists Trager and Smith to represent the vowel pronunciations of North American English. Most of the symbols that deviate from the keys are footnoted in the text.

In addition to the IPA, most formally prepared teachers are familiar with consonant and vowel charts that display the criteria for describing each consonant and vowel sound. Consonant sounds, made by constricting the airstream, have three criteria: the place in the oral cavity where the airstream is constricted, the manner in which the airstream is constricted, and whether sound is voiceless or voiced. Both manner of articulation and voicing are shown in Table P.3. Vowel sounds, on the other hand, are produced by a freely flowing airstream. Essentially, we create different vowel sounds by using the mouth as a resonance cavity and changing its size and shape. Vowel sounds are typically classified by lip position (rounded or unrounded), tongue height (high, mid, or low), and tongue position (whether the front, central or back part of the tongue is in a high, mid, or low position). Relative tongue height and position are represented in the vowel sound part of Table P.3.

Consonant and vowel charts have been commonplace in training programs for quite some time. They are available in several of the teacher resource books listed in Appendix 7.2 of Myth 7 (e.g., Avery &

TABLE P.3: IPA Symbols and Key Words for the Sounds of North American English[1]

Consonant Sounds		
Manner of Articulation	**Unvoiced**	**Voiced**
Stops or plosives (air is stopped and then released)	/p/ *pie* /t/ *ten* /k/ *key*	/b/ *boy* /d/ *day* /g/ *go*
Fricatives (air is forced through a narrowed or constricted passage creating a friction-like sound)	/f/ *fan* /θ/ *think* /s/ *so* /ʃ/ *shoe* /h/ *house*	/v/ *van* /ð/ *that* /z/ *zoo* /ʒ/ *usual*
Affricates (stop plus a fricative creates one sound)	/tʃ/ *chip*	/dʒ/ *job*
Nasals (air is redirected through the nose)	/m/ *my* /n/ *new*	/ŋ/ *sing*
Liquids (air is not constricted; air is directed around the tongue and is free flowing)	/l/ *late* /r/ *rain*	
Glides (air is not constricted; air glides over the top of the tongue and is free-flowing)	/w/ *week* /y/ *yes*	

Vowel Sounds			
	Front Part of Tongue	**Central Part**	**Back Part**
High position in mouth	/iy/ see /ɪ/ sit		/uw/ do /ʊ/ put
Mid position	/ey/ may /ɛ/ met	/ə/ about /ʌ/ cup	/ow/ no
Low position	/æ/ bat	/ɑ/ father	/ɔ/ law

Diphthongs (two vowel sounds considered to be one): /ay/ my   /aw/ now /ɔy/ boy

---

[1]Variants of **North American English (NAE)** are spoken in the United States and Canada.

Ehrlich, 1992; Celce-Murcia, Brinton, & Goodwin, 2010) and, for the most part, are self-explanatory. Once phonemic charts have been covered in teacher training programs, however, orientation to segmentals often comes to a grinding halt. Because these charts describe the articulation of abstract sounds in isolation, it is easy to see how teachers might walk away with the idea that segmentals are static, stand-alone bits that we string together into words. This is a fictionalized view and partially underlies Myth 3 challenged by Field—that L2 learners have to internalize a set of distinct phonemes in order to recognize and produce them in spoken English. Field makes it clear that how teachers conceptualize the segmental system and teach it to L2 learners is not nearly as clear-cut as we might have thought.

If consonant and vowel sounds in spoken English were indeed discrete and unvarying, rhythm and fluency would be disrupted, and our speech would sound unnatural. Or we might sound perpetually irritated, much like a father I recently overheard trying to corral his three high-spirited children into an airport elevator. Each sound he spoke was clearly articulated, each word was uniformly stressed, and each word formed its own sentence: "Get. Into. The. Lift." Needless to say, the children did not hesitate.

It is important to realize that there is not just one pronunciation or realization of each sound. If a speaker were to say the word *cat* /kæt/, for instance, the same three sounds could not be sequenced in reverse order to form the word *tack*. First of all, in real speech, sounds spill into neighboring sounds, so it would be difficult to determine where one sound ended and the next one began. Second, a sound changes each time it is produced. It differs in its physical production (i.e., exactly where in the mouth it is produced) and in the way it sounds depending on its neighboring sounds, its position in a word, the relative importance of that word, and the role of that word in discourse. Even the speed of speech, the individual speaker, and the formality of the situation are factors.

Sound Variation in Spoken English

When considering sounds and how they vary in spoken English, a helpful analogy is a bulls-eye or dart board. The target consonant or vowel sound as produced in isolation is located in the center or the eye. In the circle or ring around the eye are all of the acceptable variants of the target sound as they occur in spoken English. Some variants diverge from the target more than others, but all of the sounds falling within that first circle are acceptable pronunciations. Why are some sounds and words more precise and closer to the citation form of the target sound than others? Is there any predictability to the variations? Well, not all variants are patterned or predictable, but some are.

A. *Sounds are subject to change based on their position*
   in the word.

>   Example: Consider the /k/ as produced in *come* and in
>   *sky*

The initial /k/ in the word *come* is spoken with a puff of air or aspiration. The /k/ in the blend /sk/ in the word *sky* is unaspirated and sounds more like /g/. This may be one reason why native listeners sometimes misperceive the lyrics in "Purple Haze" by Jimi Hendrix as follows:

LYRIC:	'Scuse me while I kiss <u>the sky</u>.
MISHEARD AS:	'Scuse me while I kiss <u>this guy</u>.

The two sounds (i.e., [kʰ] in *come* and the [k] in *sky*) are so-called **allophones** of /k/, that is, they are different versions of the phoneme /k/ by virtue of their position within a word. The two sounds are phonetically different—one is aspirated and the other is unaspirated, yet native speakers of English perceive them to be the same sound. What complicates learning the sounds in an L2 is the fact that allophones are language specific. For example, allophones in English, such as the versions of /k/, might be two distinct phonemes in another language and vice-versa. Two distinct phonemes in English, like /p/ and /b/, are classified as allophones in some other languages, such as Arabic. Consider, for example, an Arabic learner who produces what English speakers perceive as two separate phonemes: /p/ in *pan* and /b/ in *ban*. To many Arabic learners, however, /p/and /b/are indistinguishable, and there would be no difference in meaning between *panning a program* and *banning a program*.

After considering allophones, I hope it is clear that L2 pronunciation learning involves more than articulating sounds. Granted, a certain sound might be hard for a learner to say, but the inability to pronounce a sound is usually not the primary problem. What makes pronunciation learning a gradual, and slightly more complex process, is that learners ultimately have to re-categorize phonetic contrasts in the new language at a conceptual level so that they can automatically monitor their use of the new sound or the new distinction.

*B. Sounds are subject to change based on the influence
of adjacent sounds.*

Example: Consider the pronunciation of /n/ in *in
Boston*

All speakers, no matter what their L1, take articulatory short cuts as they move from one sound to the next. In the process, the placement of a consonant sound can vary (e.g., notice the difference in tongue placement for the /k/ sound in the words *call* and *keep*); sounds can be omitted (e.g., *accepts*); and, sounds can take on characteristics of adjacent sounds. In the example above, most proficient English speakers would take an easier, more effortless route from the /n/ in *in* to the /b/ in *Boston*. In a process called **assimilation**, the /n/ would become more like the neighboring sound /b/ (i.e., *im Boston*).

Assimilation often causes learners significant problems as listeners. Several years ago, one of my graduate students at Georgia State University, also a full-time English teacher, recounted a misunderstanding that had occurred in her ESL class that day. Her story was timely because, in our Teaching English Pronunciation as a Second Language class the week before, we had discussed assimilation in the context of connected speech phenomena.

Example: Teacher: "No homework <u>since you</u> did it
last night."
Learner: "Who is <u>Sinshoo</u>?"

The words *since* and *you* would no doubt have been recognized by this learner if each word had been spoken in citation form, but these common words were not understood in connected speech due to another prevalent type of assimilation termed **palatalization**. In this case, the final /s/ in *sin<u>c</u>e* followed by the initial /y/ in *you* merged into a third sound /ʃ/as in *Sin<u>sh</u>oo*.

C. *Sounds in words are subject to change based on the relative importance of those words in the utterance.*

Example: The pronunciation of *two* and *to* is the same
in citation form (i.e., /tuw/) but different in
these contexts.

1. *two* /tuw/—3 2 5 (*two* is a number, a content word)

2. *to* /tə/—3 to 5 (*to* is a preposition, a grammatical
function word)

Vowel sounds tend to be full and clear in stressed content words, like the number *two*, and shortened and reduced in unstressed function words, like the preposition *to*. This example represents an authentic interaction in which an ESL student attempted to tell his teacher the time of an upcoming meeting. The student, however, said, "*The meeting is three* /tuw/ *five.*" Because the student used the full, citation form of *to* rather than the reduced form of *to*, the teacher perceived the student to be reporting the room number (3-2-5) as opposed to the meeting time (3 to 5). Reducing vowel sounds to schwa enables speakers to maintain the rhythmic pattern of English by squeezing the less meaningful bits of the message between the parts that carry more meaning.

D. *Sounds are subject to change based on the role of the word in discourse.*

> Examples: Consider the pronunciation of *leave* in these
> two contexts.
>
> 1. I'm trying to study. Leave me a<u>LONE</u>!
>
> 2. I still love you! Don't <u>LEAVE</u> me!

In the first example, *leave* is non-prominent and more susceptible to phonological processes like assimilation (i.e., *leave me alone* = *leamme alone*). In the second example, *leave* is the most important word in the utterance. As such, it is more likely to approximate the **citation** or dictionary pronunciation. As Caldwell (2012) says, "The listener's experience of normal speech . . . is of a stream, words flow into each other in patterns . . . in which some words retain resemblance to the citation form and others are pulled out of shape" (p. 1).

With so much variability associated with segmentals, Field (see Myth 3) questions the nature of the consonant and vowel sounds that learners need to internalize when they acquire the pronunciation of a second language. He also looks at evidence for the possibility that learners decode speech by relying on units larger than the phoneme—syllables, words, and high-frequency phrases.

THE INTERSECTION OF THE SEGMENTAL AND SUPRASEGMENTAL SYSTEMS

Dickerson (2009) cautions us that even though we may teach the suprasegmental and the segmental systems separately, we cannot view them separately. He explains that the two systems are "woven into a single system" with pieces that interrelate (p. 2). Indeed, the final two examples of sound variation (see Sections C and D) point up this interrelationship. In both cases, the clarity of the segmentals was dictated by the relative importance of the words to the message. In essence, the suprasegmental system was "calling the shots." Kjellin (2004) describes the nature of the segmental/suprasegmental relationship this way: "Segmentals must be somehow very underspecified until their exact places and roles in the discourse have been determined, and only then do they get their final characteristics" (email communication). Related research by Zielinski (2008) indicates that the clear, accurate production of segments within the prominent word (or syllable) contributes to intelligibility and serves as an important source of information for native listeners. For a visual depiction of this relationship between prosody and speech sounds, see Gilbert's pyramid diagram, Figure 4.1.

Levels of Pronunciation Teaching and Learning

At the beginning of the Prologue, I shared a story about the first pronunciation class I ever taught, which proved to be something of a disaster. I am happy to report that most of the pronunciation classes I have taught since then have been somewhat more successful. In fact, in the early '90s, I began to organize my classroom materials into a textbook format and subsequently published the first edition of *Well Said: Pronunciation for Clear Communication*, now in its third edition. That text was followed by *Well Said Intro* in 2007. For many reasons, however, I am still learning about what works and what does not: (1) there is neither one instructional approach nor one pronunciation syllabus that serves all students in all contexts; (2) as research evolves, I continue to look over the shoulders of researchers and recalibrate my classroom teaching accordingly; and (3) adult language learners are changing long-standing, deep-seated pronunciation patterns, so our instruction and expectations of progress need to take into account that pronunciation change is gradual and multi-layered. No matter what the instructional context or specific needs of the student, L2 pronunciation teaching needs to address the many levels on which pronunciation change occurs.

- **Motor or physical level:** Learners need easy descriptions of sounds and patterns in order to produce them. For new sounds not in the first language, they also need a considerable amount of practice to overcome long established articulatory movements.

- **Perceptual level:** Research by Werker (1989) indicates that all infants are born with a universal sensitivity to perceive all sounds from all languages, but, by the age of about 10–12 months, that sensitivity becomes limited to the sounds and patterns that carry meaning in the child's mother tongue. Thus, features of L2 pronunciation that are not meaningful in the L1 are likely to elude adult learners. Werker (1989), however, points out that the ability to perceive sounds and develop perceptual models not in the L1 is recoverable. To develop sensitivity to sounds in the L2, adult learners need to be guided through focused perceptual training to attend to sounds and sound distinctions they have not noticed since childhood.

- **Cognitive level:** Perceptual training along with considerable exposure to and practice with the target language ultimately leads to a mental reorganization of the sound system or the formation of new perceptual categories on which learners base their pronunciation of the new language. This level of acquisition can be thought of as learning the array of sounds or forms that represent the category or family of sounds called /p/, for example. As Fraser puts it, many teachers assume "that pronunciation is something that happens in the mouth. . . . Much better if teachers can recognize that pronunciation is something that happens in the mind" (Fraser, email communication, 2010).

- **Psycho-social level:** As important as what happens on the perceptual, motor, and cognitive levels are the conscious and unconscious attitudes of adult learners toward pronunciation change. Are they concerned about being intelligible? Do they have personal or professional reasons for improving pronunciation? Are they positively inclined toward the host culture? Do they want to integrate socially? Because pronunciation is a central aspect of personal and cultural identity (Schumann, 1986), progress in pronunciation hinges in part on the answers to these questions. See Grant, Myth 5, for a discussion of psycho-social factors and other learner variables that influence ultimate attainment in L2 pronunciation.

Thanks to Tracey Derwing and John Murphy for their helpful comments on an earlier draft of this prologue.

References

Avery, P., & Ehrlich, S. (1992). *Teaching American English pronunciation.* Oxford, U.K.: Oxford University Press.

Abercrombie, D. (1949). Teaching pronunciation. *English Language Teaching 3,* 113–122.

Bradlow, A. R., Pisoni, D. B., Akahane-Yamada, R., & Tokhura, Y (1997). Training Japanese listeners to identify English /r/ and /l/: IV. Some effects of perceptual learning on speech production. *Journal of the Acoustical Society of America, 101*(4), 2200–2310.

Brown, S. (2011). *Listening myths: Applying second language research to classroom teaching.* Ann Arbor: University of Michigan Press.

Cauldwell, R. (2012). The two-sides rule in teaching listening and pronunciation. http://www.developingteachers.com/articles_tchtraining/two_sides1_richard.htm

Celce-Murcia, M., Brinton, D., & Goodwin, J. (2010). *Teaching pronunciation: A coursebook and reference guide* (2nd ed.). New York: Cambridge University Press.

Dalton, C., & Seidlhofer, B. (1994). *Pronunciation.* Oxford, U.K.: Oxford University Press.

Deng, J., Holtby, A., Howden-Weaver, L., Nessim, L., Nicholas, B., Nickle, K., Pannekoek, C., Stephan, S., & Sun, M. (2009). *English pronunciation research: The neglected orphan of second language acquisition studies?* (PMC Working paper WP O5-09). Edmonton, AB: Prairie Metropolis Centre.

Derwing, T.M., & Munro, M.J. (1997). Accent, intelligibility, and comprehensibility: Evidence from four L1s. *Studies in Second Language Acquisition, 19*, 1–16.

Derwing, T. M., & Munro, M. J. (2001). What speaking rates do nonnative listeners prefer? *Applied Linguistics, 22*, 324–337.

Derwing, T. M., & Munro, M. J. (2005). Second language accent and pronunciation teaching: A research-based approach, *TESOL Quarterly, 39*, 379–397.

Derwing, T. M., & Munro, M. J. (2011). Intelligibility, comprehensibility and accent: Their relevance to pronunciation teaching. *Speak Out! IATEFL Pronunciation Special Interest Group Newsletter,* (X) 1–5.

Derwing, T. M., Munro, M. J., & Wiebe, G. E. (1998). Evidence in favour of a broad framework for pronunciation instruction. *Language Learning, 39*, 393–410.

Derwing, T. M., Rossiter, M. J., & Munro, M. J. (2002). Teaching native speakers to listen to foreign-accented speech. *Journal of Multilingual and Multicultural Development, 23*, 245–259.

Dickerson, W. (2010). Walking the walk: Integrating the story of English phonology. In J. Levis & K. LeVelle (Eds.), *Proceedings of the 1st Pronunciation in Second Language Learning and Teaching Conference.* Ames: Iowa State University, 10–23.

Esling J. H., & Wong, R. (1983). Voice quality settings and the teaching of pronunciation. *TESOL Quarterly, 17*, 89–95.

Field, J. (2005). Intelligibility and the listener: The role of lexical stress. *TESOL Quarterly, 39*, 399–423.

Foote, J. A., Holtby, A. K., & Derwing, T. M. (2011). Survey of the teaching of pronunciation in adult ESL programs in Canada, 2010, *TESOL Canada Journal, 29*, 1–22.

Fraser, H. (2001). *Teaching pronunciation: A handbook for teachers and trainers.* Sydney: AMES NSW. helenfraser.com.au/downloads/HF%20Handbook.pdf

Gass, S., & Varonis, E. M., (1984). The effect of familiarity on the comprehensibility of nonnative speech. *Language Learning, 34*, 65–89.

Gilbert, J. B. (1984, 1993, 2005, 2010). *Clear speech.* New York: Cambridge University Press.

Gilbert, J. (2010). Pronunciation as orphan: What can be done? *Speak Out! IATEFL Pronunciation Special Interest Newsletter, 43,* 3–7.

Grant, L. (2010). *Well said: Pronunciation for clear communication* (3rd ed.). Boston: National Geographic Learning Cengage.

Grant, L. (2007). *Well said intro.* Boston: National Geographic Learning Cengage.

Hahn, L. D. (2004). Primary stress and intelligibility: Research to motivate the teaching of suprasegmentals. *TESOL Quarterly, 38,* 201–223.

Jenkins, J. (2000). *The phonology of English as an international language.* Oxford, U.K.: Oxford University Press.

Jones, R., & Evans, S. (1995). Teaching pronunciation through voice quality. *ELT Journal, 49,* 244–251.

Kanellou, V. (2009). The place of pronunciation in current ELT manuals: a review. *Speak Out! IATEFL Pronunciation Special Interest Newsletter, 41,* 4–7.

Keys, J. K. (2000). Discourse level phonology in the language curriculum: a review of current thinking in teaching pronunciation in EFL courses. *Linguagem & Ensino, 3*(1), 89–105.

Lacey, M. (2011, Sept. 24). In Arizona, Complaints That an Accent Can Hinder a Teacher's Career, *The New York Times,* p. A18.

Levis, J.M. (2005). Changing contexts and shifting paradigms in pronunciation teaching. *TESOL Quarterly, 39,* 369–377.

Lindemann, S. (2010). Who's "unintelligible"? The perceiver's role. *Issues in Applied Linguistics, 18,* 223–232.

Lippi-Green, R. (2012). *English with an accent: Language, ideology, and discrimination in the United States* (2nd ed.). New York: Routledge.

Morley, J. (1991). The pronunciation component of teaching English to speakers of other languages. *TESOL Quarterly, 25*(3), 481–520.

Munro, M. J., & Derwing, T. M. (1995). Processing time, accent, and comprehensibility in the perception of native and foreign-accented speech. *Language and Speech, 38,* 289–306.

Munro, M. J., & Derwing, T. M. (2001). Modeling perceptions of the accentedness and comprehensibility of L2 speech: The role of speaking rate. *Studies in Second Language Acquisition, 23,* 451–468.

Munro, M. J., & Derwing, T. M. (2006). The functional load principle in ESL pronunciation instruction: An exploratory study. *System, 34,* 520–531.

Murphy, J. M., & Baker, A. A. (forthcoming). History of ESL pronunciation teaching. In John Levis and Marnie Reed (Eds.), *Wiley-Blackwell Handbook of English Pronunciation.*

Rubin, D. (1992). Nonlanguage factors affecting undergraduates' judgments of nonnative English-speaking teaching assistants. *Research in Higher Education, 33,* 511–531.

Swan, M., & Smith, B. (2001). *Learner English: A teacher's guide to interference and other problems* (2nd ed.). Cambridge, U.K.: Cambridge University Press.

Walker, R. (2010). *Teaching the pronunciation of English as a lingua franca.* Oxford, U.K.: Oxford University Press.

Wang, X., & Munro, M. (2004). Computer-based training for learning English vowel contrasts. *System, 32,* 539–552.

Werker, J. F. (1989). Becoming an active listener. *American Scientist, 77,* 54–59.

Wong, R. (1993). Pronunciation myths and facts. *English Teaching Forum* (October), 45–46.

Zielinski, B. (2008). The listener: No longer the silent partner in reduced intelligibility. *System, 36,* 69–84.

MYTH **1**

Once you have been speaking a second language for years, it's too late to change your prounciation.

Tracey Derwing and Murray J. Munro
University of Alberta and Simon Fraser University

In the Real World

David Nguyen, originally from Vietnam, moved to Canada in 1980, a time when many Vietnamese people were fleeing their country. David was an engineer and, although it took a long time and a lot of hard work, his credentials were eventually recognized, and he was hired in a large engineering firm. His professional skills were very strong, but his employers often complained that they had difficulty understanding him, despite the fact that he had taken several ESL courses when he first arrived and had a good grasp of both spoken and written English. The problem, as they put it, was his "heavy accent."

Sixteen years after his arrival in Canada, David enrolled in a Clear Speaking course offered two evenings a week for twelve weeks at a local college. Along with his classmates, he received instruction intended to make him more intelligible. On the first night, the students were invited to participate in a study that would entail collecting samples of their English pronunciation at the beginning and end of the course. Like David, the other students had all been in Canada for extensive periods of time; the average length of stay was ten years. They were all well educated and ranged from high intermediate to very advanced in terms of English proficiency. Each student agreed to record speech samples in the first and last weeks of the course; they were offered an honorarium at the end of the study.

What the Research Says

What could David, after 16 years of living in an English-speaking city in Canada, realistically expect from thirty-six hours of instruction over twelve weeks? The conventional wisdom about immigrants like David is quite discouraging. A widespread assumption is that he would have *fossilized*, a term coined by Selinker (1972) to describe the process undergone by a second language (L2) speaker who is unlikely to show improvement in certain forms of the target language, regardless of instruction. Selinker's proposal is supported by a number of early pronunciation studies. Oyama (1976), for instance, examined the pronunciation of 60 Italian immigrants to the United States. Their ages on arrival ranged from six to twenty years, and they had lived in the U.S. for five to eighteen years. Two linguistically trained judges assessed their accentedness on a five-point scale. Oyama found that the immigrants who arrived at later ages had much stronger foreign accents than those who had come at an earlier age. Interestingly, length of time in the U.S. made no significant difference to degree of accentedness. Oyama concluded that pronunciation instruction in an L2 should take place when learners are young. Her finding has often been interpreted as indicating that older learners don't benefit from pronunciation instruction; in other words, they have "fossilized."

Another interpretation of fossilization is connected to the length of time an L2 learner has spent in the target language community. Research on naturalistic development of L2 pronunciation patterns has shown that experience in the second language environment does indeed have some impact on pronunciation, even though it is quite small. Moreover, most changes in the direction of the target language tend to occur within the first year in the second language environment (Flege, 1988; Munro & Derwing, 2008). These findings, along with those of Oyama (1976), suggest that L2 learners' productions will fossilize after even a relatively short period of residence in their new language environment. Thus, fossilization has been tied to both age and length of residence. Older learners are considered to have more difficulty modifying their L2 speech, and learners who have resided in the target language community for more than a year are considered to be likely candidates for fossilization.

Is Fossilization Restricted to L2 Speakers?

Although the concept of fossilization is usually discussed as an unwanted aspect of second language learning, even native speakers of a language often demonstrate a comparable resistance to change, despite extensive exposure to accepted norms. English language prescriptivists are fond of complaining about the "deterioration" of the language, citing mispronunciations that they find egregious. Some of these mispronunciations arise when a native speaker first encounters a word in written form and attributes a pronunciation to it that may conform with other similarly spelled words. For example, some people pronounce *epitome* with three syllables (/ˈɛpətom/), rather than with four (/əˈpɪtəmi/).[2] Another common mispronunciation is the word *heroine*, the second syllable of which is mistakenly pronounced to rhyme with *groin*. Reading pronunciations like these seem remarkably resistant to change. Even after hearing the more accepted pronunciation, some

---

[1] /ˈɛpətom/ is also represented as /ˈɛpətowm/.
[2] /əˈpɪtəmi/ is also represented as /əˈpɪtəmiy/.

speakers persist in using the one they learned on their own. Uneducated speakers may produce innovations such as *drownded* for *drowned* and *spayeded* for *spayed*. Other non-standard forms become so widespread that eventually they are accepted as alternative pronunciations. Some dictionaries, for instance, list *expresso* as an acceptable alternative to *espresso* and *heighth* as an alternative to the more common *height*. In the most extreme cases, a word can actually change in response to the new pronunciation. For example, *apron* came into existence because people interpreted *a napron* as *an apron*. The point to all of these examples is that native speakers, in spite of ongoing exposure to accepted forms, sometimes do not notice that these differ from their own productions. Thus, although fossilization is often regarded as a process restricted to L2 speakers, it appears in native speaker speech as well. In the absence of overt correction, native speakers do not necessarily change their mispronunciations.

The main fossilization difference between native speakers and second language speakers is the level of the errors. Native speaker mispronunciations are usually restricted to specific words. The same can happen with L2 learners, but they are also subject to systematic grammatical and phonological fossilization. A Japanese speaker who is unable to produce English /ɹ/[3] (the first sound in the word *run*), for instance, will extend the error across a wide range of contexts.

Why Don't More Teachers Address Fossilized Pronunciation in Their L2 Classrooms?

Many researchers have bemoaned the fact that language instructors tend to shy away from teaching pronunciation. One key reason is the belief that pronunciation teaching is not effective. A discouraging study conducted by Purcell and Suter (1980) reinforced this sentiment. They examined the speech of 61 English learners from a variety of first language backgrounds. The authors collected information on several factors including age of arrival, length of residence in an English-speaking

---

[3] /ɹ/ is also represented as /r/.

country, amount of English used in conversation, motivation, aptitude for oral mimicry, strength of concern for pronunciation, amount of general English instruction, and number of weeks focused specifically on pronunciation instruction. In their correlational analyses, Purcell and Suter (1980) concluded that four factors accounted for accuracy of pronunciation: first language, aptitude for oral mimicry, residency, and strength of concern for pronunciation. Notably, pronunciation instruction did not correlate significantly with accent. The authors concluded that the contributors to pronunciation accuracy are largely out of the control of a second language teacher, which led to the interpretation that formal pronunciation instruction is largely ineffective.

Second language instructors may also be reluctant to devote class time to pronunciation because of pedagogical theory regarding second language acquisition. During the audiolingual era of the 1950s and 1960s, pronunciation skills were a central aspect of L2 classrooms. Students were taught to mimic native speaker models as accurately as possible as a means of developing good habits of oral language production. The publication of Purcell and Suter's (1980) study coincided with a major shift in second language classrooms across North America from audiolingual and 'designer' methods to communicative language teaching (CLT). A basic premise of CLT was that with enough input, learners would gradually develop acceptable English pronunciation, but that any special pronunciation instruction was not only unnecessary, but unlikely to be effective. The CLT approach emphasized authentic use of language and moved away from repetition and mimicry and minimized corrective feedback, which was seen as disruptive to communication. Without formal pronunciation instruction, students in CLT classrooms were left to their own devices to change their oral productions in the direction of the target language. In the absence of explicit correction, many students exhibited fossilized patterns. It seemed, then, that pronunciation fell outside the responsibilities of the CLT classroom. A decade later, in a detailed overview of what research revealed about classroom teaching, Pica (1994) agreed with Purcell and Suter: "Precise pronunciation may be an unrealistic goal for teachers to set for their students and in their teaching" (p. 73).

A third reason for the neglect of pronunciation in the language classroom is the lack of formal training in pronunciation pedagogy available to teachers (see Murphy, Myth 7, for more on this topic). In the post-audiolingual period, only a handful of researchers and practitioners promoted the view that adult learners could indeed benefit from explicit pronunciation instruction. Acton (1984), for example, described the approach he used in working with "fossilized" adult learners. Similarly, Ricard (1986) outlined strategies and techniques used in an English pronunciation course for adults that she argued were successful. Meanwhile, pronunciation specialists such as Gilbert (1984) developed materials that could be used within the CLT framework. The impact on teaching, however, appears to have been somewhat limited, right into the twenty-first century, in part because second language instructors generally had little or no training in how to teach pronunciation and were therefore uncomfortable using these materials (Burgess & Spencer, 2000; Breitkreutz, Derwing, & Rossiter, 2002; MacDonald, 2002). Furthermore, articles that were accessible to teachers, such as those of Acton (1984) and Ricard (1986), were based on personal experience rather than empirical evidence that could be replicated by others.

In summary, research and pedagogical practice over the last two decades of the twentieth century conspired to marginalize pronunciation instruction. The empirical studies of pronunciation learning had a negative message. Language teaching shifted to an approach that seemed incompatible with pronunciation instruction, and publications with a positive message for teachers were based on the authors' personal experiences rather than verifiable data.

Is Pronunciation Instruction Effective?

When we began our own program of research on second language pronunciation in the 1990s, we were taken aback at the paucity of empirical research on the effectiveness of explicit instruction for adult learners on pronunciation. At that time, we could identify only a handful of published studies, many of which were relatively inaccessible to second language instructors (Derwing & Munro, 2005). One of the very few before and after studies was an investigation by Perlmutter (1989), suggesting benefits of pronunciation instruction for international teaching assistants in their first six months in the U.S. Regrettably, the lack of an uninstructed comparison group meant that the improvement noted in pronunciation may have been due to overall exposure within the English-speaking community rather than to the teaching intervention.

Since that time, other studies that have included non-instructed comparison groups have been conducted. Couper (2003, 2006) investigated the benefits of explicit pronunciation instruction aimed at certain features that he deemed most problematic for listeners. He administered pre- and post-tests to international university students who were enrolled in his pronunciation courses. Couper found in both cases that the overall number of errors was reduced as a result of the instruction. In his 2006 study, he included an uninstructed comparison group; that group showed no improvement over time. These studies suggest that second language learners' speech can be changed in reaction to targeted instruction.

If we consider second language learners' pronunciation to have a propensity to "fossilize" within the first year of residence in target language community (Flege, 1988), then the studies by Couper (2003, 2006) can be understood as applicable to improving fossilized pronunciation. In both studies, the learners' mean length of residence in New Zealand was 2.5 years, ranging from 0–8 years. Derwing, Munro, and Wiebe (1998) assessed the pronunciation improvement of three groups of high-intermediate ESL learners in Canada over a 12-week period. Most of these individuals had been in the country for longer than one year (on average 3.4 years with a range of 7 months to 15 years). One group received suprasegmental (prosodic) training, while a second group received instruction focused only on individual vowels and consonants (segmentals). The third group had no pronunciation-specific instruction. An important aspect of this study was the evaluation of progress in comprehensibility (how easy or difficult listeners perceived the second language speech to be) as well as accent (how much the second language speech differed from the listeners' own native variety of English) and flu-

TABLE 1.1: Perceptual Dimensions for L2 Speech Evaluation

Dimension	Measurements (Listeners' Tasks)
Accentedness *How different is the speech from a local variety?*	9-point rating scale (not accented to very heavily accented)
Comprehensibility *How easy is it to understand the speech?*	9-point rating scale (very easy to very difficult)
Fluency *To what degree is the speech free of pauses, repetitions, hesitations, false starts, etc.?*	9-point rating scale (very fluent to very dysfluent)
Intelligibility *How much does the listener actually understand?*	Number of words correct in a dictation task, true/false verifications, summaries, comprehension questions

ency (how smooth and hesitation-free the speech flow was). When the speakers described a picture story, the suprasegmental group showed improvement in both comprehensibility and fluency, whereas the other groups did not; however, the suprasegmental group did not show any change in accent ratings, despite their improvement on the other dimensions. This outcome supports our multi-dimensional approach to L2 speech (Munro & Derwing, 1995; Derwing & Munro, 1997), which regards accent as only partially connected to factors such as comprehensibility and intelligibility (how understandable speech actually is). Table 1.1 illustrates the definitions of these speech dimensions and gives examples of how these dimensions can be measured.

What Really Matters in Pronunciation Instruction?

The findings of this study help us sort out some of the complexities that arise in understanding pronunciation research in general. Despite its possible usefulness for theoretical purposes, the study of accentedness is not very relevant to second language teaching. Far more important are the concepts of intelligibility and comprehensibility, both of which are strongly connected to communicative success. After all, the primary goal of most language learners is to make themselves understood and to understand other speakers. As our research has shown (Munro & Derwing, 1995), it is possible to have even a heavy accent and still be relatively easy to understand. Moreover, comprehensibility and intelligibility can improve even when there is no noticeable improvement in degree of accentedness. Seen in this light, the somewhat pessimistic view held by researchers and theorists who are concerned with the acquisition of native-like accuracy is essentially immaterial to second language teachers. What is important is to help learners to develop a comfortable intelligibility (Abercrombie, 1949), not the elimination of a foreign accent per se.

What Are the Mechanisms That Make Pronunciation Instruction Effective?

Because we do not yet fully understand all the factors that make second language instruction difficult for adults, we also do not have a complete grasp of the most effective techniques for teaching pronunciation. However, research has provided us with several useful insights. Some studies have indicated a relationship between learner perception and production. For instance, when Bradlow, Pisoni, Akahane-Yamada, and Tohkura (1997) trained Japanese speakers to perceive the English /ɹ/ versus /l/ distinction, their production also improved, even though there was no oral component to the training. Thomson (2011) found a comparable effect of perceptual training on the production of English vowels.

The choice of focus in the second language classroom is also important, such that those elements that are known to interfere with intelligibility should be highlighted first. Aspects of accent that may be noticeable but that have a negligible effect on intelligibility and/or comprehensibility can be left aside until greater intelligibility is achieved. For example, several studies have pointed to the importance of stress to intelligibility, whether at the level of the word or in larger units (Hahn, 2004; Field, 2005; Zielinski, 2008). On the other hand, research on certain individual segments, such as the notorious English interdental fricatives (/θ/ and /ð/), indicates minimal importance for comprehensibility (Munro & Derwing, 2006). Although there is still much work to be done in testing these expectations (that is, which factors affect intelligibility and comprehensibility the most), the available research provides some tentative guidelines to teachers.

A promising new line of work applies concepts from grammar teaching to pronunciation. In a study of Japanese speakers' production of English /ɹ/, Saito and Lyster (2012), using communicative language tasks, showed that an explicit focus on form with corrective feedback (recasts, in this case) led to improvement. Focus on form alone in the absence of corrective feedback (that is, tasks requiring productions of many instances of /ɹ/, which was both italicized and printed in red on prompting materials) did not result in changes in the speakers' productions. This study suggests that the provision of corrective feedback is vital to successful pronunciation instruction. Indeed, many students complain that interlocutors, including their teachers, do not correct their pronunciation enough (Derwing, 2010). In summary, learners' perceptions of target language phenomena are important, as is the instructor's choice of aspects of the learners' speech that challenge intelligibility and comprehensibility; finally, explicit corrective feedback is valuable.

An Empirical Study of Pronunciation Instruction for "Fossilized" Learners

Let us return to our discussion of a typical "fossilized" learner, David Nguyen. Along with 12 other students representing a variety of language backgrounds (Mandarin, Cantonese, Farsi, French, Spanish, and Ukrainian, in addition to Vietnamese), he took part in our before-and-after study of the effectiveness of a Clear Speaking course (Derwing, Munro, & Wiebe, 1997). The students were enrolled in two small classes with the same content. The instructors focused on general speaking habits and on suprasegmentals. They used the same materials (Gilbert, 1993; Grant, 1993; Matthews, 1994) and very similar teaching strategies. Their course notes indicated that they followed the "Zoom Principle," identified by Firth (1992) as an approach whereby the instructors begin with overarching issues that affect all parts of the speaker's message (e.g., body language, voice quality, speaking volume, rate, and discourse markers) and then zoom in on suprasegmentals, such as intonation, rhythm, and stress. Little emphasis was placed on individual vowels and consonants, it turned out, because the students shared very few problems at the level of the segment.

David, like his fellow students, met individually with two researchers on the first and last evenings of class to record an extensive list of true/false sentences that we have used in a number of studies (e.g., *Many people drink coffee for breakfast. Spaghetti grows on tall trees.*). We randomized a balanced selection of sentences taken from both time periods from all of the participants and played them to 37 native speakers of English. The listeners' task was to write in standard orthography exactly what they heard. The recordings were then played a second time, sentence by sentence, so that the listeners could judge each one for comprehensibility on the 9-point scale previously described. To assess intelligibility, we examined the listeners' renditions of the sentences and counted the number of words they transcribed correctly. We then calculated a percentage correct for each sentence. As can be seen in Figure 1.1, there was a statistically significant improvement on the sentence task for both true/false items from Time 1 to Time 2. In other words, the speakers' true/false sentences were more understandable after the instruction was completed.

The speakers' true sentences were also judged to be easier to understand (comprehensibility) at Time 2 (see Figure 1.2). The false sentences, although more intelligible at Time 2, were not perceived by the listeners to be easier to understand. This makes sense, because the false sentences had such unexpected, unpredictable content.

These findings are important because they show that even people who have been living and working in English for an average of ten years can make changes to their speech that noticeably improve listeners' comprehension and ease of understanding. Of course we don't know to what extent the learners were able to implement their new knowledge in their day-to-day speaking activities, but at least they became aware of what their main difficulties were. A breakdown in communication caused by a common problem is much easier to repair if the speaker is aware of what the problem is. Another important observation is that not all the students showed significant improvement, but this is not surprising given that the course was only two evenings a week for 12 weeks.

FIGURE 1.1: Significant Improvement in Intelligibility after 12 Weeks Instruction, True and False Sentences Combined (Mean LOR = 10 years), *p* < .01 (see Derwing, Munro, & Wiebe, 1997)

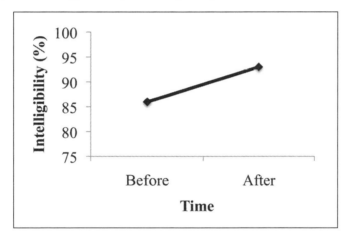

FIGURE 1.2: Significant Improvement in Comprehensibility on True Sentences, *p* < .01 (see Derwing, Munro, & Wiebe, 1997)

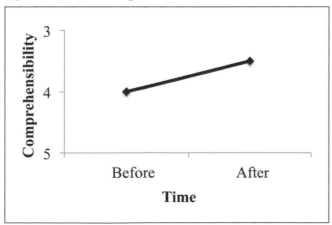

These individuals had been speaking English in a particular way for a very long time; thus a short intervention is unlikely to benefit everyone to the same degree. In this case, motivational factors may have played a role. Three of the learners did not self-select for the course but were required to take it by their PhD supervisor. One of these individuals did not show any significant improvement in either intelligibility or comprehensibility, but he was quite upset at having to attend and was not open to participating in the course activities.

In summary, this study indicates that so-called "fossilized" speakers can improve their pronunciation in a relatively short period of time, despite many years of producing some aspects of their second language incorrectly.

What We Can Do

1. Teach perception.

Students who have been speaking their L2 for a long time are their own most frequent source of input; they hear their own speech more than that of any other person. Years of input from their own speech patterns contributes to fossilization because the learners come to establish their own perceptual categories for segments and for prosodic phenomena. These deeply engrained representations make it difficult to change pronunciation patterns. Change seems to require drawing L2 speakers' attention explicitly to the differences between their own productions and more intelligible forms. The teacher's role in fostering new pronunciation skills is to first determine whether the speakers can perceive the target and whether they can distinguish between the target and their speech. If there is a problem with perception, then exposure to a range of suitable targets with feedback on incorrect perception is a suitable approach. For example, software such as *English Accent Coach* (www. englishaccentcoach.com) provides learners with opportunities to practice listening to acceptable variants of target sounds from multiple speakers, with explicit corrective feedback to guide perception. The prototype of this program was used in an experiment in which language learners' perception and production was shown to improve significantly over time (Thomson, 2011). For prosodic aspects of language, a resource such as Cauldwell's (n.d.) website, Cool Speech: Hot Listening, gives students opportunities to hear speech produced at a normal rate, as well as slowed down rates to help them realize their goals.

2. Give explicit corrective feedback.

Ample studies have shown that improved pronunciation can be achieved through classroom instruction (Couper 2003, 2006; Derwing, Munro, & Wiebe 1997, 1998). However, it is becoming increasingly clear that a key factor in the success of instruction is the provision of explicit corrective feedback. Contrary to ideas prevalent in the late 1970s and early 1980s, and still popular in some classrooms today, there is no indication that, after the first year in the target language country, pronunciation will improve to any significant extent under conditions of exposure alone. To defossilize speech patterns that interfere with intelligibility and/or comprehensibility, explicit corrective feedback for both perception and production tasks is required. Saito and Lyster (2012), for instance, describe an approach to teaching English /ɹ/ to Japanese learners within the context of communicative activities. Significant improvement was noted after four hours of instruction over a period of two weeks.

Feedback should be geared to those aspects of speech that have the greatest impact on intelligibility and comprehensibility. It may be best to provide a combination of metalinguistic feedback, explaining the nature of the error in question, and recasts, giving the student a model to imitate. Dlaska and Krekeler (2013) compared two groups of students. One group listened to their own productions along with a model (similar to a recast), while the other group heard their own productions and then received individualized metalinguistic information as well as a correct model. More than twice as many students improved their own productions when provided with explicit instruction.

Another source of explicit feedback is from student peers. Often in language classrooms, students tend to ignore each other's contributions in order to focus on those of the teacher. However, peer correction should be encouraged in an atmosphere of trust because students should be actively noticing differences across speakers. As they become aware of their own speech patterns, students should also be more sensitive to similar patterns in their classmates' speech. Friendly explicit correction of one's peers will benefit both students involved.

3. Choose the right focus.

Class time is at a premium, whether the course is pronunciation specific or a general skills L2 class. Therefore instructors need to be careful to prioritize pronunciation issues that will best address the intelligibility of their students. In doing so, the teacher should first consider the problem areas of the students. Individual needs should be identified by a thorough assessment of both perception and production. This assessment, together with research findings, should guide the selection of activities. If students typically assign stress to the wrong syllables, for instance, they are likely to confuse their interlocutors (Field, 2005; Hahn, 2004); thus, stress is a good candidate for prioritization. When selecting features that merit priority at the segmental level, teachers should take into consideration the concept of functional load (Catford, 1987). This principle is used to assess the amount of "work" that phonemic contrasts perform in the language. For instance, because many commonly encountered words are distinguished by the /n/ – /l/ distinction (*no/low, night/light, not/lot*), this sound pair is said to have a high functional load (e.g., 61 percent). See Column 1 in Table 1.2. Confusing the two sounds, as Cantonese speakers of English often do, is quite likely to lead to a loss of intelligibility. In contrast, the /ð/ – /d/ distinction (*though/dough*), a low functional load pair (e.g., 19 percent), is much less frequent and does not distinguish many commonly used words. As a result, confusion of these two sounds poses only minor problems for communication. Catford's functional load hypothesis was tested empirically in a study conducted by Munro & Derwing

TABLE 1.2: Relative Functional Load (Catford, 1987)

Initial Consonants	%	Final Consonants	%	Vowels	%
k/h	100	d/z	100	*bit/bat*	100
p/b	98	d/l	76	*beet/bit*	95
p/k	92	n/l	75	*bought/boat*	88
p/t	87	t/d	72	*bit/but*	85
p/h, s/h	85	d/n	69	*bit/bait*	80
l/r	83	l/z	66	*cat/cot*	76
b/d	82	t/k	65	*cat/cut*	68
t/k, t/s	81	t/z	61	*cot/cut*	65
d/l	79	l/n	58	*caught/curt*	64
p/f	77	t/s	57	*coat/curt*	63
b/w	76	p/t	43	*bit/bet*	54
d/r	75	p/k	42.5	*bet/bait*	53
h/zero	74	m/n	42	*bet/bat, coat/coot*	51
t/d	73	s/z	38	*cat/cart, beet/boot*	50
b/g	71	t/tʃ	31	*bet/but, bought/boot*	50
f/h	69	k/g	29	*hit/hurt*	49
f/s	64	t/θ	27	*bead/beard*	47
n/l	61	k/tʃ	26	*pet/pot*	45
m/n	59	b/d	24	*hard/hide*	44
d/g	56	d/g	23	*bet/bite, cart/caught*	43
ʃ/h	55	v/z, d/dʒ	22	*cart/cur*	41
s/ʃ, d/n	53	b/m, g/ŋ	21	*boat/bout*	40.5
k/g	50	b/g	20	*cut/curt*	40
g/w	49	n/ŋ	18	*cut/cart*	38
r/r	41	p/f, s/θ	17	*Kay/care*	35
t/tʃ, d/dʒ	39	dʒ/z, m/v	16	*carl/cot*	31.5
s/tʃ	37	ŋ/l	15	*here/hair, light/lout*	30
g/dʒ	31	p/b, m/ŋ	14	*cot/caught*	26
b/v	29	g/dʒ	13	*fire/fair*	25
w/hw	27	tʃ/ʃ	12	*her/here, buy/boy*	24
ʃ/tʃ	26	f/v, f/θ	9	*car/cow*	23
f/v	23	tʃ/dʒ	8	*her/hair*	21
v/w	22	b/v, s/ʃ, z/ð	7	*tire/tower*	19
dʒ/dr, s/θ	21	θ/ð	6	*box/books*	18
dʒ/y	20.5	d/ð	5	*paw/pore*	15
d/ð, tʃ/dʒ	19	v/ð	1	*pill/pull*	13.5
t/θ	18			*pull/pole*	12
tʃ/tr	16			*bid/beard*	11
f/θ	15			*bad/beard*	10
f/hw	13			*pin/pen, put/putt*	9
v/ð	11			*bad/Baird*	8
kw/hw	8			*pull/pool*	7
d/z	7			*sure/shore, pooh/poor*	5
s/z	6			*cam/calm, purr/poor*	4.5
tw/kw	5			*good/gourd*	1
tw/kw	5				
v/z	2				
θ/ð, z/ð	1				

(2006). Their study found evidence in favor of the functional load principle. To decide which segmental issues, if any, to cover in their classes, teachers can apply the functional load principle.

4. Use authentic language.

To become effective communicators, language learners need to understand speech as it is used in ordinary interactions. While it is not necessary for them to use reduced speech exactly as native speakers do, to be easily understood they should be able to produce connected utterances in ways that do not lead to ambiguity. Excessive use of citation pronunciations is a particularly unwise practice in the classroom. For instance, if students produce the auxiliary *can* /kæn/ in its citation form within a typical utterance, they are almost certain to be misunderstood. In fact, this form of the word is almost never used except in cases of contrastive emphasis and will very likely be heard as *can't* /kænt/. Learners should be taught to produce the obligatory reduced form of *can* as in *I can* /kən/ *stop at the store after work, if you like.* This example is just one of many aspects of reduction that warrant attention in the pronunciation classroom. Even people who have spent years in English speaking environments are often unsure about forms such as *gonna*, *hafta*, *wonchyu*, etc.

Sources of authentic language are readily available on the internet. Many instructors employ YouTube videos, for instance, to provide models of particular aspects of pronunciation. Such recordings can be incorporated in a range of activities, including heightening perception, serving as a catalyst for explicit explanations, as well as providing shadowing and mirroring opportunities. (Shadowing is a technique also known as echoing, in which learners repeat what another speaker says almost immediately, whereas with mirroring, students speak simultaneously with a model, while at the same time producing the same gestures and other body movements.) Levis and Pickering (2004) indicate that intonation is best taught at the discourse level, and they provide suggestions for ways in which technology can support such study. In an examination of given and new information patterns in authentic texts,

Levis and Levis (2010) argue that students should be introduced to the organizational structures in order to understand sentence focus. They make explicit recommendations for instruction of this type. Thus pronunciation instruction and discourse instruction go hand in hand, as noted by Tyler (1992).

5. Make judicious use of technology.

A tremendous advantage of technology is the opportunity it affords learners to practice on their own time (Chun, Hardison, & Pennington, 2008). This allows for individualization of instruction; the teacher can point the learner to areas of focus that are particularly troublesome. It also allows the instructor to use classroom time for problems that are shared across students and for provision of corrective feedback and novel listening and production activities. There is little point in encouraging students to use technology without guidance, however. Many options are available on the web, including, unfortunately, many poor quality offerings, some of which may actually do more harm than good. It is therefore important that the instructor examine and suggest what the students should work on at home.

In class, there are numerous options that can be both instructive and entertaining. Youtube videos from sitcoms can offer a wealth of helpful examples: For instance, a scene from the television show *King of Queens* depicting the rhythm and appropriate word stress needed when giving a telephone number provides useful illustrations (www. youtube.com/watch?v=RW7iB2iOTKw).

6. Don't wait for fossilization to happen.

Finally, as previously noted, much of the development of a learner's L2 phonological system takes place within the first year. An explicit focus on pronunciation in language classes, based on intelligibility priorities during that first year, may help learners to become sufficiently comprehensible that intervention for fossilized patterns several years later may not be necessary.

Now, let us return to David Nguyen. At the end of the research period, David, like his peers, was offered a modest honorarium for his participation in the study. He refused the money, insisting that it should go toward more research. David stated that advances in L2 pronunciation instruction were crucial, and he wanted to make a direct contribution to that. When native speakers assessed David's before-and-after speech samples (in a blind, randomized rating task), they detected a significant improvement in intelligibility, even though he had spent 16 years using his L2 English speech patterns before taking the course. As an old dog, David had learned new tricks, and he wanted to be sure that others like him would learn new tricks as well.

References

Abercrombie, D. (1949). Teaching pronunciation. *English Language Teaching, 3*, 113–122.

Acton, W. (1984). Changing fossilized pronunciation. *TESOL Quarterly, 18*(1), 71–85.

Bradlow, R. R., Pisoni, D. B., Akahana-Yamada, R., & Tohkura, Y. (1997). Training Japanese listeners to identify English /r/ and /l/: Some effects of perceptual learning on speech production. *Journal of the Acoustical Society of America, 101*, 2299–2310.

Breitkreutz, J., Derwing, T. M., & Rossiter, M. J. (2002). Pronunciation teaching practices in Canada. *TESL Canada Journal, 19*, 51–61.

Burgess, J., & Spencer, S. (2000). Phonology and pronunciation in integrated language teaching and teacher education. *System, 28*, 191–215.

Catford, J. C. (1987). Phonetics and the teaching of pronunciation: A systemic description of English phonology. In J. Morley (Ed.). *Current perspectives on pronunciation: Practices anchored in theory* (pp. 87–100). Alexandria, VA: TESOL.

Cauldwell, R. (n.d.). *Cool speech: Hot listening, cool pronunciation.* Retrieved from www.speechinaction.com/

Chun, D. M., Hardison, D. M., & Pennington, M. C. (2008). Technologies for prosody in context: Past and future of L2 research and practice. In J. G. Hansen Edwards & M. L. Zampini (Eds.). *Phonology in second language acquisition* (pp. 323–346). Amsterdam: John Benjamins.

Couper, G. (2003). The value of an explicit pronunciation syllabus in ESOL teaching. *Prospect, 18*(3), 53–70.

Couper, G. (2006). The short and long-term effects of pronunciation instruction. *Prospect, 21*(1), 46–66.

Derwing, T. M. (2010). L2 speakers' impressions of the role of pronunciation after 7 years in an ESL environment. Paper presented at the 2nd Annual Conference on Pronunciation in Second Language Learning and Teaching. Ames, Iowa, September 11.

Derwing, T. M., & Munro, M. J. (1997). Accent, intelligibility, and comprehensibility: Evidence from four L1s. *Studies in Second Language Acquisition, 19,* 1–16.

Derwing, T. M., & Munro, M. J. (2005). Second language accent and pronunciation teaching: A research-based approach. *TESOL Quarterly, 39,* 379–397.

Derwing, T. M., Munro, M. J., & Wiebe, G. E. (1997). Pronunciation instruction for "fossilized" learners: Can it help? *Applied Language Learning, 8,* 217–235.

Derwing, T. M., Munro, M. J., & Wiebe, G. E. (1998). Evidence in favor of a broad framework for pronunciation instruction. *Language Learning, 48,* 393–410.

Dlaska, A., & Krekeler, C. (2013). The short-term effects of individual corrective feedback on L2 pronunciation. *System, 41,* 25–37.

Field, J. (2005). Intelligibility and the listener: The role of lexical stress. *TESOL Quarterly, 39,* 399–423.

Firth, S. (1992). Pronunciation syllabus design: A question of focus. In P. Avery & S. Ehrlich (Eds.) *Teaching American English pronunciation,* (pp.173–183). Oxford, U.K.: Oxford University Press.

Flege, J. E. (1988). Factors affecting degree of perceived foreign accent in English sentences. *Journal of the Acoustical Society of America, 84,* 70–79.

Gilbert, J. B. (1984). *Clear speech: Pronunciation and listening comprehension in North American English.* New York: Cambridge University Press.

Gilbert, J. B. (1993). *Clear speech* (2nd ed.). New York: Cambridge University Press.

Grant, L. (1993). *Well said: Advanced English pronunciation.* Boston: Heinle & Heinle.

Hahn, L. (2004). Primary stress and intelligibility: Research to motivate the teaching of suprasegmentals. *TESOL Quarterly, 38,* 201–223.

Levis, G. M., & Levis, J. (2010). Authentic speech and teaching sentence focus. In J. Levis & K. LeVelle (Eds.), *Proceedings of the 1st Pronunciation in Second Language Learning and Teaching Conference,* Iowa State University (pp. 135–144). Ames: Iowa State University.

Levis, J., & Pickering, L. (2004). Teaching intonation in discourse using speech visualization technology. *System, 32,* 505–24.

MacDonald, S. (2002). Pronunciation—Views and practices of reluctant teachers. *Prospect, 17*(3), 3–18.

Matthews, C. (1994). *Speaking solutions: Interaction, presentation, listening, and pronunciation skills.* Englewood Cliffs, NJ: Prentice Hall Regents.

Munro, M. J., & Derwing, T. M. (1995). Foreign accent, comprehensibility and intelligibility in the speech of second language learners. *Language Learning, 45,* 73–97.

Munro, M. J., & Derwing, T. M. (2006). The functional load principle in ESL pronunciation instruction: An exploratory study. *System, 34,* 520–531.

Munro, M. J., & Derwing, T. M. (2008). Segmental acquisition in adult ESL learners: A longitudinal study of vowel production. *Language Learning, 58,* 479–502.

Oyama, S. (1976). A sensitive period for acquisition of a non-native phonological system. *Journal of Psychological Research, 5*(3), 261–283.

Perlmutter, M. (1989). Intelligibility rating of L2 speech pre- and post-intervention. *Perceptual and Motor Skills, 68,* 515–521.

Pica, T. (1994). Questions from the language classroom: Research perspectives. *TESOL Quarterly, 28,* 49–79.

Purcell, E., & Suter, R. (1980). Predictors of pronunciation accuracy: A re-examination. *Language Learning, 30,* 271–287.

Ricard, E. (1986). Beyond fossilization: A course on strategies and techniques in pronunciation for advanced adult learners. *TESL Canada Journal, Special Issue 1,* 243–253.

Saito, K., & Lyster, R. (2012). Effects of form-focussed instruction and corrective feedback on L2 pronunciation development: The case of English /ɹ/ by Japanese learners of English. *Language Learning, 62,* 595–633.

Selinker, L. (1972). Interlanguage. *International Review of Applied Linguistics and Language Teaching, 10,* 209–231.

Thomson, R. I. (2011). *English accent coach.* Retrieved from www.englishaccentcoach.com/

Thomson, R. I. (2011). Computer assisted pronunciation training: Targeting second language vowel perception improves pronunciation. *CALICO Journal, 28,* 744–765.

Tyler, A. (1992). Discourse structure and the perception of incoherence in international teaching assistants' spoken discourse. *TESOL Quarterly, 26,* 713–729.

Zielinski, B. W. (2008). The listener: No longer the silent partner in reduced intelligibility. *System, 36,* 69–84.

Pronunciation instruction is not appropriate for beginning-level learners.

Beth Zielinski and Lynda Yates
Macquarie University

In the Real World

Most learners at every level are keen to learn how to speak as well as how to read and write in English, and beginners are no exception. But learning how to speak a language successfully involves learning how to make what you say intelligible to others. It is therefore difficult to imagine teaching beginning-level learners how to speak in English without teaching them pronunciation. Most important, beginners themselves are very keen to learn how to pronounce English in a way that makes them easier to understand. This became very clear to Vicki, a colleague of ours with considerable experience teaching adult learners. At the time, Vicki was working with a class of beginning-level learners from very diverse backgrounds. Because she is always conscientious about meeting the needs of her students, she decided to collect feedback about different aspects of her classes on a regular basis. This feedback consistently indicated that her students were pleased with her teaching but they wanted to learn how to speak in their daily lives. At first, she responded to these requests by not only increasing the opportunity for her students to speak in class, but also devising assignments that encouraged them to speak outside the class and advising them of community-based facilities where they could practice . However, even after these changes, the students still reported that they wanted to learn to speak in their daily lives.

Vicki gradually came to understand that what the students really wanted was not an increased opportunity to speak, but explicit instruction on how to speak, that is, explicit instruction in pronunciation. She realised she had been avoiding actually teaching pronunciation because she was a little unsure how to go about it. Once she started to incorporate pronunciation instruction into her classes, however, the need to learn to speak no longer featured in the feedback from students. In addition, former students who had moved to higher levels came back to attend her beginner classes, so much so that, at times, her classes would be overflowing with past students as well as current class members. They obviously felt they were learning to speak!

When teaching beginner adult learners of English, we are faced with a seemingly daunting task. On the one hand, we want to provide these learners with a strong foundation for their continued English learning. On the other hand, we need to equip them with those language skills that are currently important to them in their everyday lives. There are so many things they need to learn! They need to learn how to speak, listen, read, and write in English, and proficiency in each of these skills requires the mastery of many different sub-skills. It can therefore be difficult to establish priorities when deciding what to teach in a beginning-level classroom. Unfortunately, pronunciation is often overlooked as a teaching priority at this level because other aspects of English are deemed to be more important. Some teachers may even feel that instruction in pronunciation is too threatening or challenging for beginners who are already struggling with so many different aspects of English. Other teachers may have the idea that pronunciation is too difficult or complicated for them to teach. We disagree! Such views are based on misconceptions of pronunciation and its role in how we learn to speak a language. It is not only essential for beginners to attend to pronunciation, but it can also be engaging and fun.

This chapter looks at why pronunciation instruction is not only appropriate but also crucial for beginning-level learners. We consider why teaching pronunciation should be a priority in the beginning-level classroom, demonstrate that learners can start learning pronunciation from the first day, and suggest practical ways of integrating pronunciation into basic English instruction simply and easily.

What the Research Says

Pronunciation Difficulties Affect Intelligibility and Confidence to Speak

Even if all other aspects of spoken English are perfect, learners at any level of language learning may find that they are not understood because of their pronunciation. This can be frustrating and demotivating. Such negative experiences have the potential to undermine students' confidence and willingness to speak, which in turn can affect the amount of English they speak in everyday life and thus how much English they eventually learn (Yates, 2011).

Zielinski (2011, 2012) explored the perceptions of recently arrived migrants to Australia who were taking or had taken classes with the Adult Migrant English Program (AMEP). [1] Drawing on data from interviews conducted as part of a larger longitudinal study involving newly arrived migrants to Australia (see Yates, 2010), she explored 26 participants' perceptions of the impact of their pronunciation skills on their interactions in English. The participants were interviewed four times over a 12-month period and on each occasion were asked about their

---

[1] The AMEP is the national on-arrival English language program for migrants in Australia funded by the Australian Government Department of Immigration and Citizenship.

use of English. Fourteen of the 26 participants were beginning-level learners, and all but one (92.9 percent) commented at some stage during the interviews that pronunciation difficulties had a negative impact on their interactions in English (Zielinski, 2012). For example, some participants indicated that pronunciation difficulties affected their confidence to speak or caused them to avoid speaking altogether, as in the excerpts from Zielinski (2011) shown in Figure 2.1.

When pronunciation difficulties lead to a reticence or loss of confidence to interact in spoken English, beginning-level learners have limited opportunities for practice, which, in turn, can affect further language development. This lack of progress in L2 acquisition can ultimately contribute to social isolation and limit educational and work opportunities (Derwing, Thomson, & Munro, 2006; Fraser, 2000; Yates, 2011). It is, therefore, of utmost importance that pronunciation instruction be an integral part of the process of learning English from the beginning and not regarded as an option added at a later stage. As Chela-Flores (2001) argues, it makes little sense to immerse beginning learners into the grammar and vocabulary of English but then leave them to struggle on their own with the pronunciation. She maintains that learners should be gradually immersed into the grammar, vocabulary, and pronunciation of English simultaneously from the very beginning. Darcy, Ewert, and Lidster (2012) agree and claim that pronunciation instruction should start in beginning-level classes and be embedded within the curriculum so that it is a constant and fundamen-

FIGURE 2.1: Impact of Pronunciation Difficulties on Interactions in English

Because of my pronunciation . . . I have no confidence at all. Once I try I wanted to speak out or read it loud but . . . the poor pronunciation and the people would just laugh at me.
(Interpreter for a 52-year-old female from China)

She scared of speaking English because she is afraid yeah she's . . . saying wrong . . . . Her pronunciation is not right . . . . She . . . avoid talking.
(Interpreter for a 28-year-old female from Vietnam)

tal part of every English lesson. In this way, learners accept from the very beginning that working to develop pronunciation skills in order to improve intelligibility is a normal and necessary part of learning English. Plus they benefit from explicit pronunciation instruction in their English classroom from the first day. As Yates (2002) maintains, "Pronunciation teaching should not be seen as 'fixing problems' but rather as 'teaching how to speak'" (p. 1)—a view, it seems, also held by beginners themselves.

Pronunciation Is Important to Beginning-Level Learners

Research indicates that beginners themselves are convinced of the need to improve their pronunciation skills in their English classes. As described, our colleague found that her beginning students equated learning to speak with pronunciation instruction and repeatedly asked for guidance in this area in their English classes (see Hambling, 2009, for details). As part of a larger study, Baker (2011) investigated ESL learners' beliefs about pronunciation learning and teaching. At the time of the study, the learners were enrolled in oral communication courses in an Intensive English Program in the U.S. and were at the beginning, low-intermediate, intermediate, or high-intermediate levels. They were asked to complete questionnaires in which they indicated their responses to statements related to pronunciation teaching using one of five categories: strongly agree, agree, maybe, disagree, or strongly disagree. All of the beginning-level participants either agreed or strongly agreed that they wanted to improve their pronunciation and wanted their teachers to teach pronunciation. The majority also indicated that they wanted feedback on their pronunciation and valued their teachers' corrections, whether they occurred in private, in small groups in class, or even in front of the class when other class members could hear what the teacher said.

Without Pronunciation Instruction, Improvement May Be Limited

Research tells us that it may be difficult for many beginners to improve their pronunciation without explicit pronunciation instruction. As part of a larger longitudinal study, Derwing, Thomson, & Munro (2006) reported on the progress of 40 beginning-level learners from Mandarin and Slavic (Russian and Ukrainian) language backgrounds over a 10-month period while they attended a full-time ESL program for newcomers to Canada. Pronunciation instruction was not specifically emphasized in this program, and changes in pronunciation over the period of the study were found to be minimal. Listeners, who were native speakers of Canadian English, were asked to rate samples of the learners' connected speech collected on three different occasions: at the onset of the study, after two months, and after ten months. Their ratings for accent, from 1 (no accent) to 7 (very strong accent), indicated that for both groups of learners there was very little change in accentedness over time. In addition, on each of the three different occasions, the majority of the learners themselves reported dissatisfaction with their pronunciation skills.

Derwing, Munro, & Thomson (2008) looked at, among other things, the development of comprehensibility over time in 32 of the same group of learners who were followed up on one year later in the longitudinal study. A different group of listeners, again native speakers of Canadian English, rated samples of the learners' connected speech collected over a period of 22 months on three different occasions: 2 months and 10 months after the onset of the study, and then one year after that. The ratings for comprehensibility, from 1 (very easy to understand) to 7 (extremely difficult to understand), showed that although the learners from Slavic language backgrounds had become easier to understand over this period of time, those from a Mandarin language background made no such improvement. The comprehensibility of the Slavic group improved from two months to ten months but showed no further improvement from then on, while that of the Mandarin group did not change at all over the 22-month period. It seems, therefore, that in the absence of formal pronunciation instruction, improvement in pronunciation was not guaranteed for the learners in this study. Such findings highlight the importance of pronunciation instruction for beginning-level learners.

Beginning-Level Learners Can Improve with Pronunciation Instruction

Studies that look at the effect of different approaches to teaching English pronunciation have chiefly investigated gains among intermediate or higher-level learners, and the findings have largely supported the benefits of explicit pronunciation instruction for learners at these levels (see, for example, Couper, 2006, 2011; Derwing, Munro, & Wiebe, 1997, 1998; Hincks & Edlund, 2009; Saito, 2011; Saito & Lyster, 2012; Tanner & Landon, 2009). In contrast, learners at lower levels of proficiency have received little attention in the research literature. However, a number of studies by individual teachers using an action research approach (see Burns, 2010) have illustrated how important and powerful attention to pronunciation can be for beginning-level learners.

The action research study by Hambling (2009) noted above documented an experienced teacher's increasing awareness of the kind of instruction her beginning-level learners needed in order to feel satisfied that they were learning how to speak English. Another action research study conducted by Springall (2002), also a teacher with the AMEP, focused on the kinds of pronunciation activities that would both be useful and fit comfortably within the competence of a group of 21 beginning-level migrant learners from nine different language backgrounds and a range of socio-educational backgrounds. Her study not only found that beginners needed and enjoyed pronunciation instruction, but also that they could be introduced to a basic pronunciation metalanguage for extending their understanding of how English pronunciation works and how it differs from the pronunciation of their languages. As part of the study, Springall devised materials and activities designed to develop the learners' awareness of key pronunciation features including individual sounds, syllables and stress, sentence stress and rhythm, linking, and vocal expression (i.e., the use of intonation for the expression of different feelings). Pronunciation instruction was integrated into the regular twelve-hour per week beginning-level curriculum for nine weeks and included the following:

- activities to raise awareness of pronunciation features
- both a segmental and suprasegmental focus
- activities and practice that were sometimes explicit (i.e., the focus on pronunciation was overt), sometimes implicit (i.e., the focus on pronunciation was present but not obvious), and sometimes incidental (i.e., attention to the pronunciation feature had not been planned, rather the feature surfaced in the context of the lesson).

From the diary Springall kept of her activities and reflections, it is clear that initial student reaction to an explicit focus on pronunciation varied. At first, some learners were mystified by concepts such as a set of symbols to represent sound rather than spelling (i.e., the International Phonetic Alphabet or IPA), whereas those who had had prior exposure to the idea of an IPA were relieved to re-connect with it and immediately found it helpful. By the end of the course, however, the whole class felt comfortable with the new pronunciation concepts and terms they were learning, and were able to accurately complete a worksheet demonstrating their understanding of the metalanguage that had been presented (see Figure 2.2). Springall found that, although learners were not consistently able to apply all they had learned in spontaneous speech, improvement was evident in their awareness of sound-spelling relationships and in their understanding of how various features of pronunciation worked.

The findings from Springall's action research study are important because they illustrate how pronunciation teaching and learning involve much more than the concrete, measureable gains in the production of particular sounds or features that are more often the focus

FIGURE 2.2. Basic Pronunciation Terms and Concepts—Student Worksheet (from Springall, 2002)

letters	• • ● • • **na-tion-AL-i-ty**
vowels	Some meat and some eggs and some fish la LA la la LA la la LA
consonants	**abcdefghijklmnopqrst uvwxyz**
sounds	ba–na–na = 3 tel-e-vi-sion = 4
syllables	**What‿is‿it?**
word stress	B C D F G H J K L M N P Q R S T W X Y Z
rhythm	happy/sad/ excited/angry/ bored
linking	A E I O U
voice-expression	/tʃ/ /dʒ/ /iː/[1] /θ/ /e/[2]

[1] /iː/ is also represented as /iy/
[2] /e/ is also represented as /ɛ/.

of studies designed to investigate the benefits of instruction (e.g., Couper, 2006, 2011; Derwing, Munro, & Wiebe, 1997, 1998). While measurable improvement is, of course, important, it is underpinned by gains in understanding and confidence that are not as easy to measure. If pronunciation learning is to have lasting effects, the learning—particularly for adults—must encompass more than mechanical expertise. This means that, besides being explicit, instruction should allow students to play an active part in their own learning and facilitate understanding without recourse to long theoretical explanations that intimidate and bore learners and teachers alike. Action research studies such as Springall's, if tackled in an integrated and student-sensitive way, highlight how beginning-level learners—even older learners without strong educational backgrounds—can enjoy and benefit from consistent, explicit attention to pronunciation. Specific activities that worked well with this group are discussed in the next section.

What We Can Do

As we have indicated, pronunciation can and should be taught in beginning-level classes and can be usefully integrated into the curriculum at that level. Advice on exactly what should be taught and when varies. This is hardly surprising. Learners, teachers, and contexts vary enormously, so there is unlikely to be one size that fits all. What is critical is that the approach to teaching pronunciation is systematic and that pronunciation instruction becomes an integral part of the process of learning English from the very beginning.

1. Take a systematic approach to pronunciation instruction.

As with the teaching of other aspects of English, it is important that the approach we take when teaching pronunciation allows learners to advance through a series of developmental stages so that they have ample opportunity to practice at a level they can handle before moving

TABLE 2.1: A Systematic Approach to Pronunciation Instruction

Stage of Development	Aims
1. Listening and awareness	**To develop learners' awareness of the target pronunciation feature and how it differs from the feature in the L1.** Learners need this exposure in order to discover the physical and perceptual aspects of the target English sound or pattern. At this stage learners might, for example, develop their ability to identify words that start with the target sound, words that have the same stress pattern, or words that are emphasized in a particular phrase.
2. Control	**To develop learners' physical control over the pronunciation of the target feature.** At this stage learners might, for example, work on a particular sound at the beginning of words, the production of words with a particular stress pattern, or the emphasis of the appropriate word in a phrase.
3. Practice	**To develop learners' ability to produce the target feature in a range of different and increasingly difficult structured contexts.** For example, learners might start by practicing a pronunciation feature in single words and then progress to pronouncing that feature in short phrases and then longer sentences.
4. Extension	**To develop learners' ability to apply their new skills in a range of contexts.** At this stage, learners might practice the target sound or pattern in somewhat less structured activities such as answering questions or participating in short scripted dialogues. They might then progress to using that feature in slightly more spontaneous classroom contexts (e.g., asking for directions, making appointments, or participating in everyday conversations).

on to the next. Table 2.1 presents a systematic sequence from Yates & Zielinski (2009, 2011) that recognizes stages in the acquisition of a new feature of pronunciation. Sample activities that are effective with beginners at each of the stages are provided later in this section.

2. Separate written practice from spoken practice.

When conducting speaking/pronunciation activities like those in Table 2.1, it is important to remember the differences between written and spoken language. Depending on the context and the activity, we vary vocabulary and grammatical structure when we speak and when we write. For that reason, care should be taken that spoken language, including pronunciation, is taught as a spoken skill and not confused with learning to read or write. Practicing reading aloud, for example, while useful for developing sound-symbol relationships, is not the same thing as learning to use pronunciation in spoken communication. Vocabulary teaching is another example. Although most learners eventually want to know how to write a new item of vocabulary, they also need to know how to perceive the word when spoken by others and how to say it intelligibly. But literate learners, particularly those who have been formally educated, are often so keen to learn the written form of the word that they miss the opportunity to hear the word spoken or practice saying it themselves. Teachers and learners alike can be tempted to rush straight for the board or the book without taking the time to learn it as a spoken item in its own right. This does not help with the development of their pronunciation since once learners have seen a word written down, there is a tendency for them to pronounce it as it is spelled or say it using the sounds of the letters as they would be pronounced in their L1, rather than being guided by the rhythms and sounds of the L2. Consider, for example, how misleading it is for learners to be guided by the spelling of words like *comfortable* or *taught*.

It is therefore important that when focusing on pronunciation, the activity types in Table 2.1 are conducted as far as possible without too much reference to the written word. When practicing basic dialogues, for example, ask learners to listen without reading and practice speaking without relying on written text. In this way, they will learn to trust their ears and develop not only a sense of the musicality of English but also the confidence to launch out into the interactive world of speaking without relying on written text. Be warned: learners may resist at first because they are so familiar learning a language through reading and writing. But it is well worth persevering, and soon learners will be taking the lead and learning this way by themselves.

3. Use different modalities to demonstrate features of pronunciation.

Beginning-level adult learners may find it difficult to hear particular features of English pronunciation and may not understand how these characteristics differ from those in their first languages. As we move through the stages of instruction in Table 2.1, it is therefore useful to demonstrate features of speech in ways that do not rely entirely on "listening carefully" to a model. Techniques that tap into the auditory, visual, and kinaesthetic modalities call attention to aspects of English pronunciation that might otherwise go unnoticed. For example, stretching a rubber band on the stressed syllable of a word highlights the fact that length or duration is a primary component of English stress. More techniques of this type can be found in Table 2.2 and in Yates & Zielinski (2009).

4. Provide targeted feedback.

As noted earlier, Baker (2011) found that the beginning-level learners in her study wanted feedback from their teachers on their pronunciation and liked being corrected, even if this occurred within earshot of their classmates. It is crucial that we provide feedback for beginners sensitively and judiciously so that we don't undermine their confidence. Students need to know when their pronunciation is intelligible and when it is not. If they do need to change some aspect of their pronunciation, they need to know *what* to change and how to change it. Feedback therefore needs to be targeted to the learners' needs. For example, students in learning to produce words with a particular stress pattern (e.g., *to-MA-to; po-TA-to*) might have different challenges at the *control* stage of development. Some students might misplace stress (e.g., *TO-ma-to; PO-ta-to*) and need feedback on the syllable that receives primary stress, whereas other students in the same class might produce all syllables with equal stress and need feedback on how to make English stressed syllables relatively longer than unstressed ones.

TABLE 2.2: Techniques for Demonstrating Stress Patterns in Words (adapted from Yates & Zielinski, 2009)

Stage of Development	Technique	Modality and Examples
1. Listening and awareness	When providing examples of target words, students listen to the teacher and watch the accompanying movements. They observe the teacher using movement (e.g., clapping, snapping the fingers, tapping the desk, stretching a rubber band, taking a step, opening a fist, etc.) to correspond with the production of stressed syllables in the words	Visual/Auditory. For example, the teacher closes fist next to face and opens fist when saying the stressed syllable in va-CA-tion.
	Stress patterns of target words are represented using dots or Cuisenaire rods above the syllables.	Visual. For example: • ● • to MA to
2. Control	Learners use movement to correspond with stressed syllables of the target words.	Visual/Kinesthetic. For example, the learner stretches a rubber band and watches movement while saying the word and stressing the appropriate syllable in va-CA-tion.
	Learners use dots or Cuisenaire rods as a guide to the stress patterns of the target words as they say them aloud.	Visual. • ● • va CA tion
3. Practice	Learners practice using the target words in context. At first, stressed syllables might be capitalized, marked with dots, or accompanied by movement (as described above), but cueing decreases as students progress.	Auditory/Visual/Kinesthetic
4. Extension	Learners use words in less structured activities such as dialogues or role plays. The teacher uses various modalities to provide reminders or feedback to the learners if they have difficulty with particular stress patterns. Learners might also use various multimodality techniques to reinforce stress patterns for themselves as they practice words in different contexts.	Auditory/Visual/Kinesthetic

Feedback also needs to be systematic and relevant to the learners' stage of development. That means if learners are at a control stage of instruction, expecting error-free production in spontaneous speech would be unrealistic. Plus, in order for feedback to be effective, teachers need to limit comments and corrections to features that have been taught rather than to those learners may not yet have covered in their English lessons and therefore may not be familiar with.

When providing feedback to beginners, it is useful to think in terms of both immediate and delayed feedback—that is, to decide when to comment immediately on pronunciation strengths and weaknesses and when to overlook phonological form and return to it later. For example, at the control or practice stage, when a new word has just been introduced or the class is revisiting an item that has recently been taught and practiced, it may be useful to give immediate, explicit feedback because the student stands a reasonable chance of remembering the correct pronunciation and will no doubt take pride in improving his or her production. On the other hand, at the extension stage, if learners have been constructing their own dialogues and are performing them in front of the class with some trepidation, we would be ill-advised to shatter their confidence or potentially embarrass them in front of the class by drawing attention to incorrect pronunciations. However, there may be some scope for providing delayed feedback on previously taught issues when the rest of the class is usefully engaged in another activity. Both approaches to providing feedback have their advantages and disadvantages, and the successful learner usually benefits from both to some extent.

Of course, learners respond differently to feedback on their pronunciation. While some readily accept and incorporate teacher feedback, others—often those more timid about speaking in groups—may be less than enthralled by such direct feedback. Learners also vary in how precise and accurate they would like to be in the way they pronounce English. Some like to speak regardless of any errors they may make; others will not speak until they are confident that what they are going to say is completely accurate. Ultimately, successful teachers know their students and are best able to judge when an intervention is likely to be useful and when it may be counter-productive.

When providing feedback to beginning-level learners about their pronunciation attempts, it is useful to have a common language—a way of referring to or talking about different features of pronunciation. As discussed earlier, Springall (2002) successfully introduced a metalanguage to her beginners so they had a shared understanding of different features of pronunciation. In addition, teachers can provide feedback to beginning-level learners by cueing correction non-verbally through gestures, hand signals, auditory cues (e.g., tapping, clapping) and written symbols. In fact, any of the techniques in Table 2.2 can be used to provide feedback on learners' attempts. As an alternative to those techniques, teachers and learners can devise their own prompts for feedback purposes. For example, a teacher may notice that several students in the class are not stressing the right syllable in a word or phrase and indicate the problem by making a strong downward fist movement on the appropriate syllable to be stressed. Beginning-level students soon get the implication of these invented and sometimes idiosyncratic gestures and usually enjoy working out the desired responses.

5. Integrate pronunciation into every lesson and always have a pronunciation goal.

One way to ensure that we consistently include pronunciation instruction in our classes is to always have a pronunciation goal in mind, regardless of what we are teaching. Integrating pronunciation is most effectively achieved when the selected pronunciation target relates to our learners' needs and occurs naturally in the particular classroom activity. Some classroom activities are more suited to pronunciation instruction opportunities than others. For example, introducing new vocabulary for beginner topics (e.g., health, public transport, personal information, etc.) is compatible with teaching stress patterns in words because students need to learn the stress pattern for every new multi-syllable word they acquire. Table 2.3 illustrates a systematic approach

TABLE 2.3: Incorporating Pronunciation Instruction into a Typical Beginning-Level Classroom Activity: Learning New Vocabulary

Class activity: Dialogue with new vocabulary (buying vegetables in a small shop) Pronunciation goal: Stress patterns in words	
Stage of Development	**Suggested Activities**
1. Listening and awareness	Teacher uses props / pictures for the different items that learners can ask to purchase (e.g., cucumber, broccoli, tomato, potato, artichoke). Learners listen to teacher say each item. Teacher emphasizes the stressed syllable in some (non-written) way while saying each word out loud, for example, by patterns of claps with a loud clap on the stressed syllable, etc. Learners direct teacher to place items / pictures in one of two groups depending on their stress pattern, as in: ● **●** ● (to-MA-to, po-TA-to) **●** ● ● (AR-ti-choke, CU-cum-ber)
2. Control	Learners say the words in each group out loud following the teacher's model (using movement or visual cues for additional support as needed). Learners say the words out loud without the teacher's model and without the items grouped by stress patterns.
3. Practice	Learners listen to dialogue prompts and practice short utterances in the dialogue (e.g., *Can I have a . . . please?*).
4. Extension	Learners act out the dialogue making their own choices as to which item they are ordering, first in closed pairs and then in front of the class. Learners think of other items that can be bought and suggest which stress pattern grouping they should go into. In groups, learners consider the stress patterns of items found in a different kind of shop and then role play a similar dialogue, with different sets of vocabulary but with a continuing focus on stress in words.

to integrating a focus on word-level stress into the teaching and learning of new vocabulary.

In contrast to the shopping activity in Table 2.3, a reading and writing task like completing a form with personal information does not seem, on the surface, particularly conducive to pronunciation practice. Such an activity does, however, provide the perfect opportunity to raise awareness of stress patterns in words and short phrases and practice exchanging personal information in spoken English using those stress patterns in ways they might outside the classroom. A pronunciation activity from Yates (2002) that could be integrated with the written personal information is presented in Figure 2.3.

By developing our beginning-level learners' pronunciation along with other aspects of their English, we are not only making it more rel-

FIGURE 2.3: Practicing Word Stress while Exchanging Personal Information (adapted from Yates, 2000)

Names/places
The teacher writes his/her name on a card and marks the stress pattern. For example:

Jacky

Then the learners each take a card, write their names, work out the stress pattern, and mark the stress on the card. For example:

Maria

When the cards are completed, the students find classmates whose names have the same pattern and stand in groups by stress patterns.. Then they secure the cards to a whiteboard under headings of the stress patterns (● ●/● ● ● and so on). The class can repeat the activity with the names of neighborhoods.

Extension: The teacher and learners throw a beanbag around the circle. The person holding the beanbag tells the class his or her name and where she or he lives. (I'm _____ . I live in _____.)

evant, but we are also providing learners with a sound foundation on which to build their future English language learning.

6. Use activities that have proven successful with beginning-level adult learners.

Springall (2002) found a range of activities successful in tackling different aspects of pronunciation with her beginners. Some were designed to raise awareness, and others provided the opportunity to reinforce and practice pronunciation features that had previously been covered in class. Since beginners may find some of the new sounds they encounter in English confusing—particularly the vowels—Springall found it useful to select a "sound of the week"—that is, a particular consonant or vowel sound that was the focus of instruction in any one week. She was able to introduce symbols representing the sounds using an IPA wall chart without overwhelming the students because she focused on only one or, at most, two sounds at a time, starting with sounds that were not too problematic and working toward sounds that she judged from her experience to be more challenging as the course progressed. Here are various ways teachers can encourage learners to focus on the "sound of the week" in conjunction with other classroom vocabulary/activities:

- Say a group of words that learners are familiar with and that have one sound in common and ask the class to work out what it is (for example, *ship, Lynda, little,* etc.). Learners can then think of their own words containing this sound. They will need plenty of opportunity to listen to the sound being said before they will be able to say it accurately themselves either in isolation or in a word. (See Field, Myth 3, for additional practice with segmentals at the word level.)

- Put learners into groups and ask them to brainstorm as many words as they can in two minutes with the sound(s) of the week. If your class enjoys competition, you can award one point for each word and bonus points for words containing two target sounds. Learners can then write them up on the board, and the class can check the meanings of the words, their pronunciations, and how to use them in simple sentences.
- Give small groups sets of simple written words with one word in each list that does not have the sound of the week (for example, *ship, Lynda, (line)*). Each group has to circle the odd word out and explain why it does not belong.

Additional activities that teachers have found useful with beginners can be found in online resources developed through the AMEP Research Centre in Australia (Yates, 2002; Yates & Zielinski, 2009). Because there is insufficient space to describe these in detail, representative suggestions are included in Table 2.4.

Whatever the activity, central to the success of pronunciation instruction is the value placed on intelligibility in the classroom. Without clear models and clear feedback on pronunciation, it will be difficult for learners to understand how they need to modify their speech in order to be intelligible in the world outside the classroom. And intelligibility is particularly important for beginning-level learners. If they cannot make the few words that they know in English intelligible to others, they will lose confidence and motivation. The challenge for teachers is therefore to integrate pronunciation into every class in ways that are systematic (but non-threatening), engaging, and confidence-building so that the students will be motivated to improve their pronunciation throughout their learning.

TABLE 2.4: Useful Activities for Pronunciation Instruction with Beginning-Level Learners

Activity Type	Pronunciation Feature	Brief Description
Matching games	word stress	Learners match stress patterns to words that they hear (or see). Stress patterns to be matched can be clapped by teacher (one clap for each syllable with louder claps on the stressed syllable) or presented visually in the form of small dots for unstressed syllables and large dots for stressed syllables.
Stepping out	rhythm	Learners decide which words are stressed in a phrase they are practicing. Holding hands, they step forward together as they say each stress in the phrase. For the phrase, *What time are they coming?* (e.g., what TIME are they COMing), students would step in synchrony with TIME and COM.
Sound stories	sounds	Teacher tells a short story in which the sound of the week frequently occurs. For example, if the sound of the week is /ɜ:/ (as in g__ir__l and sh__ir__t), a sample story might begin as follows: "The girl in the blue shirt was the first in the world to learn the song. She . . . ." Learners identify the sound. Then in small groups, they make up their own stories/sentences using the same sound. Groups can compete both in composing a story and in saying it correctly.
I went to the store *. . .*	final sounds	A theme-based activity with a focus on final sounds in words begins with the following prompt: *I went to the store and I bought _____.*" The first student fills in the blank (e.g., *a cat*), and the next student chooses a word that starts with the final sound of the previous word (e.g., __t__omato), and so on around the class.

References

Baker, A. A. (2011). *Pronunciation pedagogy: Second language teacher cognition and practice.* Unpublished doctoral dissertation, Georgia State University, Atlanta.

Burns, A. (2010). *Doing action research in English language teaching: A guide for practitioners.* New York: Routledge.

Chela-Flores, B. (2001). Pronunciation and language learning: An integrative approach. *International Review of Applied Linguistics in Language Teaching, 39*(2), 85–101.

Couper, G. (2006). The short and long-term effects of pronunciation instruction. *Prospect, 21*(1), 46–66.

Couper, G. (2011). What makes pronunciation teaching work? Testing for the effect of two variables: Socially constructed metalanguage and critical listening. *Language Awareness, 20*(3), 159–182.

Darcy, I., Ewert, D., & Lidster, R. (2012). Bringing pronunciation instruction back into the classroom: An ESL teachers' pronunciation "toolbox." In J. Levis & K. LeVelle (Eds.). *Proceedings of the 3rd Pronunciation in Second Langauge Learning and Teaching Conference,* (pp. 93–108). Ames: Iowa State University. Retrieved from: http://jlevis.public.iastate.edu/Proceedingsfrom3rdPSLLT%20up dated.pdf

Derwing, T. M., Munro, M. J., & Thomson, R. I. (2008). A longitudinal study of ESL learners' fluency and comprehensibility development. *Applied Linguistics, 29*(3), 359–380.

Derwing, T. M., Munro, M. J., & Wiebe, G. (1997). Pronunciation instruction for "fossilized" learners. Can it help? *Applied Language Learning, 8*(2), 217–235.

Derwing, T. M., Munro, M. J., & Wiebe, G. (1998). Evidence in favor of a broad framework for pronunciation instruction. *Language Learning, 48*(3), 393–410.

Derwing, T. M., Thomson, R. I., & Munro, M. J. (2006). English pronunciation and fluency development in Mandarin and Slavic speakers. *System, 34*(2), 183–193.

Foote, J. A., Holtby, A. K., & Derwing, T. M. (2011). Survey of the teaching of pronunciation in adult ESL programs in Canada, 2010. *TESL Canada Journal 29*(1), 1–22.

Fraser, H. (2000). Coordinating improvements in pronunciation teaching for adult learners of English as a second language. Canberra: Department of Education, Training and Youth Affairs (Australian National Training Authority Adult Literacy National Project).

Hambling, V. (2009). We want to speak. Paper presented at the AMEP Research Centre National Forum, Macquarie University, NSW, Australia. Available at: www.ameprc.mq.edu.au/events/ameprc_national_forums/2009_forum_3

Hincks, R., & Edlund, J. (2009). Promoting increased pitch variation in oral presentations with transient visual feedback. *Language Learning & Technology, 13*(3), 32–50.

Saito, K. (2011). Examining the role of explicit phonetic instruction in native-like and comprehensible pronunciation development: An instructed SLA approach to L2 phonology. *Language Awareness, 20*(1), 45–59.

Saito, K., & Lyster, R. (2012). Effects of form-focused instruction and corrective feedback on L2 pronunciation development of /ɹ/ by Japanese learners of English. *Language Learning 62*(2), 595–633.

Springall, J. (2002). *Pronunciation project*. Unpublished manuscript.

Tanner, M.W., & Landon, M.M. (2009). The effects of computer-assisted pronunciation readings on ESL learners' use of pausing, stress, intonation, and overall comprehensibility. *Language Learning & Technology, 13*(3), 51–65.

Yates, L. (2002). *Fact sheet—Teaching pronunciation: Approaches and activities*. Sydney, Australia: AMEP Research Centre, Macquarie University. Retrieved from http://www.ameprc.mq.edu.au/resources/amep_fact_sheets

Yates, L. (2010). Language training and settlement success. Sydney: AMEP Research Centre.

Yates, L. (2011). Language, interaction and social inclusion in early settlement, *International Journal of Bilingual Education and Bilingualism, 14*(4), 457–471.

Yates, L., & Zielinski, B. (2009). Give it a go: Teaching pronunciation to adults. Sydney: AMEP Research Centre. Retrieved from www.ameprc. mq.edu.au/__data/assets/pdf_file/0011/157664/interactive_sm

Yates, L., & Zielinski, B. (2011). Teaching English pronunciation for adult learners. Eight reasons not to teach pronunciation (and why they are all wrong). In H.P. Widodo & A. Cirocki (Eds.), *Innovation and creativity in ELT methodology* (pp. 109–120). New York: Nova Science Publishers.

Zielinski, B. (2011). The social impact of pronunciation difficulties: Confidence and willingness to speak. Paper presented at the 3rd Pronunciation in Second Language Learning and Teaching Conference, September 2011, Ames, IA.

Zielinski, B. (2012). The social impact of pronunciation difficulties: Confidence and willingness to speak. In J. Levis & K. LeVelle (Eds.). *Proceedings of the 3rd pronunciation in second langauge learning and teaching conference* (pp. 18–26). Ames: Iowa State University. Retrieved from: http://jlevis.public.iastate.edu/Proceedingsfrom3rd PSLLT%20updated.pdf

Pronunciation teaching has to establish in the minds of language learners a set of distinct consonant and vowel sounds.

John Field
CRELLA, University of Bedfordshire, U.K.

In the Real World

Consider this real-life encounter between a waitress and four diners in a restaurant in an English-speaking country: The waitress is a native speaker of Russian who has been working in the restaurant for some three months. Her English is heavily influenced by her first language, and three of the four diners cannot understand what she says to them about the dishes on the menu. The fourth, who happens to be a specialist in the teaching of ESL/EFL, has to act as interpreter. After this problematic start, the diners order, and the waitress has no difficulty taking down what they want.

   This simple incident raises issues that are of importance to pronunciation instructors but tend to get sidelined or overlooked. Let us first consider the TESOL specialist. What is it that enables him (none other than the author of this chapter) to understand the Russian-accented English of the waitress when his friends cannot? One could say that he has a trained ear that is sensitive to the sounds of speech across languages and across speakers. More concretely, he has been exposed to many speakers of Russian origin through his work, and, over a period of time, has learned to decode what they say. The interesting questions are: What form does that knowledge take? How long did it take him to acquire it? How many Russian speakers of English did he need to meet before he accommodated to their speech?

Now—and more to the point—consider the waitress. She has been exposed daily to native speakers of English; indeed, she has had far greater exposure than a student learning English in an EFL classroom would have. She is capable of understanding native speakers in order to take their orders and respond to their enquiries, but her English is not intelligible to them. Is it possible that she does not hear the sounds of English distinctively enough to reproduce them? That she does not 'notice' (Schmidt & Frota, 1986) the difference between the sounds she produces and those that native speakers produce? Or is it that she has two systems: one for the sounds that others utter and one for the sounds that she utters herself?

This simple example has drawn attention to an area of pronunciation teaching that is largely neglected in teacher manuals. We tend to take it for granted that the first step in introducing learners to the speech sounds (phonemes) of a new language is ear training in distinguishing the sounds. We also tend to take it for granted that this ear training (possibly accompanied by the demonstration of mouth positions) will enable learners to internalise the sounds so that they can make them for themselves. But these assumptions beg two important questions.

Firstly, what is it that we expect learners to store in their minds during ear training? Surely it has to be more than an echo of the teacher's voice, which is likely to be short-lived? Does repetition help? And is it safe to assume that, as a result of instruction or exposure to the second language, learners will end up storing a set of precise phonemes in their minds to which they can refer?

Secondly, how confident are we that storing a phoneme in the mind in some way enables the learner to recognise it when it is heard again in connected speech? How confident can we be that this stored memory will assist the learner in producing it? The case of the waitress suggests that the first may not necessarily lead to the second.

The purpose of this chapter is not to question the importance of familiarising learners with the phonemes of a second language. To be sure, there are other features of pronunciation that need to be taught—especially suprasegmental features such as stress and intonation; but ensuring that learners are able to identify and produce the sounds of the language is an obvious priority. The aspect of the myth that is questioned here is the idea that we can firmly establish these phonemes in the minds of learners. Precisely what are the consonant and vowel sounds that they have to internalise when acquiring the sound system of an L2? And how do they manage to store them in such a way that they can recognise them and produce them when called upon to do so?

What the Research Says

Traditional phonology tells us that what a learner has to acquire is not a set of individual sounds, but a complete system, in which sounds operate in contrast (Cruttenden, 2008). It is a question not just of mastering sounds such as /p/ and /b/ in isolation, but also of mastering the distinction between them. This is true in speaking, where a learner has to recognise the different timings and configurations of the articulators (tongue, lips, jaw, vocal cords, soft palate) that produce the target sounds. It is similarly true in listening, where the learner has to learn to distinguish *pill* from *bill* and *cap* from *cab*. The acquisition process is not problematic if a similar contrast exists in the learner's L1, but it is indeed difficult if one of the two sounds is not present in it. Taking Arabic as an example, standard dialects of the language have the sound

/b/ but not the sound /p/. An Arabic-speaking listener is accustomed to accepting quite a wide range of sounds as /b/, and, in learning English, faces the task of redistributing these sounds between /b/ and /p/.

A learner of English as a second language thus has to internalize, not simply the separate sounds of the English system, as the myth suggests, but also the contrasts between the sounds. As already noted, ear training has traditionally formed an important part of this process. It is assumed that the first step in pronunciation instruction is to learn to identify the sounds when they are heard, and that being able to distinguish them from each other assists the learner in reproducing them. There is a lot of sense in this. When we speak, even in our L1, we monitor what we say to ensure that it conforms to what we planned and gets our intended meaning across (Levelt, 1989). In principle, L2 learners have the same mechanism available to compare their pronunciation of a word against their recall of how the word is pronounced by an expert speaker of the language. But, of course, this only works if their record of the spoken form of the word is an accurate one.

Many teachers conclude, quite reasonably, that the best way of establishing the sounds of a second language in the minds of a group of learners is to demonstrate each in turn, contrasting them where necessary. We no longer feel obliged to demonstrate all the phonemes of the target language as some teachers did 50 years ago. Instead, we focus on those that are not present in the learners' first language and, within them, those that are most easily confused.

Unfortunately, this operation is not quite as straightforward as it seems. Firstly, many consonants cannot be pronounced in isolation. This is true of plosives such as /p/ and /b/, of fricatives such as /f/, and of affricates such as /tʃ/ (the initial sound of *choose*), which have to be uttered with a weak schwa sound after them: [pə, bə, fə, tʃə]. The only way one can demonstrate them is within a word; hence the widespread use of minimal pairs (Cruttenden, 2008) to contrast easily confused sounds: *pea/bee, pin/bin, pack/back*. But here already established practice raises issues of representation. When instructors use minimal pairs in this way, precisely what is it that they expect learners to store: a recall of the phonemes that differentiate the words or a recall of entire words with the phonemes in them? Teacher's manuals tend to assume the former.

This is where a second complication comes in. The fact is that phonemes (whether vowels or consonants) do not have a standard form. They vary according to where in a syllable or word they occur. The /p/ in *pot* is not quite the same as the /p/ in *top*: The first is likely to be more strongly aspirated (followed by a brief puff of air—[pʰ]) than the second. Phonemes also vary according to the sound that precedes them and the sound that comes after them—a phenomenon known as co-articulation and the inevitable result of a speaker moving his/her articulators as efficiently as possible from one position to another. Try saying *keep-card* several times and compare the position of your tongue when making the initial /k/ sound. You will note that it changes, anticipating the vowel that comes after it. In short, there is no such thing as a single form for /k/ in English. To make matters worse, the /k/ in *card* approximates to a sound which, in Arabic, is a distinct sound in its own right (/q/) and in contrast with /k/. Similarly, Thai treats the [pʰ] at the beginning of *pin* as a different sound from the [p] at the end of *top*.

Once researchers were able to represent speech on the printed page by means of spectrograms, they discovered another uncomfortable fact. Phonemes do not just influence their neighbours within the syllable; they blend together. The word *this* does not consist of three separate units: /ð/ + /ɪ/ + /s/. The features that mark out each phoneme overlap with those of adjacent ones (Delattre, Liberman, & Cooper, 1955).

What this demonstrates is that it is wrong to think of the material we use for phoneme practice as a set of stable sounds. To fully acquire the English consonant sound /k/, learners have to come across it at the beginning, middle, and end of words (*can, packet, back*) and before different vowels, including those made at the front of the mouth (*kid, keep*) and those at the back (*card, coop*). Something similar can be said for vowels, which are partly shaped by the consonants that occur before and after them within a syllable. They can be subject to nasalisation when they are preceded by /m/ and /n/ in words like *meet* or *neat* or followed by /m/, /n/ and /ŋ/ (*ham, ran, rang*). They can also vary in duration according to the consonant that follows (compare the length of the vowel sounds in *hard* and *heart*).

The point at issue is that ear-training has to accustom L2 learners not just to a single unique form of a phoneme as the myth of our title suggests, but to a range of sounds that can represent a phoneme. An expert English listener recognises the sound at the beginning of *cook* as equivalent to the rather different sounds at the beginning of *kick* and at the ends of both words. A novice listener may not.

But the variability of phonemes raises an even bigger and more intractable question for pronunciation teachers. It is clear that the process of acquiring pronunciation in a new language cannot be anything as simple as the type of mastery suggested by the myth. What precisely is it that the language learners learn when they acquire the ability to recognise a new sound in the L2? What kind of information do they need to store in their minds? These questions are very rarely asked in manuals for language instructors—leaving some uncertainty about what it is that pronunciation classes aim to achieve. Teachers become reliant upon protracted modelling of L2 sounds in the belief that practice will make perfect.

Research on Standard Phonemes

The limited discussion of these issues in the TESOL domain is curious because a great deal of work on precisely this area has been done by speech scientists and cognitive psychologists over the past 60 years. In the early days of listening studies, researchers considered two possible solutions for how an L1 speaker manages to recognise phonemes despite multiple forms. They were based on the kinds of assumptions that tend to be made about the phoneme in second language contexts:

- *Theory A.* Although phonemes vary a great deal, any example of a given phoneme has characteristics that distinguish it from all others.

- *Theory B*. We store a set of 'ideal' phonemes in the mind, against which to match what we hear.

If either of these theories could be demonstrated, they would support the received view among many instructors of ESL/EFL that learners can be taught to recognise certain basic distinguishing features of the sounds of a language and that these features can then be stored in the learner's memory. Let us examine what the researchers discovered.

THEORY A: ALL VARIANTS OF A GIVEN PHONEME HAVE CERTAIN FEATURES IN COMMON.

It is important to realise that the raw speech reaching the listener's ear is not a string of phonemes but a series of acoustic cues that the listener has to match to phonemes. It would seem logical that each phoneme of the language is associated with a particular combination of these cues—making the set associated with the phoneme /k/, for example, quite distinct from the set associated with any other. This was the assumption that underlay much of the early work on L1 speech perception at the Haskins Laboratories at Yale University. Researchers (e.g., Liberman, 1957) made use of synthesised speech that enabled them to manipulate the cues in a piece of speech, deleting some and preserving others. They analysed the acoustic features of a number of English phonemes but could not find any which were exclusive to one phoneme and not present in the realisations of at least one of the others. To complicate the situation further, it was later discovered that our recognition of phonemes is partly influenced by the speed at which somebody is speaking (Miller, 1981). By splicing words said at a slow speech rate into a piece of fast speech and vice versa, it was discovered that a sound that is taken to be /b/ in a fast speaker is heard as /w/ in a slower one (Miller & Liberman, 1979).

It was also discovered that consonants and vowels are processed differently. Consonants are perceived categorically: in other words, listeners make quite sharp distinctions between them. Again using synthesised (or artifically produced) speech, researchers (Abramson & Lister, 1967) were able to create a continuum of sounds that went from a clear example of /pa/ to a clear example of /ba/. They discovered that there was a point between the two at which there was a high level of agreement between the listeners that they had stopped hearing /pa/ and had begun to hear /ba/.

The situation with vowels was found to be quite different. What distinguishes vowels is a set of three formants, or bands of intensity at different frequencies. But, of course, every speaker's voice is different in terms of its pitch level. Peterson & Barney (1952) tracked the position of the first (lowest) and second (next to lowest) formant in a range of American English vowels spoken by 33 men, 28 women, and 15 children. They found that the formants varied enormously in their frequencies. The redeeming feature was that the relationship between the first formant and the second remains relatively constant. If the first formant is high, the second will be high in proportion. It is this relationship that seemed to provide a key to how we identify vowels across different speakers. The point is that a particular vowel has no constant value, as is commonly thought; it can simply be characterised as falling within a general area. In addition, listeners, quite early on in a conversation, have to establish a benchmark frequency level for a speaker's voice to assist them in recognising vowels accurately.

What all these findings demonstrate very conclusively is that there is no simple one-to-one match between a group of acoustic cues and a phoneme in the language. It would seem that a checklist approach to the presentation of phonemes will not suffice—especially if it is linked to the notion of learners committing a system of sounds to memory.

THEORY B: WE STORE A SET OF IDEAL PHONEMES IN THE MIND.

Much advice given to L2 pronunciation instructors appears to be based on the established idea that listeners deal with the various forms of a given phoneme by comparing what they actually hear against some kind of 'ideal' version of the phoneme in their minds. On this assumption, listeners recognise the sounds of a language by cancelling out any features that appear to be unusual and going for the best phoneme match to what they have heard. If one adopts this view, then pronunciation training should aim to ensure that L2 learners construct a set of these templates at an early stage. Instructors might present standard[1] versions of phonemes along the lines of the citation forms used by vocabulary teachers. In this way, they lay down models against which natural speech can be matched.

A more nuanced argument might draw on the notion of a *prototype* (Rosch, 1975). The L2 learner (or indeed the child acquiring its first language) is exposed to multiple examples of a particular phoneme in many different contexts and many different voices and speech rates and, gradually, from these experiences, constructs some kind of central version against which he/she can in future match all variants. Such an account goes a long way toward explaining how we manage to recognise vowels. There is some supporting evidence in that L1 listeners find it easier to distinguish between two non-standard forms of a vowel than between a non-standard one and one they earlier characterised as a 'good' example of the vowel (Kuhl & Iverson, 1995). See Pickett (1999, pp. 249–255) for a detailed discussion.

The attraction of any template account is that it is very economical in terms of how much has to be stored in the mind—just one prototype per phoneme. Conversely, it is quite demanding in the operation required of the listener, who needs to make a series of judgments about how closely each real-life speech sound matches one of these prototypes. As we shall see, thinking has now rather moved on, as neuroscientists have gained more and more evidence that the human mind has much more storage capacity than was previously assumed but is quite slow to perform elaborate local operations like making comparisons.

Another argument against the template idea is that the variation caused by co-articulation is not random: Much of the variation in the sound of the /k/ in *car* is caused by the /aː/[2] sound that follows, and much of the variation in the /aː/ is caused by the /k/ that precedes it. So is it not making rather heavy weather of the operation to assume that these phonemes have to be matched individually against an idealised version, regardless of their context? As Nygaard and Pisoni (1995) put

---

[1] Term taken from Wells, 1982, pp. 280–283, and Cruttenden, 2008, p. 78.

[2] /aː/ represents the vowel sound in *car*, where /r/ is dropped in certain post-vocalic positions and the vowel is lengthened.

it: "It appears that no one unit can be processed without consideration of the context in which it is embedded" (p. 67).

Research on More Recent Theories

Researchers have therefore moved on to three rather different theories about how we manage to recognise the sounds of our own language or those of a foreign one. They have not, to be sure, come up with a clear and definitive solution (for a review of the difficulties of accounting for speech perception, see Nygaard & Pisoni, 1995), but each of the possible theories deserves mention as each has different implications for the way in which we present the sounds of an L2 to learners. These theories, and the evidence that supports them, form the basis of the discussion that follows.

- *Theory C.* We do not use the phoneme as a unit of representation when we listen.
- *Theory D.* The phoneme is one of several cues that serve to identify words, and perhaps not the most important.
- *Theory E.* Our minds store many variants of each phoneme heard in different contexts and different voices.

THEORY C: THE PHONEME DOES NOT EXIST AS A UNIT OF REPRESENTATION IN OUR MINDS.

Some commentators have suggested that the solution to the variability of the phoneme is that listeners do not use the phoneme at all when they are analysing a piece of spoken input, or may only use it when particular attention is needed to what has been said. This is not as radical as it might seem. As Coleman (2002) points out, students of phonology usually experience difficulty in recognising how many sounds are represented by a written form such as *x* as in *fix* (corresponding to the two phonemes /ks/) or *ng* as in *sing* and *ch* as in *chair*.

Evidence supporting the idea that the phoneme may not play a part in how we normally analyse speech comes from a study of

Portuguese illiterates (Morais et al., 1979) who were asked to perform a simple phoneme manipulation task. To give an English equivalent, they were asked what word would remain if they took away the /g/ sound at the beginning of the word *gold*. Many of them proved to be incapable of doing this, suggesting that our awareness of phonemes may be the product of acquiring literacy rather than part of our listening ability that is present from infancy onward. This finding has been supported by several recent neurological studies of individuals performing a task that involves listening for the occurrence of a particular phoneme in a piece of speech. These studies (e.g., Mummery et al., 1996; Zattore et al., 1996) show that the task activates an area of the brain that is often associated with speech production but not usually with speech perception. In addition, brain imaging evidence from Démonet, Thierry, & Nespoulos (2002) indicates that deconstructing a nonsense word into its consonants and vowels is a slower task than connecting spoken input to a word in one's vocabulary. This suggests that a listener has to first access the word before being able to identify its phonemes, rather than the other way around.

Instead of the phoneme, it has been argued that listeners use a larger unit such as the demi-syllable[3] (Dupoux, 1993), the syllable (Mehler et al., 1981), or even the word or clause (McNeill & Lindig, 1973). The syllable presents a particularly attractive option. It is a much more constant unit than the phoneme, which, as we have seen, varies according to adjacent phonemes. Information at the syllable level plays an important part in dividing up connected speech; for example, in English, stressed syllables provide important cues to where each new content word begins (Cutler, 1990). Grosjean & Gee (1987) even suggest that stressed syllables provide a vital cue to identifying content words—that is, /sɪl/ would be an important key to recognising the word *SYLLable* and /zi:n/[4] would serve the same function for *magaZINE*.

---

[3] A syllable can be divided into its onset and rime, with a word like *train* providing *trai + ain*.

[4] /i:/ is also represented as /iy/.

The number of syllables in any language is more limited than one might suppose. It has been calculated that for French a set of 6,000 could represent the entire vocabulary (Cerf et al., 1989). Partial syllables would be even more efficient as a unit, requiring perhaps 2,000 forms in French (Dupoux, 1993). Coleman (2002) calculates that there are 1,409 possible phoneme pairs in English that potentially form parts of a syllable and argues that L1 listeners have learned over time to recognise the likelihood of any two phonemes occurring together in a syllable, as opposed to on either side of a syllable boundary.

One solution to the doubtful status of the phoneme might thus be for pronunciation instructors to focus much more heavily on high-frequency syllables as units of perception and articulation rather than on individual sounds.

THEORY D: THE PHONEME IS ONE OF SEVERAL CUES THAT SERVE TO IDENTIFY WORDS, AND IT IS PERHAPS NOT THE MOST IMPORTANT CUE.

There is a small problem with the analysis just presented. The syllable in English is not as neatly bounded a unit as it is in some other languages such as French. Consider the English word *lemon*. It is very difficult to tell whether the middle phoneme /m/ belongs to the first syllable or the second. Indeed, it appears to belong to both: /lem/[5] + /mən/. This feature (known as ambisyllabicity) affects only a small number of words, but it rather complicates matters if we want to think of the syllable as a consistent and reliable unit when L1 or L2 listeners are mapping from speech to words. Some words like *lemon*, it seems, have to be handled in terms of a larger unit than the syllable.

In addition, not all of the evidence supporting the role of the syllable has been unequivocal. Research in the 1970s and 1980s (Mehler, 1981; Segui, 1984) appeared to demonstrate that listeners responded faster to syllable-sized units in speech than to phonemes, but doubt was cast by other research that showed similar effects for words and even phrases. For a review, see Goldinger & Azuma, 2003, pp. 306–307.

---

[5] /e/ is also represented as /ɛ/.

A criticism sometimes levelled against these studies is that they tended to focus listener attention at the particular level of analysis they were interested in and so may have ended up getting the results that they expected.

This suggests another possible solution: It may be that the syllable is just one unit among several to which the listener is sensitive. Current models of how we recognise words in connected speech assume that L1 listeners draw on a variety of different cues (see McQueen, 2007, for an overview). Instead of building words phoneme by phoneme, as we tend to assume, a listener takes account simultaneously of incoming information at the level of the phoneme, the syllable, the whole word, and the lexical chunk. The listener also uses the knowledge that particular phonemes very often occur together and draws on world knowledge, the general context, and the surrounding words. The accumulating evidence suggests a number of possible word matches for what has been heard (some of them likely candidates and others less likely). The possibilities are then reduced to one when one of them emerges as the most strongly supported. All of this happens, of course, very rapidly.

How does this work in practice, given that an utterance reaches our ears over a period of time? It seems that we process speech as we hear it at a delay of about a quarter of a second behind a speaker (Marlsen-Wilson, 1975). A quarter of a second is about the length of a syllable, but it has been demonstrated (Pollack & Pickett, 1963) that, if syllables and even words are excised out of a piece of natural speech, listeners often fail to recognise them. What seems to happen is that we hear a syllable and make a first guess as to what it is (and even what word it belongs to); we then revise the guess when we hear the next syllable and the next. It may take several syllables before we are sure of what the speaker has said so far (Grosjean, 1985). Viewed this way, listening is a very tentative process, where we are constantly adjusting what we think we have heard.

This process particularly makes use of larger units such as the word and the lexical chunk to overcome problems with smaller ones. Field (2008a) explains it as follows:

Let us suppose that you hear somebody say the word *veshtables* ['veʃtəblz] and succeed in matching it to a word in your vocabulary. How did you do it? If you had proceeded in a bottom-up way you would have been fazed by the presence of the unexpected sound [ʃ]. To resolve the issue, you might have drawn on co-text, for example: *cabbages, carrots and other*. . . . Or you might have drawn on context (the fact that you are in a greengrocer's or ordering a meal in a restaurant). But you might equally well have drawn upon your knowledge of a familiar chunk of language (*fruit and vegetables*) or just of the word *vegetables*. You might even have drawn on the knowledge that the syllable *vesh* is not used in English . . . all of [these examples] involve using larger units to resolve a decoding problem that concerns a smaller one in the form of the unorthodox sound [ʃ]. (p. 133)

This explanation has been quoted at some length because it illustrates the important fact that a failure of phoneme-level pronunciation or a failure to recognise a phoneme may not be a major obstacle to communication. Findings from research suggest that, up to at least intermediate level, second language listeners have a strong tendency to listen out for units at word level—even if it involves overruling phonological evidence. Field (2008b) reported on data obtained during a paused transcription task, in which participants transcribed the last five words heard whenever there was a pause in a recording. Confronted with an unknown word, one third of respondents ignored both phoneme-level evidence and contextual evidence and instead made a rough match with a known word. Similar findings were obtained in a recent protocol study of test takers' behaviour in an international test of listening (Field, 2012), where 13 out of 20 respondents reported relying on words because they were perceptually salient, regardless of the fact that they did not constitute appropriate answers to the test items.

This reliance on word-level matching, often approximate, is partly the by-product of tasks such as transcription and gap-filling, but it also appears to be prevalent in less constrained listening conditions. Because the phoneme varies so much and because L2 phonology is insufficiently familiar, it seems that learners do not trust their perceptual skills in relation to smaller units of language. Instead, they prefer to rely on a unit that they regard as more constant and that they learned as a discrete form—namely, the word. The conclusion for a pronunciation instructor is that it may be more useful to focus on word-level recognition and even to incorporate a degree of pronunciation practice into the teaching of oral vocabulary than to dwell too long on phoneme-level inventories. The problem here, of course, is that word units are themselves subject to variation and are very often assimilated to adjoining words or heavily reduced if they are not prominent in an utterance. This suggests the value of ear-training practice in relation to an even larger unit than the word, namely the recurrent lexical chunk (*just a moment, on the other hand, couldn't help it*, etc.)

It might seem that the discussion has moved rather far from the traditional content of programs that train learners to produce the individual sounds of a second language. But the point is that the sounds of speech are so variable that it may only be through learning to identify them in larger units that the learner can come to terms with the many different forms a particular phoneme is likely to take. The lexical chunk and the syntactic chunk (*I should have done/I wish I'd known/I'd have liked to*) are phonological phenomena as well as useful groups of words. By training learners to recognise and produce them, one is embedding that inconstant feature, the phoneme, in an environment where it is much less subject to variation.

THEORY E: OUR MINDS STORE MANY VARIANTS OF EACH PHONEME HEARD IN DIFFERENT CONTEXTS AND DIFFERENT VOICES.

At the outset, it was suggested that the biggest challenge to the myth of simply learning to recognise and produce a set of discrete L2 consonants and vowels lies in the fact that in any language these sounds vary enormously according to where they occur in the word and according to the sounds that occur before and after them. It is also worth noting that they vary in the mouths of different speakers—reflecting the fundamental pitch of the speaker's voice (clearly there is a big difference between male and female and infant speakers), the rate of speech, the formality of the context, and the speaker's accent. We have not yet fully addressed the question of how it is that we manage to store these elusive forms in our minds, whether we are acquiring our first language as an infant or whether we are acquiring a second language.

An interesting recent development in the way science views the operations of the human mind may help to shed some light. Researchers have come to realise that our minds are enormous storage devices and capable of holding much more than was previously supposed. Conversely, those minds do not seem to operate quite as rapidly when handling pieces of information as was once assumed. For an excellent discussion of the issues, see Dąbrovska (2004, pp. 17–27). This insight calls into question the template view discussed in Theory B, which is based on the idea that we need to minimise the information we need to hold in the mind, even if that means a complex editing operation.

Taking account of this, psychologists of language have increasingly argued that, instead of storing a single perfect version of a phoneme (or even a word) in our minds, we store a very large number of examples encountered over the years. Those examples will have occurred in different contexts, but they will also have occurred in different voices. What this enables us to do is to map directly from an example of a phoneme or word in speech to a memory of having heard that phoneme or word spoken in the same way before. See Bybee (2001) for a well-argued and comprehensive account of how this multiple trace theory can be applied to our understanding of phonology. For applications to L2 listening, see Field (2008a, pp. 165–167).

The scenario just suggested may sound improbable. But it is a more plausible way than any other of accounting for how we recognise phonemes despite their many different forms and despite the many different voices in which we hear them. It also accounts for the way we are able to adjust to unfamiliar varieties of our own language. Many individuals report that there are certain accents of their L1 that they have great difficulty in understanding. What seems to make the difference is being exposed, over time, to multiple speakers of that variety. In terms of the theory just outlined, this entails laying down traces of voices speaking with the accent in question, to which listeners can refer on future occasions when they encounter it.

Here, the implications for the teacher of pronunciation are rather different from those associated with some of the other theories examined. This multiple trace account places weight on exposing learners to the phonemes of a second language in many different realisations. Teachers will need to rethink the received wisdom that learners must spend a lot of time internalising the sound system of the target language in the form of 'pure' phonemes. They will also need to recognise the limitations of learning and storing words in their citation forms. A primary requirement will be for the listener to encounter the same words in a wide range of contexts and voices.

The precept is well supported by experimental findings from Pisoni, Lively, & Logan (1994). They demonstrated that exposing language learners to multiple examples is especially helpful with consonants because it makes it easier for them to form robust categories of the kind that were discussed at the outset (e.g., the sharp distinction between /pa/ and /ba/). Pisoni et al. also demonstrated that pronunciation training of this kind was more effective if it involved labelling the variant forms that were heard (i.e., identifying one stimulus as containing /p/ and one as containing /b/ in the way a minimal pairs task would demand) rather than simply saying whether they were the same or different.

However, a note of caution is needed. In recent years, there has been a great deal of pressure on teachers and testers to introduce a range of varieties of the second language into their listening programs (see, e.g., the *ELT Journal* discussion between Jenkins and Taylor, 2006). In general, the arguments put forward have not been underpinned by any established body of theory or evidence as to how the ability to understand different varieties is acquired. If one accepts the multiple trace version of events, then it suggests that it is more demanding and more time consuming than is generally supposed for L2 learners to lay down traces of the phoneme system of even a single variety of English.

It would seem advisable to postpone the introduction of others until at least the intermediate level. We also need to recognise that the receptive acquisition of a new variety of a second language will take place over some time and only by dint of sustained exposure. From this point of view, it is arguably unfair to test learners at lower levels on their ability to recognise varieties other than two or three standard ones (General American, Australian, General British RP[6]) or the variety of the community within which the learner is studying.

What We Can Do . . .

In sum, the current state of theory lends support to three different ways of looking at the acquisition of the vowels and consonants of the second language. Let us briefly consider how each might enable teachers to add usefully to their present range of pronunciation tasks. In line with much of the discussion in this chapter, the suggestions for activities relate specifically to ear training as the first step in familiarising learners with English sounds, syllables and words. They are drawn from or based upon Field (2008a), where further auditory exercises of this type will be found.

1. Focus practice at the level of the syllable.

Theory C (the reliable unit view) indicates the value of focusing pronunciation practice at the level of the monosyllabic word or the syllable, since these units are not subject to the same variation as the phoneme. Some doubt was cast earlier upon research that claimed to show that the syllable is used as a unit of analysis. However, recent studies (e.g., Cholin, Levelt, & Schiller, 2006) have demonstrated that L1 speakers recognise and assemble the frequent syllables of their language more easily than the infrequent ones. So there is certainly value in exposing L2 learners to them.

---

[6] Term taken from Wells, 1982, pp. 280–283, and Cruttenden, 2008, p. 78.

Possible exercises include the following;

- Rime recognition. In addition to practising minimal pairs, the teacher dictates rimes that are highly frequent in the target language and asks learners first to write them and then to suggest known words of which they are part. English has common rimes ending in /p/, /t/, /d/, /k/, /f/ /v/, /s/, /z/, and /n/. By way of example, those ending in /t/ include:

Rimes	Common Words
/aɪt/[7]	*night, might, fight*
/eɪt/	*great, date, late, weight, wait*
/ɔt/	*taught, thought*
/ot/	*coat, vote*
/iːt/	*feet, meet, compete*

- Syllable recognition. Instead of practising individual phonemes, the teacher dictates the most common syllables of English. Learners try to write them. They then read them aloud and indicate whether they form complete words or suggest words that include them. English syllables fall into several patterns; those within the most frequent words (more than 500 in the spoken corpus of Leech, Wrayson, & Wilson, 2001) are listed:

	One-Syllable Words	Multi-Syllable Words
VC:	*in, up, out*	*oth(er), on(ly)*
CV:	*no/know, go, now, too, see, say, so*	*peo(ple), rea(lly)*
CVC:	*here, there, where, then, get, said, mean, right, which, time, like, come, put, not, good, need*	*(be)cause, some(thing), nev(er), mon(ey), sev(eral), num(ber), diff(erent)*
CVCC:	*want, think, last*	
CCVC:	*still*	*twen(ty), prob(ably)*

---

[7] /aɪt/, /eɪt/, /ot/, and /iːt/ are also represented as /ayt/, /eyt/, /owt/, and /iyt/.

The recognition and production of more complex and less frequent patterns (see Roach, 2008, Chap. 8) can be practised at higher levels.

- Stressed syllables. Teacher tells students that sometimes a stressed syllable is the only part of a word that a listener hears clearly. Students listen to the teacher saying stressed syllables and guess what the full word is. The box shows the stressed syllable and the word students should say.

[*Initial syllable*] /twen/ (twenty) /mɔ:n/ (morning), /brek/ (breakfast), /nʌm/ (number), / mʌŋ/ (monkey), /dɪs/ (distant / distance)

[*Internal or final syllable*] /mem/ (remember), /hæps/ (perhaps), /twi:n/ (between), /nʌf/ (enough)

---

2. Take instruction beyond the syllable level.

While there is certainly value in syllable level practice, we noted above that syllable boundaries in English are not always clear-cut. This led us to a second position. Theory D (the 'cue-trading' view) sees word recognition as based upon information at several levels (phoneme, syllable, word, etc.). It suggests the usefulness of hearing and practising larger units (the word and the lexical and syntactic chunk) where phoneme forms are embedded in familiar co-texts. Here are some exercises that take us beyond syllable level.

- **Word activation.** Learners are told that they will hear a recording on a certain general knowledge topic. They are asked to predict the words they will hear; the teacher writes the words on the board. Learners then listen to the recording. They do not need to understand

everything in the recording; all they have to do is to
note if and how often the predicted words occur.
Where the class disagrees, teacher replays parts of the
recording.

- **Gap filling.** The teacher gives students a transcript in
  which complete lexical chunks or syntactic chunks of
  up to five words have been omitted. Students listen to
  the recording and fill in the missing words. Examples
  of commonly occurring lexical chunks include lexical
  phrases such as *instead of, so long as, anything else, on the
  other hand, quarter past (three), in other words, from time
  to time,* or *in a hurry.* They include collocations such as
  heavy smoker or *low frequency noise;* they also include
  complete expressions like *I can't get used to it* or *I'm
  running short of money* and (at higher levels) metaphors
  and idioms such as *burn the candle at both ends, What
  did you make of the film?* or *can't get his head round the
  problem.* Examples of commonly occurring syntactic
  chunks are *should have done, I wish I'd known, if you ask
  me, I wouldn't have thought, took (hours) to do, spent
  (hours) doing, had (the car) repaired,* etc.
- **Focus on chunks.** Similarly, after a general listening
  lesson using an authentic recording, the teacher should
  replay sections of the recording that contain lexical and
  syntactic chunks that occur frequently in natural
  speech. Learners are asked to transcribe these chunks
  and then to practice saying them. Examples are: fixed
  formulae (*You all right?*), longer fillers (*do you know
  what I mean?*), and syntactic patterns (*I should have
  done*). Examples of some highly reduced formulaic
  chunks appear in the Appendix.
- **Identifying function words within a group.** Learners
  often find it hard to recognise and reproduce
  unstressed syllables, especially those that represent
  function words. The teacher dictates a phrase or sen-

tence and asks learners to write only the prominent stressed words (e.g., *box match*). The teacher then repeats the phrase or sentence, and learners add in function words (e.g., *box of matches*) and learners add in function words. Examples are given.

BOX of MATCHes	PLACes in SPAIN
WAITed at HOME	WANTed to KNOW
WENT to the BANK	PIECes of CAKE
LOOKing at the SKY	RULES for DRIVers
GUESSes the TIME	The GLASS is BROKen.

3. Expose learners to a variety of contexts, voices, and accents.

Perhaps the most persuasive of the three accounts presented here of how L2 pronunciation is stored in the mind is Theory E (the multiple-trace view). This theory highlights the importance of exposing learners to a very wide range of contexts and voices, in order to ensure that multiple traces are established, to which they can later refer.

A multiple-trace view would seem to endorse the use of the traditional approach to listening instruction, using mid-length recordings that feature a range of voices and contexts. But we must recognise that there needs to be more to this type of exercise than just answering comprehension questions. We need to be sensitive to the fact that learners need time and support to adjust to new voices that they have not heard before. We need to vary recordings not just in terms of topic but also in terms of speech rate, voice pitch, regularity of delivery, and the precision with which the speaker is speaking. Within listening practice, we need to provide replays so that listeners can come to terms with features such as these, going beyond the information that is being conveyed. One way of achieving this is to ask learners to transcribe short sections of a recording; another is to give them a transcript towards the end of a listening lesson so that they can match to words any passages they find difficult. In the early stages of listening instruction, it is also useful to play examples of the same set of sentences said by different speakers (e.g., three or four colleagues) at different speeds. Learners should first report what they have heard and then imitate the speakers.

The most important message of all to be derived from the multiple trace view is perhaps that the acquisition of a repertoire of voices, styles of speech and accents takes time. Field (2008a) suggests a gradual progression in the demands imposed by speakers, beginning with a reliance on the voice of the teacher and building up variety in voices and styles before variety in accents. But the quantity of exposure to L2 should also be increased. With the availability of downloadable MP3 files and with an enormous choice of spoken material on the internet, instructors now have the opportunity to extend listening practice by assigning homework and by encouraging learners to listen autonomously. By stepping up exposure in this way, we enable learners to lay down memories of words and phrases in L2, said in various ways in various contexts by various voices. Those memories will assist their ability to recognise words in future—and feed into their ability to produce the words within their own connected speech.

The discussion of this myth has raised a curtain upon the insufficiently discussed issue of how second language learners represent the phoneme system of the L2 in their minds. The reader will draw his or her own conclusions, but the point should be made that it is Theories D and E that are most strongly supported by psycholinguistic thinking. It is also those two viewpoints that are most likely to encourage teachers to rethink some of their priorities when introducing learners to the sounds of a second language.

References

Abramson, A.S., & Lister, L. (1967). Discrimination along the voicing continuum: Cross language tests. Status report on speech research. Stanford, CT: Haskins Laboratories.

Bybee, J. (2001). *Phonology and language use*. Cambridge, U.K.: Cambridge University Press.

Cerf, H., Danon, T., Derouault, A.M., El Beze, M., & Merialdo, B. (1989). Speech recognition in French with a very large dictionary. *Proceedings of Eurospeech, 89,* 150–153.

Cholin, J., Levelt, E.J.M., & Schiller, N.O. (2006) Effects of syllable frequency in speech production. *Cognition, 99,* 205–235.

Coleman, J. (2002). Phonetic representations in the mental lexicon. In J. Durand & B. Lacks (Eds.), *Phonetics, phonology, and cognition* (pp. 96–130). Oxford, U.K.: Oxford University Press.

Cruttenden, A. (2008). *Gimson's introduction to the pronunciation of English* (7th ed.). London: Hodder Education.

Cutler, A. (1990). Exploring prosodic possibilities in speech segmentation. In G. T. M. Altmann (Ed.), *Cognitive models of speech processing* (pp. 105–121). Cambridge: MIT Press.

Dąbrovska, E. (2004). *Language, mind and brain.* Edinburgh: Edinburgh University Press.

Delattre, P., Liberman, A.M., & Cooper, F. (1955). Acoustic loci and transitional cues for consonants. *Journal of the Acoustical Society of America, 27,* 769–773.

Démonet, J.-F., Thierry, G., & Nespoulous, J.-L. (2002). Towards imaging the neural correlates of language functions. In J. Durand & B. Laks (Eds.), *Phonetics, phonology, and cognition* (pp. 244–253). Oxford, U.K.: Oxford University Press.

Dupoux , E. (1993). The time course of prelexical processing: The syllabic hypothesis revisited. In G. Altmann & R. Shillcock (Eds.), *Cognitive models of speech processing* (pp. 81–111). Hove, U.K.: Lawrence Erlbaum.

Field, J. (2004). An insight into listeners' problems: Too much bottom-up or too much top-down? *System, 32,* 363–377.

Field, J. (2008a). *Listening in the language classroom.* Cambridge, U.K.: Cambridge University Press.

Field, J. (2008b). The L2 listener: Type or individual? *Working papers in English and applied linguistics in honour of Gillian Brown* (pp. 11–32). Cambridge, U.K.: RCEAL.

Field, J. (2012). The cognitive validity of the CAE listening test as a predictor of academic performance. Internal report. Cambridge, U.K.: Cambridge ESOL Research and Validation Unit.

Goldinger, S.D., & Azuma, T. (2003). Puzzle solving science: The quest for units in speech perception. *Journal of Phonetics, 31,* 305–320.

Grosjean, F. (1985). The recognition of words after their acoustic offset: Evidence and implications. *Perception and Psychophysics, 38,* 299–310.

Grosjean, F., and Gee, J. (1987). Prosody structure and spoken word recognition. *Cognition, 25,* 135–155.

Jenkins, J. (2006). The spread of EIL: A testing time for testers. *ELT Journal, 60*(1), 42–50.

Kuhl, P.K., & Iversen, P. (1995). Linguistic experience and the perceptual magnet effect. In W. Strange (Ed.), *Speech perception and linguistic experience: Theoretical and methodological issues in cross language speech research* (pp.121–154). Baltimore, MD: York.

Leech, G., Wrayson, P., & Wilson, A. (2001). *Word frequencies in written and spoken English.* London: Longman.

Levelt, W. J. M. (1989). *Speaking.* Cambridge: MIT Press.

Levelt, W. J. M., & Wheeldon, L. (1994). Do speakers have access to a mental syllabary? *Cognition, 50,* 239–269.

Liberman, A. M. (1957). Some results of research on speech perception. *Journal of the Acoustical Society, 29,* 117–123.

Marlsen-Wilson, W. D. (1975). Sentence perception as an interactive parallel process. *Science, 189,* 226–228.

McNeill, D., & Lindig, K. (1973). The perceptual reality of phonemes, syllables, words and sentences. *Journal of Verbal Learning and Verbal Behavior, 12,* 419–430.

McQueen, J. (2007). Eight questions about spoken word recognition. In G. Gaskell (Ed.), *The Oxford handbook of psycholinguistics* (pp. 37–54). Oxford, U.K.: Oxford University Press.

Mehler, J. (1981). The role of syllables in speech processing. *Philosophical Transactions of the Royal Society of London, Series B, 295,* 333–352.

Mehler, J., Dommergues, J. Y., Frauenfelder, U., & Segui, J. (1981). The syllable's role in speech segmentation. *Journal of Verbal Learning & Verbal Behaviour, 20*, 298–305.

Miller, J.L., & Liberman, A. M. (1979). Some effects of later occurring information on the perception of stop consonant and semivowel. *Perception and Psychophysics, 25*, 457–465.

Miller, J.L. (1981). Effects of speaking rate on segmental distinctions. In P. D. Eimas & J. L. Miller (Eds.), *Perspectives on the study of speech* (pp. 39–74). Hillsdale, NJ: Lawrence Erlbaum.

Morais, J., Carey, L., Alegria, J., & Bertelson, P. (1979). Does awareness of speech as a sequence of phonemes arise spontaneously? *Cognition, 50*, 323–331.

Mummery, C. J., Paterson, K., Hodges, J. R., & Wise, R. J. S. (1996). Generating 'Tiger' as an animal name or a word beginning with T: Differences in brain activation. *Proceedings of the Royal Society of London, B263*, 989–995.

Nygaard, L. C., & Pisoni, D. B. (1995). Speech perception: New directions in research and theory. In J. L. Miller and P. D. Eimas (Eds.), *Speech, language and communication* (pp. 63–96). San Diego: Academic Press.

Peterson, G.E., & Barney, H.L. (1952). Control methods used in a study of the vowels. *Journal of the Acoustical Society of America, 24*, 175–184.

Pickett, J. M. (1999) *The acoustics of speech communication*. Needham Heights, MA: Allyn & Bacon.

Pisoni, D. B., Lively, S. E., & Logan, J. S. (1994). Perceptual learning of nonnative speech contrasts: Implications for theories of speech perception. In J. Goodman & H. C. Nusbaum (Eds.), *Development of speech perception: The transition from recognizing speech sounds to spoken words* (pp. 121–166). Cambridge: MIT Press.

Pollack, I., & Pickett, J. M. (1963). The intelligibility of excerpts from conversation. *Language and Speech, 6*, 165–171.

Roach, P. (2000) *English phonetics and phonology*. Cambridge, U.K.: Cambridge University Press.

Rosch, E. H. (1975). Cognitive reference points. *Cognitive Psychology, 7,* 532–547.

Schmidt, R., & Frota, S. (1986). Developing basic conversational ability in a second language: A case study of an adult learner of Portuguese. In R. R. Day (Ed.), *Talking to learn: Conversation in second language acquisition* (pp. 237–326). Rowley, MA: Newbury House.

Segui, J. (1984). The syllable: A basic perceptual unit in speech processing. In H. Bulmer & D. G. Bauhaus (Eds.), *Attention and performance* (pp. 125–149). Hillsdale, NJ: Lawrence Erlbaum.

Taylor, L. (2006). The changing landscape of English: Implications for language assessment. *ELT Journal, 60(1),* 51–60.

Wells, J. (1982). *Accents of English 3: Beyond the British Isles.* Cambridge, U.K.: Cambridge University Press.

Zattore, R. J., Meyer, E., Gjedde, A., & Evans, A. C. (1996). PET studies of phonetic processing of speech: replication and re-analysis. *Cerebral Cortex, 6,* 21–30.

Appendix: Frequent Formulaic Chunks[8]

Standard	Reduced	Standard	Reduced
There isn't any	[ˈðɹɪznenɪ]	*Would you like*	[dʒəˈlaɪk]
got any	[ˈgɒtnɪ]	*How much*	[hʌˈmʌtʃ]
I've already	[vɔːˈredɪ]	*How are you?*	[haːˈjuː]
I don't know	[dəˈnəʊ]	*More and more*	[mɔːˈmɔː]
I'll be	[ˈʌbɪ]	*Just a moment*	[dʒəsˈməʊmənt]
Do you like	[dʒəˈlaɪk]	*in a week or two*	[nəwiːkətuː]
What do you mean?	[wɒdʒəˈmɪːn]	*Let's see*	[leˈsiː]
Half-past	[hʌˈpɑːs]	*Are you all right?*	[jəʊˈraɪ]
pair of	[ˈpeərə]	*If I were you*	[faɪwəˈjuː]
this morning	[ˈsmɔːnɪŋ]	*Never mind!*	[neˈmaɪn]

(Source: Field, 2008a, p. 156)

---

[8] The pronunciation of these formulaic chunks would vary according to speaker, situation, speed, and dialect.

Intonation is hard to teach.

Judy Gilbert
Author of Clear Speech

In the Real World

In the real world, pronunciation misunderstandings happen—sometimes funny and sometimes not. I've experienced many awkward language miscommunications, usually by unintentionally using the wrong word or sound in a word. But sometimes the misunderstanding is based on something different, something not easily recognized. Here are a few examples of this unrecognized problem.

Tom Scovel, a teacher who lived in Thailand for seven years, told me a story about his experience with a confusion that occurred because of intonation.

A Thai colleague had asked me why, when she told her American students to repeat the words in Thai for *three* and *four*, they said the first number correctly but always got *four* wrong. I explained to her that English speakers generally use a rising tone to check if they have gotten something right. On the other hand, Thai is a tone language. That means that each word has an identifying pitch pattern. The word for *three*, /saam/, has a rising tone, but the word for *four*, /sii/, has a low falling tone. Therefore, instead of saying *four*, they were actually saying *color*, which repeatedly baffled the Thai teacher.

A second story about intonation comes from Elcio de Souza, who teaches in Brazil. He wrote:

A couple of years ago, Phil, an American citizen, came to Brazil to visit a friend of his, Renato, who was also a friend of mine. We were all invited to a welcoming party on the day Phil arrived. Even though not everyone was very fluent, we held the party in English to make Phil feel part of the group. At one point, Phil mentioned he was going to drive to a nearby town to go surfing. One of our Brazilian friends (Marcos) was surprised [that] he had already rented a car given he'd just arrived in São Paulo and showed his surprise in his pre-intermediate English with this sentence: *Do you have a car?* Unfortunately, his intonation was 100% Brazilian. This is so different from English use of intonation that it made Phil think an insult was intended.

Phil was livid. He started lecturing Marcos on the fact that he could afford a vacation trip and that even if he had less money, it would be none of Marcos' business, etc. I quickly intervened and told him that Marcos was trying to show surprise at how organized Phil was because he had already rented a car and [had] planned a trip. I also said that Marcos had talked like that because of our Brazilian way of saying that sentence, which Phil was not aware of. Phil is not a teacher. Phil apologized, and Marcos said it was OK, but neither of them ever talked to each other again, although they did meet quite often during the two weeks that Phil was here.

Notice that Elcio pointed out that Phil is not a teacher, which may be why he didn't really accept Elcio's explanation. These are examples of why teachers need to know that misunderstandings caused by unrecognized signals can have serious results.

I have one story of my own, one that happened when I was having dinner with colleagues at a conference in Spain:

> I had asked the waiter what flavors of ice cream were available and he said in Spanish *Vainilla, Sabor Naranja* . . . I waited for the next flavor. He waited. The other people at our table waited. Finally, I realized that he had ended the list, but hadn't given me the signal I automatically waited for, which in English is a falling pitch meaning "end of list." I answered, but rather late.

From the beginning of my teaching, I generally understood the principle that providing the student with too many abstract concepts was counter-productive—that is, too much information tends to blur the specific teaching point. Most of us have experienced this at one time or another. So a fundamental pedagogical principle was lightening the workload, and that required setting priorities. We cannot teach everything we know about pronunciation, so what aspects are the highest priority?

What the Research Says

What Are the Priorities?

Reviewing the literature on the topic of intelligibility, I was struck by the repeated emphasis on the role of intonation (also referred to as prosody) in communication. In 1916, Alexander Graham Bell wrote: "Ordinary people who know nothing of phonetics or elocution may have difficulty in understanding slow speech composed of perfect elementary sounds, while they may have no difficulty in comprehending an imperfect gabble if only the accent and rhythm are natural" (p. 15). And 60 years later, Darwin (1976) said, "Prosody directs [the] listener's attention toward potentially informative parts of the speech stream and segments the stream into chunks that are then candidates for higher-level units of analysis" (p. 215).

In fact, research over the past fifteen years has begun to support the importance of intonation. In a recent study, Kang and Pickering (2011) compared native speaker judgments of the comprehensibility and oral proficiency of non-native speakers with computerized measures of prosodic features. They found that " . . . prosodic features play a significant role in listener ratings" (p. 4) and explained the role of prosody this way: "Listeners use prosodic cues to confirm if an item is new or one that they are already aware of, to track important information, and to predict when one topic is ending and another is beginning" (p. 6).

Hahn (2004) investigated the reactions of three groups of English-speaking undergraduates to a Korean-accented mini-lecture. The lecturer recorded three versions of the lecture with the primary sentence stress correct, incorrectly placed, or omitted entirely. Nothing else was changed. When Hahn tested the three groups for lecture comprehension, the subjects who heard the lecture with correct primary stress showed markedly better understanding. In addition, when the primary sentence stress was correct, subjects evaluated both the speech and the speaker significantly more favorably.

The importance of prosodic instruction is further supported by Derwing & Rossiter (2003), who studied the effects of different types of English pronunciation instruction. As part of that study, one group of students was instructed in segmentals (i.e., individual consonant and vowels sounds). They were taught to distinguish between English sounds and to produce these sounds as accurately as possible. Another group was primarily taught the prosodic features of English. They learned about the rhythm and melody of the spoken language and practiced using the prosodic signals that native speakers use to guide their listeners. Derwing & Rossiter (2003) commented: "We do not advocate eliminating segment-based instruction altogether, but, if the goal of pronunciation teaching is to help students become more understandable, then this study suggests that it should include a stronger emphasis on prosody" (p. 14).

Many researchers (Anderson-Hsieh, Johnson, & Koehler, 1992; Chun, 2002; Darwin, 1976; Derwing & Rossiter, 2002, 2003; Field, 2005; Nash, 1971) have found that mistakes in suprasegmentals (word stress, for instance) can have serious effects on communication, especially when there are other problems, like grammar errors.

Failure to learn the "musical signals" of English can also have serious social consequences. An example was described by Gumperz and Kaltman (1982) in a research report about communication breakdowns in a London cafeteria between speakers of Indian English serving the food and speakers of the local variety of British English being served. The source of the breakdown was the different way in which the two languages use intonation or pitch patterns. English uses a drop in pitch to indicate "This is the end of what I have to say." In contrast, speakers of some Indian languages use a drop in pitch to indicate that they are about ready to make their main point. The authors concluded that these dissimilarities in the meaning of prosody between the two languages can cause serious problems because listeners not only misunderstand the intent of the message but also tend to make categorical judgments concerning the other group. For example, the Indian speakers may question, "Why are those people always interrupting just when I am about to make my main point?" whereas the British speakers may ask, "Why are those people unable to get to the point?" This kind of confusion can result in conflicts between personalities, as people rarely recognize the source of the misunderstanding. The reason this source of trouble is rarely understood is because the basic signals of rhythm and melody specific to one's first language are generally learned by the time a child is one year old. After that, the brain has to focus on learning vocabulary and grammar. So from this age forward, people automatically assume these musical signals are a natural part of all human speech, but the truth is that systems of melody and rhythm (intonation) are specific to each language.

About this, Chun has written:

> Prosodic errors (in word stress, for instance) can also add an
> extra burden to communication. English speakers tend to store
> lexical [word] items according to stress patterns, so that if a
> wrong pattern is perceived, listeners' comprehension is hin-
> dered because they may spend time searching for stored words
> in the wrong category. (p.196)

While it remains true that we must also help students with segmentals, especially the final sounds that are grammar cues such as a
final /s/ or /z/ signaling *plurality* (e.g., *books*) or a final /t/ or /d/ signaling past tense (e.g., *planned* or *walked*), it is also true that without a
threshold level mastery of the English prosodic system, no amount of
drilling individual sounds will increase intelligibility. The prosody
actually affects how the sounds are made in "running" English speech.
For that reason, any error in intonation can affect both intelligibility
and listening comprehension. Brown (1990) points out the adverse
effects on listening comprehension:

> If a student is only exposed to carefully articulated English, he
> will have learnt to rely on acoustic signals which will be denied
> him when he encounters the normal English of native speak-
> ers. (p. 151)

This same point was most beautifully put by E.M. Forster (1924) in his
novel, *A Passage to India*: "A pause in the wrong place, an intonation
misunderstood, and a whole conversation went awry" (p. 274).

If Intonation Is So Important, Why Are Teachers So Uneasy about It?

When I tell people outside the profession that pronunciation has
been something of an orphan in English language teaching for
almost four decades, they are astonished. It doesn't seem reasonable.

Actually, it isn't reasonable, but it's a fact. I wanted to find out what caused this dumb (literally) condition, which has basically sidelined the spoken language for so long that generations of teachers find themselves ill-prepared to teach pronunciation. This subject is the focus of Murphy's Myth 7, so I will only say here that lack of training and general inaccessibility of research on pronunciation surely affects teachers' confidence. When it comes to the specific topic of intonation, however, there is quite another source of uneasiness. Are teachers' reluctant to teach intonation because it is hard to teach, as the myth suggests? Before providing practical suggestions about how to teach intonation, an inquiry into how this myth may have originated is in order.

In my opinion, traditional approaches to teaching intonation have not been teacher-friendly (or, for that matter, student-friendly). In fact, they have been inherently discouraging. These approaches have come in three main types: (A) technical rules based on grammar, (B) technical rules based on pitch levels, and (C) subjective rules based on intuitions about attitude.

DISCOURAGING APPROACH A: TECHNICAL RULES BASED ON GRAMMAR

Over the years, many textbooks have presented elaborate technical rules for intonation, some based on grammar. Here is an example of an explanation of a rule based on grammar from a teacher's resource book. (In the following statement, note that *tonicity* refers generally to intonational emphasis and *tonic* refers to the syllable with primary stress in the focus word, that is, the most important word in the sentence.)

> In transitive clause structure tonicity distinguishes extensive from intensive clauses, since an intensive complement always carries the tonic as unmarked information point . . . . (p. 143). In both positive and negative, system (22) operates as a subsystem of the tone 1 term, although, especially in negative imperative, its marked terms thus contrast with tone 1 or with tone 3. (Halliday, 1963, p.165)

You might suppose I have chosen an especially opaque example, but Halliday was the leading British intonation analyst at the time. At first, I was disheartened by my inability to understand this sort of explanation, but, when I came across some critiques of the approach by experts, I was encouraged. As it happened, I was not just being dense. Crystal (1969), reviewing Halliday's "Intonation and Grammar in British English" wrote:

> What Halliday, and indeed all of us, should be doing is not simply imposing discrete categories, but looking at how we distort intonation by imposing such categories; not just labeling meanings, but looking to see how we distort the meanings by labeling them, and making ourselves aware of the danger due to the use of such labels. (p. 392)

DISCOURAGING APPROACH B: TECHNICAL RULES BASED ON PITCH LEVELS

Some other traditional methods for teaching intonation have been based on numerical systems or pitch levels. In British teaching, this has been expressed in terms like this:

> The falling glide may start from the highest pitch of the speaking voice and fall to the lowest pitch (in the case of the *high-fall*), or from a mid-pitch to the lowest pitch (in the case of the *low-fall*), or with variations of starting point according to the intonation context. The falling glide is most perceptible when it takes place on a syllable containing a long vowel or diphthong or a voiced continuant. (Gimson, 1980, p. 266)

With reference to explanations of this type, Esler (1978), in an article comparing German and English intonation, made the following severe comment, followed by a footnote:

. . . the development of comparatively delicate description systems has been detrimental to the learning of English intonation
abroad because these description systems constitute a teaching
aim of their own. . . . A particularly bad case of counter-intuitive
notation is the number system used by Halliday, where numbers stand in abstracts for various phonetic types of tone movement. (fn: Although many or all English seminars [in Germany]
possess his course, I do not know of one instance where his
course is actually used.). (p. 42)

The American linguistic tradition has been somewhat different but
neither clearer nor more reassuring. When I started teaching ESL in the
1970s, we were being taught to describe intonation based on a system
of four pitch levels (see Trager & Smith, 1951), which students had to
learn to produce. Because I was unable to teach this system effectively,
I found this concept with its code-like numbering system just as discouraging as and no clearer than Halliday's or Gimson's analyses. So,
again, I was reassured to find that respectable authorities were beginning to express doubts about the practical utility of the system. For
instance, one review of the Trager-Smith system said this:

Anyone who has attempted to analyze or teach the English patterns of pitch and stress knows that competent observers may
vigorously disagree and that a single observer may disagree
with himself so often as to make secure confidence in his own
judgments painfully difficult. . . . (Sledd, 1955, p. 313)

Rather conclusive negative evidence of the theoretical validity of
numerical pitch levels was provided by Phillip Lieberman. In a 1967
study on intonation, he reported that two competent linguists . . . differed in 60 percent of the cases in which they were asked to transcribe
the pitch phonemes of various utterances. He concluded that "the same
pitch contours often have rather different meanings. . . . Surely, if linguists cannot agree on the assignment of pitch levels, we cannot expect
our students to do so, let alone imitate such sequences" (p. 124).

Prator and Robinette (1985), commenting about a similar system, said that "the chief weakness of this marking system (or of any marking system) appears to be that, unless it is well explained, it may give students the impression that English intonation is much less flexible than is really the case" (p. 45).

While I was wrestling with these ideas in 1978, I complained to the professor of my Acoustic Phonetics course, John Ohala, that I was baffled by the four pitch-level system of intonation analysis. "Why bother?" he said, casually, "No one's paid any attention to Trager-Smith for twenty years." This little exchange demonstrated the difference between his world of advanced research and my own world as an ESL teacher. It was clear that in *my* world, at *that* time, people did indeed pay attention to Trager-Smith; the analysis system was accepted as simply factual. My objection was a practical one: If I couldn't understand it, how could I teach it? Professor Ohala's remark, however, suggested a second objection to the approach: perhaps the analysis itself was unsound.

In that vein, Chun more recently (2002) pointed out that "when dealing with absolute levels, there is the problem of how to explain the phenomenon that sometimes very small pitch movements convey significant differences in meaning, whereas in other cases larger pitch differences carry no unusual meaning" (p. 31).

The sharpest objection to a mechanical approach to assigning pitch levels as a reliable way to study intonation appeared in an article written by Dwight Bolinger (1972). The article had the stinging title, "Accent Is Predictable (If You're a Mind Reader)." He insisted that intonation was spoken not by pitch levels, but by a gradient: a gradual rise or fall. More importantly, he further claimed that the choice of where to place the emphasis depended on the speaker's intention in a specific context, not on mechanical rules. So I stopped trying to teach pitch levels. More fundamentally, I discarded the whole approach of mechanically based rules. But then, what *was* intonation about? Feelings?

DISCOURAGING APPROACH C: SUBJECTIVE RULES BASED ON INTUITIONS ABOUT ATTITUDE

Aside from mechanical rules, another confusing concept is the use of rules connecting attitude and intonation. There is a long tradition of advice to teachers promoting this approach. Of course, it is intuitively obvious that attitude is reflected in intonation. For instance, it is very different to say "You're so smart!" with a tone of voice suggesting approval versus a tone suggesting anger. We all know this, and actors depend on such variable nuances of tone. But this approach can also cause complications when teaching pronunciation. Roach (1991) explained, as follows:

> . . . some have claimed that, unless the foreign learner learns the appropriate way to use intonation in a given situation, there is a risk that he or she may unintentionally give offense. . . . This misleading view of intonation must have caused unnecessary anxiety to many learners of the language. (p.164)

Here is an actual example of this type of anxiety-inducing approach to teaching:

> When we say *thank you*, the voice may go from a higher note to a lower one, or it may go from a lower note to a higher one and these two different tunes show two different attitudes: higher to lower means sincere gratitude; lower to higher means that the matter is purely routine. To confuse the two would clearly be dangerous. . . . (O'Connor, 1967, p. 138)

But when I started teaching, conveying attitude seemed a useful approach to intonation. So I earnestly set up the conditions for role plays, such as a dialogue between an angry parent and a bored teenager. It was enjoyable, but there was something peculiarly difficult about it. For one thing, it actually takes a lot of time, creativity, and explanation on the teacher's part to set up the emotional situation in which the various intonations might be used. This is partly because attitudes are often culturally or contextually dependent. In addition, because time is in short supply in most ESL/EFL classrooms, an activity that does not clearly get somewhere is a poor use of time. I concluded that the reason such an activity is not apt to achieve much that is transferrable to other situations is that the basic concept is wrong. There is no question about the significance of "tone of voice" in showing the speaker's attitude. Nonetheless, rules for showing attitude through intonation seem basically flawed. In fact, research has demonstrated that there is little reliable connection between intonation patterns and attitudes. The same intonation pattern can be connected with quite different meanings, such as surprise or indignation (Levelt, 1991; Stibbard, 2010). And on the other hand, different patterrns can express the very same attitudes. Recently, Stibbard (2010) investigated whether or not links existed between perceived suprasegmental/ prosodic features and perceived emotions. Listeners were asked to assign five basic emotions (anger, sadness, happiness, fear, and disgust) to recordings of free speech that had been analyzed for phonetic qualities. He reached these conclusions:

- The attempt to discover a speaker-independent relationship between speech sounds and emotions is ill-conceived.
- Speech sounds do not alone carry systematic, reliable cues sufficient to differentiate emotions.
- The vocal cues to emotional expression are more context-bound and specific to particular types of interaction than has previously been thought. (p. 1)

In commenting on a task from a student text that asked students to distinguish among polite contradiction, doubt, or simple contrast, Dalton & Seidlhofer (1994) commented as follows:

The extract seeks to demonstrate that in a specified context, a particular tone contour [pitch pattern] may be interpreted as conveying a particular attitude. It may be valuable to be able to do this, but there are also problems: above all, the attitudes or intentions of speakers are never signaled by intonation alone. Thus, the notion of politeness is bound to be relative and situation-specific. (p. 93)

To conclude, it's no surprise that both students and teachers can become confused by these traditional rule-driven approaches. Such confusion is only too likely to make students even more insecure when speaking English. On the other hand, there is certainly a place for helping students understand some social implications of intonation. For instance, if the learner loudly emphasizes every word in an eagerness to be understood, the listener may think the speaker is just excitable. Or, if everything is said very quickly or very quietly due to uncertainty about the language, the listener may become impatient, making matters worse. In either case, the specifically English system of showing emphasis will be obscured. Or, on the interpersonal level, the listener may conclude the speaker is indifferent or unfriendly. As the Gumperz and Kaltman (1982) study of East Indian speakers in London showed, failure to follow the prosodic system of English can cause serious misunderstanding on more than one level.

Next, I will suggest ways to have good teaching outcomes. English intonation is not difficult to teach if approached as a fundamentally simple system.

What We Can Do

1. Show students the differences between how English and their languages draw attention to the speaker's main point.

In 1971, Allen advised the following:

Often there is little carry-over into real-life communication when instructors rely too heavily upon the imitation of sentences from textbook dialogs with the hope that students will somehow 'absorb' American English intonation. [I] suggest that something [better] can be achieved . . . when instruction directs attention to a very few major patterns….and teaches the student to think in terms of the speaker's intention in any given speech situation. (p. 73)

Derwing and Munro (2005) made this related point: "Students learning L2 pronunciation benefit from being explicitly taught phonological form to help them notice the differences between their own productions and those of proficient speakers in the L2 community" (p. 388).

The highest priority pronunciation concept for a student to learn to notice is how spoken English calls attention to the point that the speaker most wants the listener to focus on. This seems simple to a lot of people. Isn't it **obvious** that you emphasize the main point? Yes and no. Every language has a way to draw attention to the main or important word in each phrase, but different languages do it differently. English depends more than most other languages on musical signals (prosody) for this crucial task.

In the English examples that follow on page 121, the emphasized word is in capital letters and underlined (e.g., You _DID_ forget it!). Because it is so important that the listener notice emphasis, English has three main prosodic signals specific to English that call attention to this important word:

1. a change in pitch at the primary stressed syllable of the focus word
2. a lengthening of the vowel in that syllable
3. extra clarity of this particular vowel.

It is true that this syllable is also louder, but this comes naturally when students are trying hard; the other signals are more pedagogically important because they are not as natural for speakers born into different language systems. Some examples of ways native speakers of a few other languages call attention to the focus of meaning are given.

- special words, as in German (*doch*), or special post-word particles, as in Japanese (*-ga*)
- grammatical construction, or word order, as in Spanish, French, or Portuguese

---

English/German (use of *doch*)
You DID forget it!
Jetzt hast du es doch vergessen!

English/Japanese (post-word particle –*ga*)
THIS is my bag.
Kore-ga watashino kaban-desu.

English/Spanish (grammatical construction: mainly word order)
No, it's HIS fault.
Al contrario, la culpa la tiene él.

English/French ((grammatical construction: mainly word order)
It's MY pen!
C'est mon stylo à moi!

English/European Portuguese (grammatical construction: mainly word order)
1. *I would prefer her to COME.*
   Eu prefiro que ela venha
2. *I would prefer HER to come.*
   Eu prefiro que venha ela.

(Cruz-Ferreira, 1998, p. 173)

---

2. Make basic intonation your first teaching priority, and teach it in dialogues.

Native English–speaking listeners count on prosodic cues (rhythm and pitch change) to help them follow the meaning. These signals are important road signs to help the listener to follow what goes with what and what is most important. But if these prosodic cues are not taught, then efforts at achieving communicative competence by drilling individual sounds will prove frustrating. After all, practicing pronunciation by focusing only on individual sounds is like using only part of the language. So if there is only time to teach a threshold level of the core prosodic system, students will have achieved a great deal of communicative competence. Then if we have more time, we can add attention to certain critical sounds, such as the grammar cues at the end of words like the sound /s/ for plurals (e.g., *books*) or /d/ for past tense (e.g., *planned*). If there is even more time, more nuanced elements can be taught. But the top priority is competence with basic intonation.

When I was first trying to figure out this fundamental principle—how intonation is used as a guide for the listener—I was electrified to read Wallace Chafe's 1970 analysis, in which the important thing about intonation is distinguishing between *new information* and *old information*. This concept explained so much! Here is an example:

Jan: I lost my <u>SHOES</u>! (*shoes* is the topic)

Jane: <u>WHICH</u> shoes? (*shoes* is now understood between the speakers and therefore is old information; *which* is now the focus of attention)

This example demonstrates that practice with emphasis needs to be in dialogue form. One sentence isn't enough to activate the system because the focus of new information in a conversation changes in reaction to what was said before.

3. Teach "listener-friendly" intonation—that is, intonation that helps the listener "follow" what the speaker is saying.

In English, prosodic cues serve as navigation guides to help the listener follow the intentions of the speaker. These signals communicate emphasis and make clear the relationship between ideas (new and old information) so that listeners can readily identify these relationships and understand the speaker's meaning. Unfortunately, when English learners speak in class, they are typically not thinking about how to help their listeners follow their meaning. Instead, they are often thinking about avoiding mistakes in grammar, vocabulary, and so on. Native speakers also commonly make this error when delivering a presentation or when reading aloud in a classroom, a business meeting, or in some other setting. When nervous, they concentrate all attention on avoiding "mistakes" and may ignore the actual point of communication. Instead, they need to learn to think about their listeners, using the prosodic signals and word grouping essential to listener-friendly pronunciation.

Emphasis that conveys the wrong meaning, or thought groups that either run together or break in inappropriate places, cause extra work for the listener who is trying to follow the speaker's meaning. If the burden becomes too great, the listener simply stops listening. The principle of "helping the listener to follow," therefore, is a vital one, so time spent helping students concentrate on the major rhythmic and melodic signals of English is more important than any other efforts to improve intelligibility. These signals are also vital to improving students' listening comprehension. As Brown (1990) explained:

> It is essential in English to learn to pay attention . . . to those words in the stream of speech which are [emphasized], since these mark the richest information-bearing units. Listeners who fail to distinguish these are likely to flounder. They are likely to lose even more information if they do not know how to identify information peaks and how to use the information encoded in this distribution. (p. 151)

Morley (1992) put the same idea in different words:

> Sentence stresses may be thought of as the strong beats in the rhythm of a sentence similar to the strong beats in the rhythm of music. The speaker gives more strength to the especially important words to help the listener get the sense (or meaning) of the sentence. (p. 37)

4. Focus instruction on the main—and most teachable—functions of intonation.

There are many ways to analyze the purposeful use of prosodic signals, but for practical teaching, the main two uses of prosody are: highlighting new information and separating thought groups for listeners.

HIGHLIGHTING NEW INFORMATION

From the point of view of either intelligibility or listening efficiency, this principle may be the primary function of intonation. Grant (2010) has explained that "listeners of English expect more important words to be strong and less important words to be weak. The strong words are the ones listeners pay the most attention to. Contrasting strong and weak words is a basic part of speaking clearly" (p. 90).

SEPARATING THOUGHT GROUPS SO THAT THE LISTENER CAN MORE EASILY PROCESS THE MESSAGE

On this point, Walker (2010) has said:

> The first benefit that comes from the use of word groups is that they break the speech flow up into manageable, meaningful blocks of information. This makes the task of the listener easier for two reasons. Firstly, it provides the information in packages that bring out the meaning more clearly than if the speaker simply pauses at random. Secondly, the small pauses between each word group allow the listener time to process what he or she has heard. (p. 36)

For example, here are two sentences, made different by the use of punctuation to separate thought groups:

a. John said, "The Boss is an idiot!"

b. "John," said the Boss, "is an idiot!"

The written punctuation helps readers to know who is speaking. But in spoken English, there is no punctuation, so the prosodic signals take the place of these visible markers. Or, to be more exact, punctuation marks convey in writing what is conveyed in speech by musical signals.

5. Warning!! Students may not believe you. Because the system is apt to be foreign to students, they may not actually believe that intonation affects meaning. Convince them by providing practice with built-in feedback.

Long ago I used an exercise that depended on varying emphasis for the same sentence, *I want three dozen oranges.* Each line had a different word in capital letters, followed by the different meaning in parentheses. To me, the purpose was obvious. But after I had led the class to dutifully repeat the sentences differently, one of my students said, "This is just an exercise for the class, no?" I was angry, but then thought better of it. He was an aggressive sort of person, but he had actually done me a great favor. I truly hadn't realized that the principle was not self-evident. Students will rarely tell the teacher that they feel silly speaking this way, and the result will be that they may walk out of the class without having accepted the system at all. Or they may think intonation is simply decorative. I think the best way to handle this common doubt about the importance of the system is to use a good deal of practice in which the answer to a remark depends on the emphasis used. An example in which paired students help each other follows. The speaker chooses to say a or b. The listener must respond to the emphasis heard.

    a. I prefer beef <u>SOUP</u>. Not stew?

    b. I prefer <u>BEEF</u> soup. Not chicken?

If the speaker gets an unexpected answer, there is direct and imme-diate feedback to both students that emphasis matters. This is a warn-ing about potential communication breakdown in actual conversations with native speakers of English who depend on the prosodic cues to understand what the speaker is trying to say.

At the higher level, such simple practice should be followed up with tasks about the implication of emphasis. In the following tasks, the student is asked to guess what the emphasis implies might have been said previously. This is an important aspect of effective listening comprehension. Different answers are possible but they all must con-form to the type of word that has been emphasized:

    1. [Write what may have been said before.]

    _____

    No, today is <u>TUESDAY</u>.

    (the previous remark was probably about a
    different day of the week)

    2. [Write what may have been said before.]

    _____

    <u>BLUE</u> is the best color for a car.

    (the previous remark was probably about a
    different color)

6. Teach intonation as an interrelated system using a simple pyramid structure.

Because students need a clear framework, or scaffolding, to understand how English uses prosody/intonation in a systematic way, I divided this musical signaling system into four interrelated elements, as shown by the pyramid structure in Figure 4.1. The basic foundation of the

FIGURE 4.1: Pyramid of the Musical Signaling System

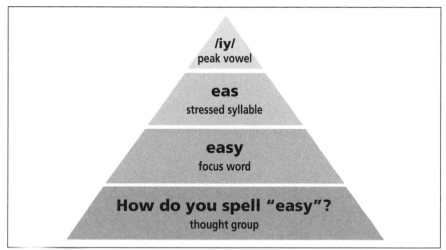

From *Clear Speech Student's Book. Pronunciation and Listening Comprehension in North American English,* 4th Edition, by Judy B. Gilbert. © 2012 CUP. Reprinted with permission of Cambridge University Press.

structure is a thought group (a short sentence, clause, or phrase). Within each thought group is one focus word. Within each focus word is one most stressed syllable. This syllable is the most important syllable in the thought group because the vowel sound at the center of this syllable is the peak of information.

This peak vowel is so important that it must have several signals to call attention to it: It must be extra long and extra clear, and it must be said on a change of pitch. The peak can go up or down, but it must have a change of pitch for it to stand out.

What is the practical effect of understanding this structure? If there has been some kind of communication breakdown with a native speaker of English, the English learner has a short window of opportunity to fix it before losing the other person's attention. Any effort to repeat the sentence, carefully trying to fix every individual sound, is likely to make the communication breakdown even worse. Speaking more loudly won't help either. A much more effective strategy is to decide which word was most important, give it emphasis, and improve the clarity of the peak vowel. Saying the sentence this way will be better understood—and more listener-friendly.

7. Teach intonation holistically. Use template sentences, taught through quality repetition.

Learning the pronunciation of a second language is something like learning to play tennis. If you concentrate too much on trying to remember what to do with your wrist and, at the same time, try to remember how to position your feet, shoulders, and knees while also trying to remember to keep your eye on the ball, the combination of too many things to think about tends to keep you from putting every-thing together in a flowing movement. Although a tennis player needs to know all of these things, it works better if all of the parts can be learned holistically or impressionistically in order to get a clear mental image of what the flow of the stroke should feel like.

Similarly, when learning pronunciation, if a student is asked to think simultaneously about where to place the tongue, whether or not to use voicing, how to let the air flow, how to link words with preced-ing and following words, as well as what stress and intonation pattern to use, the complications become so great that the student cannot be expected to produce fluent, natural-sounding speech. A more produc-tive approach is to help students form a solid acoustic impression of a short piece of language as a whole and learn it deeply, and only then to work toward understanding the specific elements that flow together to form it into English speech. These specific elements are interdependent and they tend to occur simultaneously. But how can we possibly teach all the elements at the same time with a template sentence?

Repetition, a truly ancient teaching method, fell into disfavor decades ago because teachers worried that it is boring. But the reality is that quality repetition is the opposite of boring because it helps students feel themselves growing in mastery. The basic purpose of this repetition is to give students a long-term memory resource that they can access when they need to remember how it went. Why does repetition work? The classic statement of the usefulness of repetition is sometimes referred to as Hebb's Law. Hebb (1949) has explained it this way: "The general idea is an old one, that any two cells or systems of cells that are repeatedly active at the same time will tend to become 'associated' so that activity in one facilitates activity in the other" (p. 70).

This was famously stated in a snappier way by Shatz (1992): "Cells that fire together wire together" (p. 65).

Pronunciation practice and learning is most efficient during simultaneous auditory input and production of the target words and phrases (i.e., while speaking in chorus). Group practice is also very efficient for overcoming individual psychological inhibitions. Here is Kjellin's (1999) description of the usefulness of choral practice:

> Each individual learner will be guided under the auditory pressure from the chorus to pronounce correctly. This is particularly true for the prosodic aspects of the language. Just consider how much easier it will be to learn a new song if you are allowed to sing along a number of times with someone who knows it, compared to having to try solo singing after only having listened to it a few times. This insight is important for language and speech pedagogy. (p. 14)

PRESENTING THE TEMPLATE

Many forms of repetition can be used to vary pronunciation practice in the classroom, but it is important to allow students the opportunity to listen to the template sentence many times before they actually speak it. This way, they can begin to internalize the rhythm and the melody before attempting to say the sentence themselves. At the early stages, this template should be a short sentence with just one thought group (e.g., *How do you spell* easy?). As students reach higher levels of proficiency, the template used may be a longer piece of spoken English—perhaps a longer sentence (with more than one clause) or more than one sentence (e.g., a question and response paired together). Varying the model by saying it loud, soft, low, high, whispering, squeaking, or saying it with your back to the class can keep the class amused and alert. However, remember to always remain accurate to the natural speed and melody of the template. Slowing down will distort the prosodic effect, which is crucial to making the sentence a reliable template of how authentic spoken English actually flows. Typically, after students have heard a number of renditions, they will be eager to try it themselves. At this point, students can begin saying the sentence as a class. Choral response gives support to each speaker who, if speaking alone, might falter and lose the rhythm. Such choral practice can be followed by smaller groups (e.g., opposite sides of the class) and interspersed with the listening model, all done with a strong sense of continuous rhythm. It is this rhythmic safety net that will provide students with a sense that they are mastering a chunk of spoken English.

ANALYZING THE TEMPLATE

Through quality repetition of a template sentence, students are given an opportunity to absorb into their personal long-term memory banks an accurate sample of spoken English in which all the levels of the prosodic system are present. In this way, the prosodic flow of the sentence has already been internalized before students try to understand the detailed inner workings of it. Later analysis of the various parts of the template may focus on specific topics, like emphasizing the focus word with a pitch change (For example: *How do you spell* EASY?) or reducing a vowel to nothing or to schwa (For example: *How d'yə . . .*). A solidly memorized accurate template is probably the most useful reference tool a student can possess. The template can also help with getting a firm grip on word order and grammatical elements (for example, not *How you spell easy?*).

A USEFUL IMAGE AND TWO HANDY GADGETS

It isn't enough for the teacher to be aware of the importance of rhythm and intonation; it is also necessary to have practical ways to teach these aspects of the spoken language. A few ways to add images and physical activities to lessons on suprasegmentals are presented. In Figure 4.2,

FIGURE. 4.2: Showing Contrast When Teaching Suprasegmentals

From *Clear Speech Student's Book: Pronunciation and Listening Comprehension in North American English, 4th Edition*, by Judy B. Gilbert. © 2012 CUP. Reprinted with permission of Cambridge University Press.

the butterfly on the right is easier to see. That is because when it is in contrast to the background, it is highlighted. In the same way, intonationally emphasized words are easier to hear (Gilbert, 1999).

By teaching linking, rhythm, stress, and intonation, teachers can place pronunciation teaching within a communicative setting. By using a variety of practical kinesthetic, visual, and aural teaching devices, they can help students sharpen their ability to attend to key features of spoken English.

Over many years, I've collected practical ideas to help teach intonation. Some are my own and some are suggestions from fellow teachers. Kinesthetic reinforcement is a powerful tool. For example, you can ask students to raise hands, or even raise their eyebrows with the primary stress as they say a word or sentence. Or if there is space, you can actually get them to do a "walkabout" of the room, in physical synchrony with the rhythm and emphasis of the sentence they are repeating. This has a major advantage of also being fun (Acton, 2001).

Here are two gadgets I have found especially useful for teaching the melody and rhythm that make spoken English easier to understand:

1. A kazoo. If you hum (not blow) into this toy instrument, you can reproduce the pitch pattern stripped of distractions of grammar, vocabulary, and individual sounds. This kind of presentation helps students focus their minds on the pitch pattern alone.

2. A wide rubber band. If students stretch the band while saying the crucial syllable (and let it shorten for the other syllables), you can kinesthetically reproduce the kind of effort students need to make to give a specifically English rhythm to their speech. **Warning**: This is not a suitable tool in the hands of middle school students. Also, a skinny rubber band is apt to break and be frustrating.

Here is an example of using the rubber band as a reinforcement tool: The word *banana* has three *a* letters, but one of them is said much longer because it is the primary stress of this word. This is quite different from the lengthening of a vowel in other languages. For example, a lengthened vowel in Japanese is simply a different vowel, just as the English vowel sounds in *ship* and *sheep* make different words.

The rhythm of many languages depends on a relatively **regular** length of all syllables, whereas English rhythm depends on **irregular** length. One of the most important functions of lengthening a syllable in English is give the listener time to notice the emphasis. Therefore, the English cue of lengthening must be learned, and physical practice is the best way to practice producing the variable length inherent in English rhythm. An illustration of how to practice lengthening with a rubber band while saying a word (though the same practice could apply to a thought group or sentence) is shown in Figure 4.3. <u>Note</u>: When a word is said alone, it has all the musical qualities of a whole

FIGURE 4.3: Sample of Practicing Vowel Length

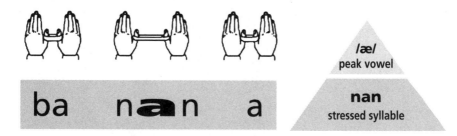

/æ/
peak vowel

nan
stressed syllable

ba na n a

From *Clear Speech Student's Book: Pronunciation and Listening Comprehension in North American English, 4th Edition,* by Judy B. Gilbert. © 2012 CUP. Reprinted with permission of Cambridge University Press.

FIGURE 4.4: Example of How Pitch Change Signals Peak of Information

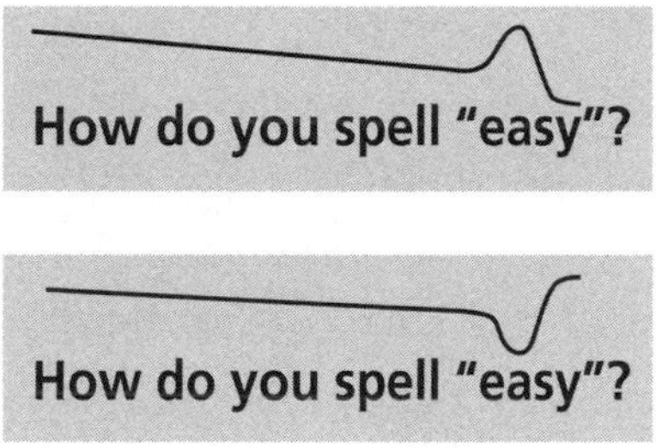

From *Clear Speech Student's Book: Pronunciation and Listening Comprehension in North American English, 4th Edition*, by Judy B. Gilbert. © 2012 CUP. Reprinted with permission of Cambridge University Press.

thought group/utterance. So the peak vowel is the peak of information, even though it is only in one word.

In a thought group of several words, there is still just one peak of information. This peak vowel is extra long and extra clear, and it also has a peak of melody. The peak can go up or down, but it must be a change of pitch to call attention to it, as shown in Figure 4.4.

Other languages use different means to make clear which word is most important: perhaps word order, or a special particle or word that alerts the listener to notice a certain part of a message. Language-specific systems for emphasis are learned so early that they are applied unconsciously to any new language, so it is necessary to train students to notice the English way of using length difference and the change of pitch on the peak vowel of the primary stress of the most important word (Gilbert, 2012b).

Intonation is NOT hard to teach if your priorities reflect the under-lying significance of the specifically English system of calling attention to the focus ideas and the grouping of words. As one teacher trainee put it, "Teaching pronunciation without prosody is like teaching ballroom dancing, only the students must practice standing still, without a partner, and without music." Once there is a threshold mastery of this system, time and energy can be spent on more subtle details.

Thanks to my long-time friend, Linda Grant, for her wise editing advice. Also thanks to Madalena Cruz-Ferreira, Laura Hahn, Anne Isaacs, Tamara Jones, Jack Windsor Lewis, Petr Roesel, Richard Stibbard, Thomas Scovel, and Elicio C. A. de Souza for generously commenting on drafts of this chapter.

References

Acton, W. (2001). Integrating focal-speak: Rhythm and stress in speech pronunciation. In J. Murphy and P. Byrd (Eds.), *Understanding the courses we teach: Local perspectives on English language teaching* (pp. 197–217). Ann Arbor: University of Michigan Press.

Allen, V. (1971). Teaching intonation, from theory to practice. *TESOL Quarterly,* 4(1), 73–81.

Anderson-Hsieh, J., Johnson, R., & Koehler, K. (1992). The relationship between native speaker judgments of nonnative pronunciation and deviance in segmentals, prosody, and syllable structure. *Language Learning, 49*(4), 529–555.

Bell, A. G. (1916). *The mechanisms of speech.* New York: Funk & Wagnalls.

Bolinger, D. (1972). Accent is predictable (if you're a mind-reader). *Language, 48*(3): 633–644.

Brown, G. (1990). *Listening to spoken English.* London: Longman.

Chafe, W. (1970). *The meaning of the structure of language.* Chicago: University of Chicago Press.

Chun, D. (2002). *Discourse intonation in L2: From theory and research to practice.* Amsterdam: John Benjamins.

Cruz-Ferreira, M. (1998). Intonation in European Portuguese. In D. Hirst & A. DiCristo (Eds.), *Intonation systems: A survey of twenty languages* (pp. 167–178). Cambridge, U.K.: Cambridge University Press.

Crystal, D. (1969). Halliday's intonation and grammar in British English. *Language, 45*(2), 378–393.

Darwin, C. (1976). The perception of speech, In E. Carterette and M. Friedman (Eds.), *Handbook of perception* (pp. 283–312). New York: Academic Press.

Dalton, C., and Seidlhofer, B. (1994). *Pronunciation.* Oxford, U.K.: Oxford University Press.

Derwing, T., Munro, M., & Wiebe, G. (1998). Evidence in favor of a broad framework for pronunciation instruction. *Language Learning, 48,* 393–410.

Derwing, T., & Rossiter, M. (2002). ESL learner's perception of their pronunciation needs and strategies. *System, 30,* 155–166.

Derwing, T., & Rossiter, M. (2003). The effects of pronunciation instruction on the accuracy, fluency, and complexity of L2 accented speech. *Applied Language Learning, 13,* 1–17.

Esler, J. (1978). Contrastive intonation of German and English, *Phonetica, 35,* 41–55.

Field, J. (2005). Intelligibility and the listener: The role of lexical stress. *TESOL Quarterly, 39,* 399–423.

Forster, E. (1924). *A passage to India.* New York: Harcourt.

Gilbert, J. (2012a). *Clear speech* (4th ed.). New York: Cambridge University Press

Gilbert, J. (2012b). *Clear speech from the start: Teacher resource and assessment book* (2nd ed.). New York: Cambridge University Press.

Gimson, A. (1980). *An introduction to the pronunciation of English.* New York: Arnold.

Grant, L. (2010). *Well said: Pronunciation for clear communication* (3rd ed.). Boston: Heinle Cengage Learning.

Gumperz, J., & Kaltman, H. (1982). *Discourse strategies.* Cambridge, U.K.: Cambridge University Press.

Hahn, L. (2004). Primary stress and intelligibility: Research to motivate the teaching of suprasegmentals. *TESOL Quarterly, 38,* 201–223.

Halliday, M. (1963). Intonation in English Grammar, *Transactions of the Philological Society,* 143–169

Hebb, D. (1949). *The organization of behavior: A neuropsychological theory.* New York: Wiley.

Kang, O., & Pickering, L. (2011). The role of objective measures of suprasegmental features in judgments of comprehensibility and oral proficiency in L2 spoken discourse. *Speak Out, 44,* 4–8.

Kjellin, O. (1999). Accent addition: Prosody and perception facilitate second language learning. In O. Fujimura, B. D. Joseph, & B. Paled (Eds.), *Proceedings of linguistics and phonetics conference 1998* (pp. 373–398). Prague: The Karolinum Press. Retrieved from www.olle-kjellin.com/SpeechDoctor/ProcLP98.html

Levelt, W. (1991). *Speaking: From intention to articulation.* Cambridge: MIT Press.

Lieberman, P. (1967). *Intonation, perception, and language.* Cambridge: MIT Research Monograph 38.

Morley, J. (1992). *Rapid review of vowel & prosodic contexts,* Ann Arbor: University of Michigan Press.

Nash, R. (1971). Phonemic and prosodic interference and their effect on intelligibility. *International Congress of Phonetic Sciences, 7,* 138–139.

O'Connor, J. (1967). *Better English pronunciation.* Cambridge, U.K.: Cambridge University Press.

Prator, C., and Robinett, B. (1985). *Manual of American English pronunciation* (4th ed.). New York: Holt, Rhinehart and Winston.

Roach, P. (1991). *English phonetics and phonology: A practical course.* (2nd ed.). Cambridge, U.K.: Cambridge University Press.

Shatz, C. (1992). The developing brain. *Scientific American, 267,* 60–67.

Sledd, J. (1955). Review of G. L. Trager and H. L. Smith, *Outline of English structure in languages, 31,* 312–335, as quoted in Liberman (1967), *Intonation, perception, and language.* Cambridge: MIT Research Monograph 38.

Stibbard, R. (2010). Vocal Expression of Emotions in Non-laboratory Speech. PhD thesis, University of Reading. www.britishschoolof phonetics.co.uk/pdf/stibbard2001.pdf

Trager, G., & Smith, H. (1951). *An outline of English structure.* Norman, OK: Battenburg Press.

Walker, R. (2010). *Teaching the pronunciation of English as a lingua franca.* Oxford, U.K.: Oxford University Press.

Students would make better progress in pronunciation if they just practiced more.

Linda Grant

In the Real World . . .

One of my favorite scenes in film occurred in *The King's Speech*. Based on a true story, this movie portrays the relationship between Albert, Duke of York (later King George VI of England), and Lionel Logue, an Australian speech therapist who treated the King for a severe stuttering problem. In spite of Logue's questionable credentials and unorthodox methods, the King made dramatic progress. At a time in history when England needed strong leadership, King George VI not only improved his fluency but also became a more confident, eloquent public speaker.

Toward the end of the movie, the King was getting ready to deliver a major radio address about England's entry into World War II. He had rehearsed his speech with Logue, inserting pauses, adding stresses, and deleting troublesome words. Logue went to Windsor Castle to listen to the live broadcast and was surprised to hear the King stumble on /w/in *weapons*. This interaction followed:

> . . . Logue shook hands with the King, and, after congratulating him, asked why that particular letter had proved to be such a problem.
>
> "I did it on purpose," the King replied with a grin.
>
> "On purpose?" asked Logue, incredulous.
>
> "Yes, if I don't make a mistake, people might not know it is me." (Logue and Conradi, 2010, p. 200)

This exchange is not directly related to L2 pronunciation learning, so I might have missed the connection if an insightful colleague had not pointed it out. Basically, long-term speech characteristics can become an integral part of who we are. In the case of L2 learners, losing a first language accent or sounding more like a native speaker of English may threaten the sense of self (Lippi-Green, 2012). Consequently, some learners elect, often unconsciously, not to change aspects of their speech even if they could (Hansen Edwards, 2008).

In pronunciation workshops, I often ask educators what bothers them the most about teaching pronunciation. Invariably, participants mention disappointing results, meaning that despite their best efforts, their learners exhibit little to no noticeable improvement in pronunciation. Some teachers hold themselves accountable—if they had only been able to give the students more individual attention. Other teachers blame the students for lack of progress—if the students had just been more diligent and devoted more time and effort to practice. There is no question that meaningful practice and constructive feedback from teachers are key elements in pronunciation progress. But teachers who are aware of the learner variables underlying ultimate attainment in L2 pronunciation are not as quick to point the finger at lack of practice when adult learners fall short.

More than in any other aspect of learning an additional language, the level of L2 pronunciation instruction success is subject to learner-based factors such as age, first language, exposure to the target language, identity, and motivation. According to Dalton and Seidlhofer (1994), "This may be the most important reason why, especially in pronunciation, there can never be a one-to-one relationship between what is taught and what is learnt. It would be self-defeating for the teacher to think or hope that there ever could be" (p. 72).

An overview of research-based learner variables that influence progress in L2 pronunciation follows. This line of research is not new. It has long been part of the second language acquisition (SLA) literature, yet it merits a review because relevant insights from these studies are seldom incorporated into classroom practice or published teaching materials. While some learner variables, such as age and first language, are beyond the influence of classroom instruction, other factors—such as attitude, motivation, and the extent of L2 use outside of the classroom—can be addressed effectively within the framework of the courses we teach. For a more complete discussion of second language acquisition research, see *Second Language Acquisition Myths: Applying Second Language Research to Classroom Teaching* (Brown & Larson-Hall, University of Michigan Press, 2012).

What the Research Says . . .

Research Related to Age

Young children seem to have an advantage when it comes to learning pronunciation. They immerse themselves in the language spoken around them and play with pitch, loudness, and the sounds of speech without inhibition. In L2 learning, if children are exposed to a language-rich environment at an early age, they seem to acquire native-like pronunciation naturally and easily. In contrast, adult learners appear to have to put forth conscious effort. Even then, adult learners rarely acquire native-like proficiency.

Observations of children and adults learning language (and recovering language ability after traumatic brain injury) gave rise to the notion of a critical period for language learning. Lenneberg (1967) was chief among the linguists who hypothesized that young children are biologically predisposed to acquire language naturally and effortlessly. At the onset of puberty, however, naturalistic language acquisition becomes more difficult due to neuro-biological changes in the brain. Lenneberg's so-called Critical Period Hypothesis (CPH) was subsequently extended to L2 pronunciation by Scovel (1969), who claimed that the maturational changes in the brain limit the ability to acquire native-like speech after the critical period. While empirical evidence clearly supports differences in pronunciation achievement related to age, whether these differences are biologically based has long been a topic of debate.

One group of studies comparing child and adult learners focuses on differences in overall accentedness. In Myth 1, the authors cited one such investigation by Asher and Garcia (1969). The researchers found that subjects who arrived in the United States before the age of six had a higher probability of ultimately being identified as native English speakers. A supporting study by Oyama (1976) found a significant negative correlation between age of arrival in the United States and pronunciation ability—that is, the younger the age of arrival, the more native-like the pronunciation was judged to be. In fact, the only speakers in the Oyama study who were deemed fully native-like had begun learning English before the age of ten.

Subsequent investigations comparing child and adult learners yielded similar results (see, for example, Flege, 1988; Flege, Munro, & MacKay, 1995; Flege, Yeni-Komshian, & Liu, 1999). One of the larger studies (Flege, Munro, & Mackay, 1995) involved more than 200 Italian immigrants who had resided in Canada for an average of 32 years, yet length of residence did not seem to be a factor in L2 pronunciation ability. Rather the results revealed a positive correlation between age at onset of learning English (AOL) and the degree of foreign accent. Another interesting finding was that the relationship between the degree of foreign accent and age was linear, and, as such, inconsistent with the CPH. If biological changes had played a major role in phonological development, researchers would have observed discontinuity resulting from a sudden increase in accentedness after the age of puberty. Another finding at odds with the CPH was the detection of accentedness in several early learners, indicating that acquiring L2 pronunciation at a young age does not necessarily ensure accent-free speech.

Another group of child-adult studies focused more narrowly on the acquisition of specific speech sounds (e.g., Flege, 1991; Kim, 1995). In the 1995 study, for example, Kim assessed Korean learners' production of two English vowel sounds, /ɪ/ as in *hit* and /iy/ as in *heat*. Subjects who arrived in the United States after the age of sixteen depended on only one acoustic dimension, vowel length, to differentiate between the two vowels. Early-arrivers, on the other hand, attended to both vowel length and vowel quality.

All in all, the age studies suggest "younger is better in acquiring the phonology of an L2" (Ioup, 2008, p. 46). There is no convincing research, however, that attributes child-adult differences to the existence of a critical period. Some researchers have claimed that the age disparity is more closely related to social and psychological factors than to neuro-biological changes. Because adults are assumed to have deeper, more enduring ties to their native culture and language, adults may be less willing than children to adopt the pronunciation patterns of the L2. In any case, children's ability to acquire native-like pronunciation more quickly and easily than adults seems to hinge on factors other than just age (Piske, Mackay, & Flege, 2001).

Before turning to those other factors, it bears mentioning that in the 1970s, when the aim of pronunciation instruction was native-like speech, age-related research gave teachers little hope that adult learners could reach their goals. This was one of several reasons why ESL programs abandoned formal pronunciation instruction at that time. Nowadays, contemporary practitioners recognize that that just because most adult learners are unlikely to eliminate an accent does not mean they are incapable of achieving intelligible speech. (See Myth 1 for more about late onset L2 learners.)

Research Related to the L1

Many years ago, Lado (1957) introduced what is known as the Contrastive Analysis Hypothesis (CAH). Ever since then, it has been generally accepted that the phonological patterns of the L1 (sounds, stresses, and intonation) influence pronunciation in the second or foreign language. According to the CAH, where the languages are similar, acquisition of features will be easier, and where languages are dissimilar, acquisition of features will be more difficult. As we will see, the relationship between the L1 and L2 sound systems is not quite as straightforward as originally proposed by the CAH.

In 1980, Purcell and Suter reconsidered data from a 1976 study by Suter. In the re-analysis of 61 adult learners, four factors accounted for variation in pronunciation accuracy: first language, aptitude for oral mimicry, length of residency, and strength of concern for pronunciation. The single best predictor of degree of accent was mother tongue. The investigators concluded that native-speakers of "favored" languages, those languages with phonologies closely related to English, were more likely to pronounce English well. A more recent study by Bongaerts, Mennen, and van der Slik (2000) rated the pronunciation ability of adults learning Dutch. The subjects represented a variety of language backgrounds, but only those speakers from first languages similar to Dutch (e.g., English and German) were judged to have native-like Dutch accents.

Studies that have singled out specific elements of pronunciation, such as consonant and vowel sounds, have produced somewhat different results. Similarities between L1 and L2 features sometimes promoted and sometimes impeded learning. In a study by Broselow, Hurtig, and Ringen (1987), the ability of adult English speakers to perceive Chinese tones was assessed. The researchers found that it was easier for English speakers to perceive the fourth Chinese tone, the falling tone, but only in positions where falling tones normally occur in English (i.e., the final positions of utterances). Another study (Lee, Guion, & Haruda, 2006) investigated the ability of Japanese and

Korean ESL learners to lengthen stressed vowels and shorten unstressed vowels in English words (as in *CA-na-da*). Despite the fact that neither Japanese nor Korean resemble English in the area of word stress, Japanese learners were better able to achieve English-like contrasts in vowel length. The researchers concluded that, because vowel length changes the meaning of some words in the Japanese language, Japanese learners were more likely than Korean learners to notice durational differences in English vowels.

When features in the L1 and L2 are quite similar, but not exactly the same, learners can easily misinterpret them as the same sound. The English phonemes /v/ and /b/, for instance, present a considerable challenge for many Spanish speakers. To native English speakers, these sounds are two separate phonemes, but to Spanish speakers, /v/ and /b/ are allophones (i.e., slightly different versions of the same phoneme) and thus perceived as the same sound. As a result, Spanish speakers may be unable to distinguish between the English /v/ and /b/ without explicit awareness-raising and focused listening practice. After many years of research on similarity (see, for example, Flege & Hillenbrand, 1987; Flege & Eefting, 1987; Flege, Munro, & Fox, 1994), Flege (1995) concluded that it is easier to learn sounds that are completely new and do not exist in the L1 because there are obvious differences, whereas it is often harder to hear subtle differences between sounds that are perceptually similar to those in the L1. Flege's conclusion was fine-tuned by Major and Kim (1996), who maintained that quite similar sounds are not necessarily more difficult to learn but may be acquired more slowly.

Suffice it to say, the influences of the mother tongue on the L2 phonology, commonly called **transfer,** is inevitable (see box on page 144). When we consider general qualities of accentedness, adult learners from L1s closely related to English appear to have an easier time learning English pronunciation. When learning specific features of the L2 sound system, however, the perceptual filter of the L1 either clarifies or confounds the process. If the L1 has a sound that is quite similar to one in the target language, it tends to be harder (or take

Positive and Negative Transfer

Positive transfer: When the phonology of the L1 facilitates L2 pronunciation learning, so-called positive transfer occurs.

Negative transfer: When the phonology of the L1 causes pronunciation errors in the L2, the result is termed negative transfer. To be sure, negative transfer is the source of many L2 pronunciation problems, frequently due to allophonic differences between the mother tongue and the target language. Not all pronunciation errors are influenced by transfer or interference from the L1, however.

Sometimes learners from different L2 backgrounds make the same types of errors. The fact that some of these errors are similar to those made by young children acquiring an L1 supports the theory that what appear to be pronunciation errors sometimes originate from universal processing constraints. An example of a universal constraint is overgeneralization. One way young learners exhibit overgeneralization in the L1 is by adding –ed to form all past tense verbs (e.g., *runned*, *ate-ed*, etc.). We see evidence of overgeneralization in L2 pronunciation also. I once tutored a Nigerian engineering professor whose students were reporting that he was difficult to understand. Among other issues, he consistently substituted /s/ for /θ/, so we dedicated a portion of one meeting to auditory discrimination between the two sounds. During the subsequent session, I was surprised to hear that the /θ/ had already begun emerging in his speech (though we had not worked on production). He was saying *think about* instead of *sink about*, *math problem* instead of *mass problem*, and *fourth-order equations* instead of *force order equations*. He was also overgeneralizing the /θ/ such that expressions like *simple solution* and *second one* sounded like *thimple tholution* and *thecond one*, respectively.

longer) for adult learners to master that sound. Clearly, we have no control over the first languages of our learners. We do, however, owe it to our students to approach pronunciation instruction with the understanding that the playing field is seldom level, especially in heterogeneous classes.

Research Related to Exposure and L1/L2 Use

About 30 years ago, in an attempt to achieve fluency in Spanish, I enrolled in a Spanish conversation course. The school was located in Atlanta, so I had few opportunities outside of class to speak Spanish. After one year of glacial progress, I was desperate for real-world interactions in Spanish, so I applied to study intensive Spanish for six weeks in Mexico. Though I made substantial progress, the students who made the most extraordinary advances in both language and pronunciation were those who had Mexican boy/girlfriends with whom they regularly communicated. I sometimes joke that my Spanish is not up to par because my marital status foreclosed the boyfriend option, but there is a grain of truth in my excuse. In fact, research indicates that exposure to and use of the target language may have a positive effect on pronunciation achievement. In the following studies, exposure refers to everyday experience with the language outside of the classroom.

In Suter's previously mentioned 1976 research, the amount of conversation with native speakers was the third strongest predictor of pronunciation accuracy. It should be noted, however, that, in the re-examination (Purcell and Suter, 1980), L2 use was no longer a significant factor and was replaced by length of residence—that is, the number of years in an environment where English is the dominant language.

Derwing, Munro, and Thomson (2007) investigated the effects of exposure to English outside the classroom. In their study, the oral proficiency of Slavic and Mandarin speakers enrolled in an ESL program in Canada was assessed by native speakers three separate times over a two-year period. Even though work and family responsibilities limited interactions in English for both language groups, the Slavic speakers reported more exposure to English outside of the classroom. That same language group also demonstrated a small but significant improvement in both fluency and comprehensibility.

In related studies, researchers have examined the effects of L1 and L2 use on pronunciation accuracy. Flege, Munro, and MacKay (1995) rated variables accounting for strength of perceived accent in the production of sentences by Italian subjects residing in Canada. A small but significant factor was length of residence (LOR). Somewhat stronger than LOR was relative use of the L2. Later studies (Flege, Frieda, & Nozawa, 1997; Riney & Flege,1998) yielded somewhat similar results. According to Flege and his colleagues, immigrants to Canada who reported frequent use of the L1 had stronger accentedness in the target language than those who reported infrequent use. Riney and Flege, who studied Japanese college students studying in the U.S., found that two of the three subjects who showed significant pronunciation improvement also reported spending the most time interacting in the L2.

The first study examining the effects of exposure on prosody was conducted by Trofimovich and Baker (2006). Analysis of suprasegmental features in the speech of 40 Korean speakers after three months, three years, and ten years of residence in the United States showed that experience with the L2 had a positive effect on what is sometimes referred to as English stress-timing—that is, the alternation of the stronger, stressed words and syllables with weaker, unstressed words and syllables.

To sum up, empirical evidence suggests amount of exposure to and experience with the L2 have a greater positive effect on various aspects of pronunciation attainment than length of residence. Fortunately, classroom teachers can effectively intervene with regard to exposure and experience.

Research Related to Psycho-Social Factors

The story about King George VI alluded to the deep-seated connection between pronunciation and identity. In that regard, many of us are familiar with the now classic study by Guiora and colleagues (1972) in which small quantities of alcohol administered to subjects improved their ability to approximate native-like pronunciation in the L2. Apparently, the alcohol temporarily lowered their affective filters (i.e., their anxiety about making mistakes), enabling them to more easily assume new language personas. What does more recent research say about affective variables like identity, motivation, and attitude and their influence on L2 pronunciation? How important is it to address these factors in the context of our pronunciation teaching?

In the 1980 Purcell and Suter study, one of four significant factors influencing pronunciation accuracy was concern for pronunciation accuracy. Various researchers have explored the driving force behind this concern. In a study of L2 German learners who intended to become teachers of German, Moyer (1999) correlated concern for pronunciation attainment with professional motivation, a form of extrinsic motivation (see box). Other studies examining personal and professional goals for studying English (e.g., Bernaus, Masgoret, Gardner, & Reyes, 2004; Gatbonton, Trofimovich, & Magid, 2005) lend support to the importance of motivation in L2 pronunciation learning. In a more recent study by Moyer (2007), the combination of two factors—experience with and a positive orientation toward the L2—appeared to be influential in the development of a more native-like accent. One finding from this study with implications for instruction was the relationship between the two factors insofar as exposure to and experience with the L2 led to a more positive orientation toward the language.

Intrinsic and Extrinsic Motivation

Motivation stems from both internal and external sources. If we more fully understand the two kinds of motivation, there is a greater likelihood we will be able to foster motivation in context of L2 pronunciation instruction.

Extrinsic motivation: Behaviors linked to practical or external outcomes, like grades on tests, are extrinsically motivated. A learner who wishes to communicate more clearly in order to succeed at school or work would be extrinsically motivated.

Intrinsic motivation: When we pursue an activity purely for the sake of personal satisfaction, we have intrinsic motivation. In L2 pronunciation, a learner who has positive associations with the target culture and wishes to learn the language in order to fit in would be intrinsically motivated.

In surveys by Timmis (2002) and Derwing, (2003), the majority of respondents reported that they aspired to sound like native speakers of English. Other learners may wish to maintain accentedness as an expression of L1 identity. Gatbonton, Trofimovich, and Magid (2005), for example, examined group engendered forces (GEFs) and their effect on degree of accent. Results indicated that L2 learners judged the degree of their peers' L2 accents as evidence of allegiance to their ethnic group. The study concluded that learners are frequently in the precarious position of weighing benefits and costs, that is, the benefits of speaking clearly in the L2 with the costs of not plainly staking out their ethnic group identity. The researchers cautioned teachers not to automatically attribute lack of pronunciation progress to learner disinterest or inability. Rather, learners may be responding, consciously or unconsciously, to social pressures in the environment. It is possible that learners will overtly express a strong desire for native-like speech as in the Derwing (2003) and Timmis (2002) surveys, yet, at the same time, be influenced by subtle social or psychological factors that inhibit progress in L2 pronunciation.

Overall, research on affective factors indicates that identity and motivation can exert a powerful influence on accent and pronunciation attainment. For many students, it is critical that we address affective variables directly in the classroom. If motivation and identity are ignored, some students may never make strides in intelligibility no matter how effective the instruction is.

More recent perspectives of affective issues that impact language and pronunciation learning (Dörnyei, 2005) hold that factors such as motivation are not necessarily static. They can vary moment to moment, depending on the situation, interlocutor, learning context, course, teacher, and even classroom activity. Such views give teachers hope that psycho-social variables can indeed be mediated in the classroom.

At this point, we have a better understanding of why some adult learners make more progress than others. To recap, pronunciation success in adult learners is a function of several learner variables: age at onset of learning, similarities between the L1 and L2 phonologies, extent of exposure to and use of the L2, and affective factors. Though we did not explore aptitude, research (Ioup, Boustagi, El Tigi, & Moselle, 1994) indicates when all other variables and opportunities seem to be equal, outstanding achievement in L2 pronunciation may be linked to a natural talent or aptitude for language learning. What we do not know from research is the relative impact of each factor on pronunciation learning (though age appears to be a primary predictor), nor do we know how the interplay of factors affects any one individual. Nevertheless, teachers have a unique opportunity to work with those learner variables that can be managed in the classroom setting.

What We Can Do . . .

Wong (1987) has pointed out that "pronunciation teaching is not exclusively a linguistic matter" (p. 17). This section explores what teachers can do in pronunciation classrooms besides teach the nuts and bolts of pronunciation. These suggestions pertain to the learner variables that are presumably under some measure of control in the instructional setting, namely identity/motivation and exposure to/experience with the target language.

1. Set realistic goals—in partnership with our learners.

The goal of pronunciation instruction for most students is clear, accented speech or comfortable intelligibility. Clarifying that goal sends several important messages to students. First, the course goals are realistic and in alignment with what can reasonably be accomplished in a classroom setting. Second, only those aspects of pronunciation that interfere with intelligibility will be addressed. Because accent is not the problem, it is not put in a negative light. It does not need to be eliminated or even reduced for students to be fully and easily understood. In this way, students sense that the L1 accent is valued and held in positive regard.

FIGURE 5.1: Scale for Goal-Setting

How clear is your speech now? In the first colum, circle the number that describes your proficiency level now.
How clear do you want or need your speech to be? In the second column, star ★ the number that describes your goal.

Now	Goal	Key
6	6	Speech sounds native-like.
5	5	Pronunciation is clear. Isolated errors occur, but they do not interfere with communication.
4	4	Patterns of error distract listeners but rarely cause misunderstanding.
3	3	Errors both distract listeners and cause misunderstanding. Listener effort is required.
2	2	Pronunciation frequently causes misunderstanding. Listeners often ask me to repeat.
1	1	Listeners understand only occasional words.

Adapted from *Well Said Intro*, Grant, L. (2010), National Geographic Learning Cengage, p. 10.

Teachers can also invite students to participate in setting personal pronunciation goals based on individual needs and purposes for studying English. A student who intends to teach English or provide call-center computer support by phone, for example, may want to attain a higher level of pronunciation accuracy than someone who expects to return to the home country and use English only occasionally with other non-native speakers. An example of a scale that can be used to establish intelligibility goals is presented in Figure 5.1. In my classroom, I generally explain the scale, assign it for homework, and then consult briefly with individual students about their ratings.

2. Set interim goals to sustain student motivation throughout the course.

Most experienced classroom practitioners know that under any circumstances "dramatic changes in student speech in 3 to 6 months are rare" (Wong, 1987, p. 8). What can teachers do to keep motivation from waning when the process takes longer than teachers or students would like?

It is easy for teachers, especially those who take the time to assess the pronunciation of their students, to feel overwhelmed by the many pronunciation variations learners sometimes exhibit. Teachers cannot possibly address all pronunciation issues in one course, nor do they have to. Besides, students have a greater chance of success if teachers limit the focus and give priority to those features with the greatest impact on overall intelligibility. Whether pronunciation is integrated or taught in a pronunciation-dedicated class, it helps each student to have a template of his or her three highest-priority pronunciation targets in view at all times. These targets can be renegotiated midway through the course. Here is an example of the information on one student's template:

1. stress in words
2. final consonant clusters and grammatical endings
3. aspiration of initial /p/, /t/, /k/

Another way to sustain student motivation is to increase their awareness of the stages of pronunciation learning. The model in Figure 5.2 depicts four levels of competence and assures students that, even if pronunciation change is not yet evident in spontaneous speech, learning is occurring.

3. Increase student engagement by individualizing assignments.

Depending on the ESL program, teachers may have a prescribed pronunciation syllabus that the class must follow. Even then, there are opportunities for tailoring pronunciation work to student needs. For

FIGURE 5.2: Four Levels of Competence

	Consciousness	Competence
Level 4	—	+
Level 3	+	+
Level 2	+	—
Level 1	—	—

Explanation of the Levels

Level 1: Prior to instruction, the student is unconsciously incompetent. He or she makes errors because the pronunciation concept has not been introduced.

Level 2: After the teacher explicitly points out the concept, the student gradually becomes aware of the new pronunciation feature but has limited ability to use the feature or correct the error.

Level 3: During controlled and guided practice, the student can use the feature and correct the error but only when conscious of it.

Level 4: Ultimately, the student is "unconsciously competent." That is, he or she can correct the error automatically—without thinking about it. It takes time to reach this point. Some students arrive at this stage after the course is over.

Adapted from *Goal-Driven Lesson Planning for Teaching English to Speakers of Other Languages*, Reed, M. and Michaud, C. (2010). University of Michigan Press, pp. 33–34.

example, we can customize some activities and exercises simply by having learners complete them twice—once to address the feature under study by the class and once to address one of the student's individual issues. An example in the form of an audiorecorded homework assignment is shown in Figure 5.3.

One more means of individualizing assignments is to use vocabulary, topics, and contexts relevant to your students. In pronunciation exercises, especially when teaching word stress and practicing minimal pair discrimination, incorporate vocabulary your students recognize and are likely to use. In 2008, Levis and Cortez analyzed minimal pairs (e.g., *late—let*) in frequent use in pronunciation textbooks and found that either or both words in each pair were rarely used in natural speech. If students don't know the meanings of the words, they will not be motivated to perceive or produce the sounds that create the distinction in meaning. Some word pairs may be useful (e.g., *fool–pool*); others are better omitted (e.g., *hooks–Huck's*).

FIGURE 5.3: Sample of Homework Assignment Adapted for Individual Learner

Directions: Is your teacher a "creature of habit"? Record yourself talking about at least three things he or she does during every single class. Listen and monitor for the features below. Listen as many times as is necessary.

1. Class feature

Words with –*s* endings omitted

2. Individual feature

Words in which you used /p/ for /f/

_____

_____

_____

_____

_____

_____

4. Ask students to maintain pronunciation logs.

Though confidence per se has not been studied by L2 researchers, it may be an important factor in pronunciation learning (Moyer, 2004). If students have too many negative interactions in the real world, they may begin to lose confidence and avoid communicating outside of class. Pronunciation journals offer an effective way to sensitize students not only to the ways in which pronunciation affects everyday communication, but also to the reality of listener bias and the fact that not all breakdowns are the fault of the students. Each week, students jot down the specifics of two or three interactions, noting the situation, what was said, and the listener's response. Students periodically volunteer their descriptions of an interaction for in-class reflection and analysis. For example, one student reported ordering *banana loap* at a coffee house. It took only a few minutes of discussion for him to realize that he had mispronounced *loaf* and used the incorrect term for *banana bread*. Another student was misunderstood when ordering lunch and assumed that she had made a pronunciation error. When she told the class exactly what she had said, however, it was clear that the listener should have understood. Perhaps it was noisy, the student spoke too softly, or the listener expected not to understand. In any case, journaling offers opportunities to reflect on verbal interactions, receive definitive feedback, and discuss strategies for negotiating misunderstandings, all of which increase the probability that students will not shrink from similar communication situations in the future.

5. Maximize student exposure to English outside of the classroom.

We are all acquainted with students who finish their English classes for the day and often do not hear or speak another word of English until their next class. If Moyer (2007) is correct about exposure to the L2 engendering a positive orientation to the language, then it behooves pronunciation teachers to do what we can to encourage exposure. Along those lines, teachers can assign simple homework assignments that require students to listen to authentic English via the Internet or other easily accessible media. Here are some examples:

- Go to www.favoritepoem.org/videos.html and select a video. Listen to the speaker read the poem and discuss why he or she loves it. Write several questions you would like to ask this speaker if you had the opportunity. Practice asking the questions.
- Go to http://english-trailers.org/index.php and select a movie trailer. Pick your favorite line in the trailer. Practice saying the line exactly like the actor. Now record yourself. Listen to your recording. Record again until you are satisfied.

Among my criteria for suitable internet sites is the availability of transcripts that students can mark and bring back to class—tangible evidence that students have completed the assignment. The audio programs and transcripts that accompany ESL listening texts are untapped resources for pronunciation work and bottom-up listening. Students can mark selected extracts of these transcripts for the feature currently under study, whether it is thought groups, focus words, past tense endings, etc. When students are ready, build in opportunities for self-monitoring and correction. Ask students to summarize the extract in their own words, transcribe it, and follow the same procedure of listening and marking for the target feature. Actively involving learners in assessing their own speech not only strengthens the perceptual skills that lead to automaticity but also validates their abilities.

These suggestions will work only if the time assigned to pronunciation in the classroom is adequate. Based on a recent survey of ESL teachers, Foote, Holtby, & Derwing (2011) expressed concern about both the quality and quantity of current pronunciation instruction. With 86 percent of respondents regularly integrating pronunciation into their classes and 73 percent regularly correcting mispronounced words, the researchers lamented that this unsystematic approach (i.e., correcting errors as they arise) may not only be ineffective but also constitutes the primary pronunciation instruction that many students receive. Foote, Holtby, & Derwing (2011) also noted that "many teachers reported spending less than 5% of their class time on pronunciation. In fact, some teachers spent as little as 1% of their time on pronunciation instruction" (p. 18).

Ultimately, if pronunciation is to be a priority to learners, then it must also be a priority to teachers, whom students assume to be experts in the field of English language teaching.

References

Asher, J., & Garcia, R. (1969). The optimal age to learn a foreign language. *Modern Language Journal, 53,* 1219–1227.

Bernaus, M., Masgoret, A., Gardner, R., & Reyes, E. (2004). Motivation and attitudes toward learning language in multicultural classrooms. *International Journal of Multilingualism, 1,* 75–89.

Bongaerts, T., Mennen, S., & van der Slik, F. (2000). Authenticity of pronunciation in naturalistic second language acquisition: The case of very advanced learners of Dutch as a second language. *Studia Linguistica, 54,* 298–308.

Broselow, E., Hurtig, R.R., & Ringen, C. (1987). The perception of second language prosody. In G. Ioup and S. H. Weinberger (Eds.),

Inter-language phonology: The acquisition of the second language sound system (pp. 350–361). Cambridge, MA: Newbury House.

Brown, S., & Larson-Hall, J. (2012). *Second language acquisition myths: Applying second language research to classroom teaching.* Ann Arbor: University of Michigan Press.

Dalton, C., & Seidlhofer, B. (1994). *Pronunciation.* Oxford, U.K.: Oxford University Press.

Derwing, T.M. (2003). What do ESL students say about their accents? *Canadian Modern Language Review, 59,* 547–566.

Derwing, T., & Munro, M. (2005). Second language accent and pronunciation teaching: A research-based approach. *TESOL Quarterly, 39,* 379–397.

Derwing, T. M., Munro, M. J., & Thompson, R.I. (2007). A longitudinal study of ESL learners' fluency and comprehensibility development. *Applied Linguistics, 29,* 359–380.

Dörnyei, Z. (2005). *The psychology of the language learner: Individual differences in second language acquisition.* London: Lawrence Erlbaum.

Flege, J. E. (1988). Factors affecting degree of perceived foreign accent in English sentences. *Journal of the Acoustical Society of America, 84,* 70–79.

Flege, J.E. (1991). Age of learning affects the authenticity of voice onset time (VOT) in stop consonants produced in a second language. *Journal of the Acoustical Society of America, 89,* 395–411.

Flege, J. (1995). Second language speech learning: Theory, findings, and problems. In W. Strange (Ed.), *Speech perception and linguistic experience: Issues in cross-linguistic research* (pp. 229–273). Timonium, MD: York Press.

Flege, J. E., Frieda, E. M., Nozawa, T. (1997). Amount of native-language (L1) use affects the pronunciation of an L2. *Journal of Phonetics, 25,* 169–186.

Flege, J., & Eefting, W. (1987). The production and perception of English stops by Spanish speakers of English. *Journal of Phonetics, 15,* 67–83.

Flege, J., & Hillenbrand, J. (1987). Differential use of closure voicing and release burst as cue to stop voicing by native speakers of French and English. *Journal of Phonetics, 15,* 203–208.

Flege, J., Munro, M., & Fox, R. (1994). Auditory and categorical effects on cross-language vowel perception. *Journal of the Acoustical Society of America, 95,* 3623–3641.

Flege, J. E., Munro, M. J., & MacKay, I. R. A. (1995). Factors affecting strength of perceived foreign accent in a second language. *Journal of the Acoustical Society of America, 97,* 3125–3134.

Flege, J., Yeni-Komshian, G., & Liu, S. (1999). Age constraints on second language acquisition. *Journal of Phonetics, 25,* 169–186.

Foote, J. A., Holtby, A.K., & Derwing, T. M. (2011). Survey of the teaching of pronunciation in adult ESL programs in Canada. *TESL Canada Journal, 29,* 1–14.

Gatbonton, E., Trofimovich, P., & Magid, M. (2005). Learners' ethnic group affiliation and L2 pronunciation accuracy. *TESOL Quarterly, 39,* 489–512.

Grant, L. (2007). *Well said intro: Pronunciation for clear communication.* Boston: National Geographic Learning Cengage.

Guiora, A. Z., Beit-Hallami, B., Brannon, R. C. L., Dull, C. Y., & Scovel, T. (1972). The effects of experimentally induced changes in ego states on pronunciation ability in a second language: An exploratory study. *Comprehensive Psychiatry, 13,* 421–428.

Hansen Edwards, J. A. (2008). Social factors and variation in production in L2 phonology. In J. G. Hansen Edwards and M. L. Zampini (Eds.), *Phonology and second language acquisition.* Philadelphia: John Benjamins.

Ioup, G. (2008). Exploring the role of age in the acquisition of a second language phonology. In J. G. Hansen Edwards and M. L. Zampini (Eds.), *Phonology and second language acquisition* (pp. 41–62). Philadelphia: John Benjamins.

Ioup, G., Boustagi, E., El Tigi, M., & Moselle, M. (1994). Re-examining the critical period hypothesis: A case study of successful adult SLA in a naturalistic environment. *Studies in Second Language Acquisition, 16,* 73–98.

Kim, R. (1995). The effect of age-of-L2 onset on L2 production: The English /i-ɪ/distinction made by Korean speakers. *English Teaching, 50;* 257–279.

Lado, R. (1957). *Linguistics across cultures.* Ann Arbor: University of Michigan Press.

Lee, B., Guion, S., & Harada, T. (2006). Acoustic analysis of the production of unstressed English vowels by early and late Korean and Japanese bilinguals. *Studies in Second Language Acquisition, 28,* 487–513.

Lenneberg, E. (1967). *Biological foundations of language.* New York: Wiley.

Levis, J., & Cortes, V. (2008). Minimal pairs in spoken corpora: Implications for pronunciation assessment and teaching. In C.A. Chapelle, Y.-R. Chung, and J. Xu (Eds.), *Towards adaptive CALL: Natural language processing for diagnostic assessment* (pp. 197–208). Ames: Iowa State University.

Lippi-Green, R. (2012). *English with an accent: Language, ideology, and discrimination in the United States* (2nd ed.). New York: Routledge.

Logue, M., & Conradi, P. (2010). *The king's speech: How one man saved the British monarchy.* New York: Sterling.

Major, R., & Kim, E. (1996). The similarity differential rate hypothesis. *Language Learning, 46,* 465–496.

Moyer, A. (1999). Ultimate attainment in L2 phonology: The critical factors of age, motivation, and instruction. *Studies in Second Language Acquisition, 21,* 81–108.

Moyer, A. (2004). *Age, accent, and experience in second language acquisition: An integrated approach to critical period inquiry.* Clevedon, U.K.: Multilingual Matters.

Moyer, A. (2007). Do language attitudes determine accent? A study of bilinguals. *Journal of Multilingual and Multicultural Development, 28,* 502–518.

Oyama, S. (1976). A sensitive period of the acquisition of a nonnative phonological system. *Journal of Psycholinguistic Research, 5,* 261–283.

Piske, T., Mackay, I. R. A., & Flege, J. E. (2001). Factors affecting degree of foreign accent in an L2: A Review. *Journal of Phonetics, 29,* 191–215.

Purcell, E., and Suter, R. (1980). Predictors of pronunciation accuracy: A reexamination. *Language Learning, 30,* 271–287.

Riney, T., & Flege, J. (1998). Changes over time in global foreign accent and liquid identifiability and accuracy. *Studies in Second Language Acquisition, 20,* 213–244.

Scovel, T. (1969). Foreign accent: Language acquisition and cerebral dominance. *Language Learning, 19,* 245–254.

Suter, R. W. (1976). Predictors of pronunciation accuracy in second language learning. *Language Learning, 26,* 233–53.

Timmis, I. (2002). Native-speaker norms and international English: A classroom view. *ELT Journal, 56,* 240–249.

Trofimovich, P., & Baker, W. (2006). Learning second language suprasegmentals: Effect of L2 experience on prosody and fluency characteristics of L2 speech. *Studies in Second Language Acquisition, 28,* 1–30.

Wong, R. (1993). Pronunciation myths and facts. *English Teaching Forum (October),* 45–46.

MYTH **6**

Accent reduction and pronunciation instruction are the same thing.

Ron I. Thomson
Brock University

In the Real World . . .

A few years ago, one of my wife's friends, whom I'll call Maritza, asked whether I thought she should enroll in an accent reduction program that was locally advertised. Maritza spoke English with a delightful Spanish accent, having emigrated from Colombia to Canada as an adult. At the time of her inquiry, she was having problems at a new job and felt her accent was to blame. It might be more accurate to say that others blamed her accent, but whatever the case, she believed what her colleagues said and noticed how they responded to her when she spoke. Maritza was already highly educated and had even obtained an MBA from a Canadian university, which in addition to my personal experience with her, I took as clear evidence that she could communicate quite effectively in her L2. She had also passed an interview for a management position with an important government agency—no small feat in itself. Despite these successes, Maritza still felt insecure about her spoken English and believed it was interfering with her job performance. After some further probing, she confided that there were also interpersonal issues at work and that the people she had other issues with were the very ones who she thought could not understand her.

Appealing to my expertise in L2 pronunciation learning, I initially managed to convince Maritza not to take the accent reduction course. I really didn't see how it could help her very much, given her current ability and my suspicions about the program's claims. Unfortunately, her workplace difficulties persisted, and she eventually succumbed to the accent reduction program's promise of a brighter, accent-free future. Later, when I asked her if she felt the program had been of benefit, Maritza confidently responded that it had. I couldn't help but notice that her response was produced using the very same easy-to-understand Spanish accent I had heard her use so many times before. Despite her motivation and financial investment, it seemed as though little had changed in her accent—or in her workplace, it turns out. Even today, Maritza experiences the same job-related frustrations, which probably never really were about accent. This episode taught me that I too have communication difficulties; I failed to dissuade someone from wasting $1,000 on a program that I knew could not solve her real problems.

Maritza's story is not uncommon. Many problems immigrants face in their new country are blamed on language, and in some cases low L2 proficiency does undoubtedly limit opportunity. The reality is, however, that many L2 learners ultimately manage to acquire the language necessary to meet their needs. Still, even among the most successful learners, few manage a convincingly native-like accent (Piske, MacKay, & Flege, 2001). This fact makes L2 English learners easily identifiable and susceptible to marketers who claim to have a magic antidote for what is often characterized as a very serious problem: a communication-inhibiting and potentially costly foreign accent. As with Maritza, L2 learners' perceived need for accent reduction is often the result of factors unrelated to pronunciation and is sometimes even manufactured by accent reduction practitioners themselves. That is, appealing to fear of discrimination, some companies or individuals help to create a need in the minds of potential clients and then conveniently offer to fill it. For example, the Faculty of Business at my university recently advertised the services of an external accent reduction instructor, stating this in its promotional material:

> The Faculty of Business, Co-op Office and Business Career Development Office believe strongly that participating in such a program will lead to:
>
> - a greater chance of securing a co-op work placement and full-time position at the conclusion of your studies.
> - stronger presentation skills for use in your graduate classes and your future work environment.

The advertisement also included the statement: "Speaking clearly and effectively in English is critical in order to achieve both professional AND social success."

This sort of promotional material for an accent reduction program is rather mild in comparison to some that will be presented later. Nevertheless, it clearly appeals to L2 learners' fear that their accent can jeopardize their studies and limit their access to employment after graduation. Furthermore, the advertisement is explicitly directed at anyone with an accent, rather than distinguishing between those whose accent might actually negatively impact their education and career and the many more for whom it will not. When the stakes seem so great, a few hundred or even a few thousand dollars can seem like a small price to pay. Front and center on one accent reduction website is a testimonial from a client who states, "This program has helped me to increase my income by more than double in a short span of three months."

It is notable that rhetoric promoting negative views of accent, along with unrealistic expectations for learners, is largely the province of "accent reduction" or "accent modification" providers. Rarely is such language associated with the term *pronunciation instruction*.

What the Research Says . . .

To understand why accent reduction and pronunciation instruction are distinct enterprises, let's begin with context and terminology. Derwing and Munro (2009) propose a three-way distinction for categorizing accent and pronunciation training programs: (1) those following a business model, (2) those following a medical model, and (3) those following an educational model. These categories are largely defined by who provides the service and in what context they do so. In the business model, anyone can provide instruction, regardless of his or her qualifications, or in many cases, despite a lack of qualifications (Lippi-Green, 2012). Under the medical model, accent is typically "treated" by speech-language pathologists (SLPs) whose education primarily equips them to assess and treat patients with speech disorders (Müller, Ball, & Guendouzi, 2000; Schmidt & Sullivan, 2003). In the educational model, pronunciation teaching is largely seen as the purview of English language teachers (ELTs), where instruction is normally provided as a small part of a broader language-learning program (Derwing, 2008). In some cases, however, English language programs may also offer pronunciation instruction as a stand-alone class. These distinctions between accent reduction and pronunciation teaching models are not hard and fast. For example, it is not uncommon for SLPs to follow a combination of both the medical and business models since in many cases SLPs own their own businesses and are engaged in private practice. Similarly, some ELTs may go into business as accent reduction specialists themselves.

In addition to these generalizable models into which most programs fit, the terms that are used to describe the services provided tend to vary across models. As Thomson (2012a) indicates, the term **accent reduction** is most commonly, though not exclusively, used in the business model and carries with it certain negative connotations about accent that are advantageous for marketing purposes. In contrast, **accent modification** is more popular in the medical model, undoubtedly because this term is recommended by governing bodies for the SLP profession, including the American Speech-Language-Hearing Association (ASHA) (2007) and its Canadian counterpart, the Canadian Association of Speech-Language Pathologists and Audiologists (CASLPA) (2011). The term **pronunciation instruction** conveys far less urgency than these other terms and is most often used by ELTs. Again, these are not absolute distinctions, but, rather, general patterns. For example, some might use the term **pronunciation instruction** to describe what takes place in accent reduction courses. Conversely, some language teachers and schools might offer a class called Accent Reduction (Lippi-Green, 2012). The distinction between business and education is increasingly murky in many other domains, so these developments in the field of language teaching are perhaps unsurprising.

The choice of terminology used by service providers can also reflect differences in orientation concerning the impact of having a foreign accent. Some who promote accent reduction or accent modification may not understand that having a foreign accent does not automatically lead to a breakdown in communication. In fact, applied linguists have long argued that intelligibility is the gold standard for pronunciation, rather than speech that is free of a detectable foreign accent (Abercrombie, 1949; Morley, 1991). Munro and Derwing (1995) confirmed this belief by explicitly examining the relationship among accent (how foreign-sounding a speaker is), intelligibility (the extent to which a speaker's utterances are understood), and comprehensibility (listeners' perceptions of how much effort is involved in processing accented speech). They found that a speaker can have a very strong foreign accent, yet still be highly intelligible and comprehensible. This led Munro and Derwing (1995) to conclude that the focus of instruction should be on those features of pronunciation that actually impact intelligibility, rather than addressing every pronunciation feature that contributes to the perception of a foreign accent.

In contrast to this view, the term **accent reduction** seems to imply that (1) accent is a liability and something that needs to be eliminated and that (2) the focus of instruction should be on every feature of a foreign accent. This would necessitate addressing features of pronunciation that, despite contibuting to an accent, may not actually lead to difficulties in communication. At the same time, the use of the term **accent reduction** does not preclude the possibility that some who use it understand that the focus of pronunciation instruction should be on those features that impair intelligibility. Some practitioners may simply use these terms because they have currency with both learners and the public. Indeed, it is because the term **accent** is popular that I have chosen to use it on my own pronunciation training website (Thomson, 2012b).

Throughout, I will use the terms **accent reduction** and **accent modification** in their most common senses, referring to their business and medical orientations. I will contrast these terms with **pronunciation instruction,** referring to the teaching of pronunciation by ELTs as one language skill among many.

Some Empirical Evidence

The accent reduction industry has been growing at an exponential rate. This is immediately evident from a quick examination of its increasing exposure on the internet. A Google search for the term *accent reduction* in early 2010 resulted in slightly fewer than 200,000 hits (Thomson, 2012a). By 2012, there were more than 400,000 hits for the same term. What is more striking is that hits related to accent reduction and accent modification far outstrip hits related to pronunciation instruction. The total number of Google hits for particular terms in the fall of 2013 are provided in Table 6.1.

To date, claims concerning differences among accent reduction, accent modification, and pronunciation instruction have largely been anecdotal. One reason for this is that while empirical research investigating L2 pronunciation within the field of English language teaching has markedly increased over the past 20 years or so (Derwing & Munro,

TABLE 6.1: Number of Hits for Google Searches Using Terms Related to Accent or Pronunciation

Term	Google Hits	Term	Google Hits
Accent	134,000,000	Pronunciation	39,000,000
English accent	1,300,000	English pronunciation	3,900,000
Accent training	738,000	Pronunciation training	54,000
Accent reduction	426,000	Pronunciation teaching	44,900
Accent modification	82,000	Pronunciation instruction	15,300
Accent instruction	9,360		

2005), academic literature related to accent reduction and accent modification is almost non-existent. At the same time, frequent media exposure and advertising by accent reduction programs have provoked some strong reactions from L2 researchers who specialize in accent and pronunciation. Derwing (2008), for example, suggests that many accent reduction programs are engaging in "hucksterism" by promising something they cannot deliver. Indeed, there is no evidence that most adult L2 learners can ever develop the ability to speak without a detectable foreign accent in spontaneous speech (Abrahamsson & Hyltenstam, 2009). Lippi-Green (2012) is more specific in her criticism, stating that:

> In any city of average size, there will be a few people who have hung out a shingle and sought clients with the claim that they can teach them to lose one accent and acquire another. There is no regulation or licensing for such businesses, in the same way that an individual can claim to have developed a miracle diet and charge money for it. (p. 229)

Furthermore, responding to criticism from Knight (2000) that Lippi-Green's own field of sociolinguistics is also unregulated, she responds:

> In fact, every academic linguist attends graduate school, passes masters and/or doctoral exams, and defends a thesis or dissertation. Any linguist on a college faculty has had to apply and

compete for that position. In short, academic linguists do not just hang up a shingle. (Lippi-Green, 2012, p. 233)

To empirically test criticism of accent reduction and accent modification programs, I conducted a search for the virtual shingles of those who provide these services. Accordingly, in the remainder of this section I report on an evaluation I conducted of the top 50 Google hits for unique companies, institutions, or individuals that offered a service under each of these two labels in late 2011. For the purpose of comparison, I also assessed 50 websites offering help with English pronunciation. Of specific interest for each type of program is the mode of delivery, the educational background of the providers, and the cost. Examples of program marketing claims are also provided. To avoid singling out specific programs, no website references are provided.[1]

MODE OF DELIVERY AND PROGRAM CONTENT

In the majority of cases, accent reduction and accent modification websites tend to be portals for obtaining clients for face-to-face coaching, both individually and in groups (see Table 6.2 on page 168). However, one-third of the programs offering accent reduction do so using web-based materials only, while only 8 percent of accent modification programs do. It is interesting to note that a sizeable number of programs in both categories also offer internet-based video-conferencing (e.g., Skype) or even instruction by telephone. Although these alternative modes of delivery are undeniably convenient, there is no known research that demonstrates the efficacy of providing remote, face-to-face instruction. In contrast to accent reduction and accent modification programs, instructional materials provided under the search term "English pronunciation" are almost exclusively web-based resources for teachers and learners as opposed to stand-alone solutions. Rarely do programs using the label "pronunciation instruction" offer face-to-face or internet-based video-conferencing instruction. As noted earlier,

---

[1] Although the rank ordering of programs evaluated as part of the 2011 survey has changed somewhat as of the fall of 2013, most of the top programs remain the same, and new hits reflect the same patterns as those reported here.

TABLE 6.2: Delivery of Accent Reduction, Accent Modification, and Pronunciation Instruction

	Limited to Web-Based Materials	In-Person Option	Online Video Conferencing	App Available (Mobile)	Other
Accent reduction	34%	62%	20%	—	8% (CD/DVD; telephone)
Accent modification	8%	90%	36%	—	10% (CD; telephone)
English pronunciation instruction	94%	2%	4%	6%	—

when what is termed *pronunciation instruction* is delivered face to face, it tends to be by ELTs and in the context of a language classroom. The web-based materials on English pronunciation websites are predominantly intended to support that classroom audience and context rather than replace it.

It is difficult to determine the precise content of many accent reduction and accent modification programs promoted on the web because prospective clients are often asked to pay for an initial assessment, only after which the course of instruction is prescribed. This may reflect a medical model, in which a plan for treatment is made only after diagnosis. Alternatively, it may reflect a business model, where the initial assessment serves as the mechanism for selling a potential client on the need for treatment. In cases where course content is made explicit on accent reduction and accent modification websites, it often reflects the same approaches used by ELTs in pronunciation classrooms, rather than offering anything innovative or proprietary. For example, there are the expected references to both segmental and suprasegmental features of pronunciation as well as examples of both auditory discrimination and articulation activities. However, it is not uncommon to also find unorthodox techniques, which have no discernable grounding in second language pronunciation literature. For example, one program links to YouTube videos demonstrating unconventional jaw and tongue rotation exercises reported to help learners lose their accent, while another suggests students strengthen the tongue for articulation of *th* sounds by pressing their tongue tip against a tongue depressor. These articulation exercises seem to be influenced by therapeutic techniques associated with the treatment of motor speech disorders, such as stroke and traumatic-brain injury, rather than by any known models of L2 speech production.

Experts in L2 speech production maintain that it is largely difficult to perceive new sounds that lead to mispronunciation (Flege, 1995; Thomson, 2011, 2012c). Production practice is only necessary in order to reinforce new articulatory gestures, not because of any weakness in the muscles used for speech. In the case of English dental *th* sounds, for example, learners have difficulty because they do not have the same sound in their L1. They must learn to perceive the difference between the English dental sounds and the similar sounds in their first language (e.g., /d/ and /t/ or /v/ and /f/) and learn the gestures associated with the new sounds. When simply relying on intuition, it may seem more plausible to assume a motor difficulty is to blame for mispronunciation of *th* sounds, since to a native speaker of English these sounds are not at all similar to /d/, /t/, /v/, and /f/. In fact, these sounds are very similar to each other, but through experience, native speakers of most dialects of English have learned to treat them as perceptually distinct. Knowing this fact about the perceptual relationship between such sounds will help instructors understand the true source of their students' difficulties. Fortunately, teachers need not be particularly concerned if learners do not pronounce English *th* sounds in a native-like fashion, since mispronouncing these particular sounds rarely leads to unintelligible speech.

TABLE 6.3: Relevant Educational Background and Qualifications Cited on Websites Offering Accent Reduction, Accent Modification, and English Pronunciation Instruction

	None Specified	Language Teaching Experience	Undergrad in TESL or Linguistics	Graduate Degree in TESL or Linguistics	Graduate Degree in SLP	Public College or University	Major Publishing House
Accent reduction	30%	16%	6%	14%	32%	2%	—
Accent modification	18%	8%	2%	6%	66%	—	—
English pronunciation instruction	44%	32%	—	8%	4%	4%	8%

EDUCATIONAL BACKGROUND OF PROGRAM OWNERS/PROVIDERS

The data summarized in Table 6.3 provides compelling support for critics' assertions that accent reduction, accent modification, and pronunciation teaching are unregulated as far as instructor qualifications are concerned. The educational backgrounds of those offering accent reduction, accent modification, and pronunciation instruction vary widely. In many cases, no background qualification of instructors is provided on the programs' websites at all. This is most common on websites offering English pronunciation instruction. However, since these materials are typically supplemental, web-based, and free (see Table 6.4), this oversight is not as disconcerting as it is for accent reduction and accent modification providers who, as noted, largely use their websites to recruit students for face-to-face instruction. When instructors' qualifications are provided for accent reduction programs, the most commonly cited credential is a degree in Speech Language Pathology. However, there are also many accent reduction programs that either omit instructor credentials or list language teaching experience or a TESL background as the qualification. A degree in Speech Language Pathology is, again, the most commonly cited credential in accent modification programs, which, as mentioned earlier, is the preferred term used by the SLP profession. For pronunciation instruction, the most common preparatory background described is language teaching experience, which may reflect not only a lack of professional regulation in the ELT field as well, but also a lingering belief that anyone who speaks the language can teach it. In each type of accent or pronunciation training program, there are also examples of instructors who boast unrelated backgrounds. For example, one instructor touts her credentials in landscape architecture, while another refers to himself as a trucker. A mathematician and a person with an MBA own another company but report no relevant credentials in pronunciation instruction.

PROGRAM COST

The absence of any coherent fee structure associated with accent reduction, accent modification, and pronunciation training programs is striking. Costs for each type of program are summarized in Table 6.4. As with other comparisons, accent reduction and accent modification programs deviate substantially from those offering pronunciation instruction. The latter largely make their web-based resources freely

TABLE 6.4: Cost of Services Related to Accent Reduction, Accent Modification, and Pronunciation Instruction

	Free Materials	Paid Materials	Programs with Prices on Website	Mean Price for Entry-Level Paid Service (Range)
Accent reduction	14%	86%	46%	$958 ($50–$10,620)
Accent modification	2%	98%	30%	$454 ($25–$1400)
English pronunciation instruction	70%	30%	100%	$116 ($6–$296)*

* Includes five programs that also use the term *accent reduction* in their advertising; when excluded, the mean price for pronunciation instruction drops to $40.

available, although in many cases some income is derived from third-party internet advertisements on their websites or through support from educational sponsors. In contrast, accent reduction and accent modification programs are predominantly fee-based. Furthermore, many of these programs do not provide pricing on their websites but require contact information or a face-to-face assessment before disclosing their fees. In cases where the cost of accent reduction or accent modification programs is provided, the entry point for service varies widely—from $25 for a one-hour session at the low end to $10,620 at the high end for a prepackaged program lasting several weeks. Interestingly, the four most expensive programs found using "English pronunciation" as the search term were four of five in the category that also used the term *accent reduction* somewhere on their websites. When these five programs are excluded from the list of programs offering English pronunciation instruction, the mean minimum cost for entry into paid pronunciation instruction programs decreases to $40. This contrasts with $958 for accent reduction programs and $454 for accent modification programs. Programs may end up costing more if the learner decides to extend training beyond what is advertised as their entry-level fee.

Many of the more expensive accent reduction and accent modification programs involve a long-term commitment to a course of instruction. However, prices on a per hour basis fluctuate dramatically, even when instructors possess the same qualification. For example, one SLP charges $1,000 per client (capped at ten clients) for a ten-hour program of group instruction in a five-week period. This amounts to $100/hour, per client. At the opposite extreme, another SLP charges $200 for 25 hours for a group of 20, which amounts to only $8/hour, per participant.

PROGRAM MARKETING CLAIMS

Program marketing claims also reveal differences among accent reduction, accent modification, and English pronunciation instruction. Having established that pronunciation instruction is largely provided by ELTs in educational settings, it is unsurprising that marketing is not a major part of their strategy. While a few ELTs make dubious claims, most say little about accent, and some even downplay its impact. For example, two free pronunciation activity websites state:

1. Don't confuse pronunciation with accent. It doesn't mean that we all have to talk like the Queen of England. As long as your pronunciation is understandable and pleasant that's fine . . . but unless you are an actor and you need to play different roles, please don't try to get rid of your accent.

2. The goal of this course isn't to force you into a certain speaking style or make you sound like me. The goal is to get you speaking clearly so your messages are understood every time.

This type of discourse helps to construct a view of accent and pronunciation that is aligned with academic research on the subject (see Derwing & Munro, 2005, for a concise and accessible overview). Accent is not the issue; intelligibility is. For example, if a learner produces a trilled *r* in place of English *r*, this will lead listeners to perceive an accent, but the trilled *r* will still be interpreted by the listener as an *r* (e.g., the *r* in *rice* can be trilled and still sound like an *r*). In contrast, if a learner substitutes *l* for *r*, this will cause a loss of intelligibility, since in many cases such a substitution will result in a different English word (e.g., substituting an *l* for *r* in *rice* will result in *lice*).

In striking contrast to the types of statements typically found on pronunciation instruction websites, accent reduction and accent modification websites often use statements that are seemingly designed to instill anxiety about one's accent. For example:

1. If you speak English as a second language and feel like your foreign accent is holding your back from jobs, promotions, and even friendships, this may be one of the most important messages you will ever read . . . .

2. Your foreign accent may be preventing others from understanding you, which makes for frustrating conversations. If you have an accent that causes an American listener to strain, eventually people will stop listening. Your accent may give Americans the

impression that you have a limited grasp of English and do not understand it well. In fact, many may believe that you are uneducated and unintelligent, and they might also have limited confidence in your overall abilities.

3. Excellent communication skills are essential in today's competitive business world. Unclear English pronunciation can: adversely influence advancement and promotion; hamper performance and productivity; be a source of concern and embarrassment; result in misunderstandings, time-consuming repetitions, and inaccurate messages; lead to poor relationships among members of your staff.

4. Typical non-native English speakers with strong foreign accents lose about 25 percent of their time and effectiveness because of unclear speech.

5. As the saying goes, *Time is money.* The more time you must spend making yourself understood, the less money you are making for yourself and your company.

Accent reduction and accent modification programs also frequently make quantitative claims regarding outcomes but offer no published evidence to support such statements. Consider these examples:

1. Past comparisons have shown that people who practice the recommended exercises for one hour every day can expect to experience at least a 50 percent change in their accent or dialect.

2. Can you really lose your accent? Yes! [In 28 days] says accent reduction expert.

3. If your accent is holding you back from communicating effectively when speaking English, then we can help you achieve significant, life-changing results in just a few hours.

4. WE WILL FIX YOUR ENGLISH PRONUNCIATION PROBLEMS PERMANENTLY IN MINUTES! Our approach is Simple, Easy, Painless and Fun!

5. Research consistently shows that business professionals who complete our program achieve a 50 to 60 percent improvement in their English pronunciation skills.

As noted earlier, there is no published evidence of any approach to pronunciation instruction that allows typical adult learners to speak a second language without an accent, while there is clear evidence that such a goal is normally unattainable (see Abrahamsson & Hyltenstam, 2009). Even improving learners' intelligibility and comprehensibility takes both extended training, as well as substantial experience in the real world (see Derwing & Munro, 2005). One possible source of the belief that improvement can be more rapid might be the form of assessment used to measure improvement. There is no doubt that learners can be taught to improve in highly controlled situations (such as on a reading or imitation task). However, the extent to which this type of learning translates to spontaneous speech outside of instruction is not well understood.

Accent reduction and accent modification programs sometimes emphasize the importance of instructor qualifications to promote their services, despite that fact that the industry is currently unregulated and no qualifications are required. Alluding to credentials that are not necessarily representative of any recognized expertise in second language pronunciation can nevertheless sound compelling to prospective clients. Here are two examples:

1. CONSUMER ALERT! A Speech Therapist, Accent Reduction Trainer, American Accent Coach or Pronunciation Specialist is NOT the same as an ASHA Certified Speech Language Pathologist with a Masters or PhD. Do not be fooled!

2. Accent reduction is a specialization within the profession of Speech-Language Pathology. Speech pathologists are specifically educated to analyze the speech sounds and train clients to modify their speech patterns.

The first example is clearly false, since despite there being no recognized credential for offering this service, it implies that only SLPs should be trusted to provide instruction. On the surface, the second claim is true but is likely to further the misconception that all SLPs are trained in this area and that non-SLPs are not. Having a degree in Speech Language Pathology does not guarantee that an SLP is equipped for teaching pronunciation to L2 learners and, in fact, the overwhelming majority of SLPs are not (Müller, Ball, & Guendouzi, 2000; Schmidt & Sullivan, 2003; Thomson, 2012a).

Providing accent reduction, accent modification, or pronunciation instruction without training specific to L2 pronunciation may be at odds with professional ethics. For example, ASHA's (2011) Code of Ethics, which governs the conduct of SLPs in the U.S., explicitly states that "individuals shall engage in only those aspects of the professions that are within the scope of their professional practice and competence, considering their level of education, training, and experience." The Code of Ethics also indicates that SLPs shall not misrepresent their credentials or competence. These ethical position statements are inconsistent with a recent ASHA publication that describes accent modification as one of the best-kept career path secrets for SLPs (Kuster, 2010). Kuster quotes a *U.S. News & World Report* article (Nemko, 2008) claiming that "SLPs are especially qualified to provide this service." The Nemko article indicates that "a license in speech-language pathology . . . or a specialty credential in accent reduction or [ELT] training" are also typical qualifications. In fact, there is no recognized qualification within either the SLP or ELT profession.

It is not only SLPs who lack specific training in how to teach L2 pronunciation. ELTs with an educational background in TESL or Linguistics may also wrongly assume that simply being a language teacher provides sufficient background to teach pronunciation. As noted in my survey of accent reduction programs, 20 percent of the programs cited an undergraduate or graduate degree in TESL or Linguistics as an instructor's qualification. Although these degree programs are more likely to include a component on teaching pronunciation than SLP degree programs, they very well may not. Again, without specific training, the stance that ELTs are qualified to provide specialized pronunciation instruction is ethically indefensible. To their credit, there is evidence that many ELTs recognize their lack of preparation. See Myth 7 for a comprehensive overview of ELT training in the teaching of pronunciation.

In summary, the results of the survey of accent reduction, accent modification, and English pronunciation programs promoted on the internet corroborates many of the concerns voiced by applied linguists and language teachers who have an interest in pronunciation instruction. The lack of standards with regards to instructor qualifications, program content, and program fees is self-evident.

In some cases, the lack of instructor qualifications is obvious. Instructor backgrounds in math, business, landscape architecture, or trucking clearly do not result in pedagogically sound approaches to instruction. Judging the legitimacy of other credentials is not as straightforward. For instance, some well-intentioned SLPs quite honestly assume that, as specialists in what is often called communication sciences, they are equipped to provide pronunciation instruction. This is no doubt due in part to accent modification being classified within the SLP's scope of practice (ASHA, 2007; CASLPA, 2011). Similarly, some ELTs may assume they are qualified simply because pronunciation is a feature of language learning.

Recognizing that this is an ethical dilemma facing their field, Müller, Ball, & Guendouzi (2000) explicitly encourage SLPs who want to enter the field of accent reduction to first "acquire additional qualifications as a language teacher," arguing that "the awareness of the specific skills and demands of language teaching . . . is in [their] opinion crucial, but not usually acknowledged in 'corporate speech pathology'" (p. 128). Müller, Ball, & Guendouzi (2000) also suggest that there is a necessary bifurcation between SLP practices that are health related and accent reduction, for which *teacher* is a more appropriate label. This seems to imply that when teaching pronunciation, an SLP is really no longer an SLP, although some of the SLP knowledge base is obviously relevant and therefore transferable. In fact, many SLPs are widely respected leaders in the field of pronunciation instruction after doing just what Müller, Ball, & Guendouzi (2000) recommend.

While SLPs are well advised to acquire additional training in language teaching before embarking on a career as a L2 pronunciation specialist, many ELTs would benefit from additional training in articulatory phonetics—something most SLPs already have. While insufficient on its own, knowledge of articulatory phonetics is an indispensable foundation for teaching pronunciation.

In addition to questions surrounding the qualification of instructors, the survey results also raise concerns regarding how some programs frame accent reduction and accent modification. Programs often follow the business and medical models described by Derwing and Munro (2009). For example, their advertising frequently highlights the negative consequences of having a foreign accent. Numerous programs also describe their instruction in terms of treatment, using language similar to that used by medical professionals. While in many cases inaccurate claims about a foreign accent may simply be advertising strategies, other inaccuracies may be based on a lack of understanding of what causes accents, and of the real impact that foreign accents have on communication. If foreign accented speech is intelligible, breakdowns in communication are likely the responsibility of the listener.

The revelations provided by the survey demand a response, but given the size of the industry and the market for these types of programs, knowing where to begin is no simple task. The next section will suggest some tentative possibilities.

What We Can Do . . .

1. Provide ethical pronunciation instruction.

The population being pursued by accent reduction, accent modification, and pronunciation programs is unquestionably vulnerable and is often the target of accent-related discrimination (Munro, 2003; Lippi-Green, 2012). Thus, a heightened concern for ethics is particularly important in contexts where pronunciation instruction is the primary focus. A teacher might quite justifiably address minor pronunciation issues as they arise in the broader context of a language classroom, but when an instructor desires to specialize in pronunciation training, ethical practice demands that they be minimally prepared.

Since there is not yet a recognized minimum qualification for entry into this field, it is impossible to describe precisely what such training should comprise. Ideally, however, it should include an entire course specifically aimed at helping prospective instructors understand how L2 speech develops and should provide them with evidence-based practices that are known to benefit L2 learners. To insure legitimacy and accountablity, such a course should be taken for credit from a recognized post-secondary institution. That is, it should not simply require paying a fee to attend a private workshop. While courses in general linguistics, articulatory phonetics, and language teaching provide an excellent foundation, they do not themselves constitute adequate preparation for teaching pronunciation.

Like Müller, Ball, & Guendouzi (2000), Derwing (2008) proposes that the ELT profession is the most natural fit for pronunciation instruction and that language classrooms, not health care facilities, are the more appropriate context. English language teachers are more likely to have an understanding of the psycholinguistic, social, and personal dimensions of foreign accent because they often have specialized training and broad experience working with this population. As noted earlier, this does not exclude SLPs or anyone else from providing pronunciation instruction; it simply demands that anyone who desires to teach L2 pronunciation should be properly equipped to do so. In Myth 7, Murphy specifically discusses the extent to which ELTs are prepared to teach pronunciation.

Professional associations in the field of English language teaching ought to follow the lead of the SLP profession and develop a detailed set of ethical guidelines for professional practice. Within these professional associations, those with a special interest in pronunciation instruction should contribute to the establishment of a professional position on the minimum requirements expected of those who offer this service.

Having a clear professional position on what constitutes ethical, evidence-based practice in pronunciation instruction will enable us to speak with authority on the topic. This in turn might increase the probability that English language programs will become the first and most obvious point of contact for companies wanting to improve the communication skills of their non–native speaking employees. Recognized professional status for ELTs who teach pronunciation may also reduce the commonly encountered practice of postsecondary programs outsourcing pronunciation instruction for their international students or International Teaching Assistants to private accent reduction providers. Ironically, many institutions do this when they have English language programs operating on the same campus.

2. Give more attention to pronunciation instruction as part of English language classes.

If ELTs are the most natural fit for providing pronunciation instruction, then there must be a return to more explicit pronunciation instruction in English language classrooms. Beginning with the advent of Communicative Language Teaching (CLT) in the 1980s and throughout the so-called post-methods era that has followed (Richards and Rodgers, 2001), pronunciation has been neglected by many ELT programs. Ostensibly, this is because many teachers now believe that a focus on form, including grammatical form, is unimportant. In truth, it might have just as much to do with the fact that with the globalization of English, the ELT profession has exploded, and thus the demand for teachers far exceeds the capacity to train them effectively (Thomson, 2012d). Consequently, while underprepared teachers may be able to manage a listening, speaking, reading, or writing activity using a textbook, focusing on form, whether it is grammatical or phonological, requires explicit knowledge of the item being taught.

Ironically, this very absence of pronunciation instruction in English language classrooms may explain the concomitant explosion of the accent reduction and accent modification industries. Sikorski (2005) argues that many SLPs began entering the field because L2 English learners were desperate for assistance and started approaching SLPs in the absence of any alternative. In fact, surveys of L2 English learners clearly support the view that both in English-speaking contexts and abroad, learners overwhelmingly desire to acquire the pronunciation of a native speaker variety of English (Timmis, 2002; Derwing, 2003). If pronunciation were more dominantly featured in English language classrooms, the appeal of accent reduction programs might be diminished. Students would not only benefit by developing more intelligible pronunciation when necessary but, in the process, teachers could also help raise learners' awareness of what is realistically possible. If students understood, for example, that native-like pronunciation is a pipedream for most adult L2 learners, they would be less susceptible to the baseless promises made by many in the accent reduction industry. Ultimately, incorporating more pronunciation instruction into language classes will require teacher preparation, which, in recent decades, has been limited (Murphy, 1997). As noted earlier, however, there is positive evidence that substantive training opportunities in teaching L2 pronunciation are on the rise (Foote, Holtby, & Derwing, 2011).

3. Urge your language program to give more explicit attention to pronunciation instruction.

Another way to obviate the lure of accent reduction for English learners is for language programs to offer more focused attention to pronunciation instruction within their existing course or to provide stand-alone pronunciation courses of their own. As has been pointed out, there is clearly a demand for this type of instruction from learners themselves. While tactics that appeal to learners' insecurities may artificially increase that demand, most prospective clients will still shop around. If they find a language program offering comparable instruction for a much smaller fee, they may consider that option first, providing another opportunity to raise this population's awareness of accent, pronunciation, and the outcomes that can be realistically expected. The fact that none of the stand-alone programs surveyed on the internet were offered under the auspices of a language training program suggests a missed opportunity.

Stand-alone pronunciation courses offered by English language programs will be more affordable than many corporate accent reduction programs because they are able to use an education-based fee structure characteristic of language instruction in general (e.g., stand-alone courses in L2 reading or writing are commonly found in many community colleges for a reasonable fee). Assigning an appropriately qualified ELT to teach a stand-alone pronunciation course would cost the same as assigning an ELT to any other class. Apart from possessing more appropriate educational background as a whole, ELTs are normally more reasonably priced relative to others offering this service.

A stand-alone pronunciation program offered by a language-training program is also more likely to be truly elective in nature since profit is less of an issue. Knight (2000) reports that some accent reduction providers behave ethically in this regard by refusing to take clients who they assess as having perfectly intelligible speech, despite an obvious accent. Language training programs can take this same ethical approach. Prospective students can be assessed to determine if they would truly benefit from pronunciation instruction. If their speech is perfectly intelligible, the difference between intelligibility and accent, as outlined earlier, can be explained, to ensure learners understand their options. In some cases, learners might have a special motivation for moving beyond intelligibility or working on pronunciation that sounds more like a particular variety of English. Again, it needs to be made clear that most adult L2 learners are limited in what they can achieve. In an educational context, it is easier to realistically assess students than it is in the corporate accent reduction world where there may sometimes be a greater tendency to accept any potential client for the sake of improving the bottom line.

Some learners have a special need or financial capacity for focused private pronunciation instruction. Again, in the context of an educational institution that provides a broader L2 English curriculum, this need can be addressed by someone who is suitably qualified, and for a far smaller fee than is often the case in the accent reduction or accent modification industries.

Finally, to reach learners who need support, it may be necessary to do what is to some unthinkable: Go against what has become accepted orthodoxy in applied linguistics circles and use the term **accent** in promotional materials. There is no escaping the fact that, rightly or wrongly, this term has greater currency among many learners than the term **pronunciation**. How foreign accent is treated is ultimately of far greater importance than what pronunciation instruction is called. From the Google hits data alone, it is clear that the term **accent** currently has the momentum.

4. In the absence of alternatives to privately offered pronunciation instruction, give students tips on how best to avoid charlatans.

Ultimately, some learners simply do not have access to language program–based pronunciation instruction and are going to look elsewhere. They may be like my wife's friend, Martiza, who was determined to do something about her accent. In such cases, there may be advice that we, as English language teachers, can give to our students to prevent them from wasting time and money. Some tips that I have begun giving learners include:

- Avoid companies that use fear-mongering in their marketing. They do not have your best interests at heart. Shy away from programs that profess to be able to eliminate foreign accents. In all but a few unusual cases, this is impossible; thus, everything else they claim should be treated with suspicion.
- Don't enroll in programs that claim that they have a magic method for improving your pronunciation. There are no shortcuts—only hard work.
- Stay away from programs that claim to be able to affect permanent change over the course of a weekend, a few

weeknights, or even a month. Progress is never that rapid. Real progress of the sort that impacts sponta-neous speech requires instruction combined with years of experience.

- Ask the programs if they focus on segmentals, supra-segmentals, articulation, or auditory training. If they don't understand the question, it's probably not because of your accent, but because they are not mini-mally qualified. Be wary! If they indicate that they focus on one or two aspects, to the neglect of the others, the approach is not very useful.

- Determine how the programs assess pronunciation, both before and after training. If they use reading out loud as their only form of assessment, be concerned. Measuring improvement in pronunciation in a reading task is not the same as measuring improvement in spontaneous communication.

- Request the instructors' qualifications. If providers sim-ply state that they have years of experience or are SLPs or ELTs, but nothing more, ask where they gained their specific knowledge of L2 pronunciation instruction.

- Verify that any claims to formal education, including content related to L2 pronunciation instruction, are in the form of credit courses from recognized colleges or universities, and not credentials from private compa-nies who are self-regulated.

- Ask programs to provide you with the title, author, and date of publication for the resources they will use. If they use self-published materials, ask why. There are many excellent materials printed by major publishing houses, and they should be able to explain why they don't want theirs published by a commercial publisher where quality is more likely to be assured.

- Don't enroll in programs that require large upfront fees or a lengthy program of instruction that offers no possibility of withdrawing or obtaining a partial refund if the program is not what you were expecting. This is not meant to imply that opting out should be a possibility for the entire duration of a long course, but there ought to be some early withdrawal deadline, as is normally the case for semester-long college and university programs.

- Read the fine print on money-back guarantees. For example, one program promises a full refund if you're not fully satisfied (as long as they monitor you using their online program for five days a week for an entire year).

References

Abercrombie, D. (1949). Teaching pronunciation. *ELT Journal, 3*, 113–122.

Abrahamsson, N., & Hyltenstam, K. (2009). Age of onset and native-likeness in a second language: Listener perception versus linguistic scrutiny. *Language Learning, 59*, 249–306.

American Speech-Language-Hearing Association (ASHA). (2011). *Code of ethics* [Ethics]. Retrieved from www.asha.org/policy

American Speech-Language-Hearing Association (ASHA). (2007). *Scope of practice in speech-language pathology.* Retrieved from www.asha.org/policy

Canadian Association of Speech-Language Pathologists and Audiologists (CASLPA). (2011). *Scope of practice for speech-language pathology.* Retrieved from http://www.caslpa.ca/english/resources/scopes.asp

Derwing, T. M. (2003). What do ESL students say about their accents? *Canadian Modern Language Review, 59*, 547–566.

Derwing, T. M. (2008). Curriculum issues in teaching pronunciation. In J. G. Hansen Edwards & M. L. Zampini (Eds.). *Phonology and second language acquisition* (pp. 347–369). Philadelphia: John Benjamins.

Derwing, T. M., & Munro, M. J. (2005). Second language accent and pronunciation teaching: A research-based approach. *TESOL Quarterly, 39*, 379–397.

Derwing, T. M., & Munro, M. J. (2009). Putting accent in its place: Rethinking obstacles to communication. *Language Teaching, 42*, 476–490.

Flege, J. E. (1995). Second-language speech learning: Theory, findings, and problems. In W. Strange (Ed.), *Speech perception and linguistic experience: Theoretical and methodological issues* (pp. 229–273). Timonium, MD: York Press.

Foote, J. A., Holtby, A., & Derwing, T. M. (2011). Survey of the teaching of pronunciation in adult ESL programs in Canada, 2010. *TESL Canada Journal, 29*(1), 1–22.

Knight, D. (2000). Standards. In R. Dal Vera (Ed.), *Standard speech and other contemporary issues in professional voice and speech training* (pp. 61–78). New York: Applause.

Kuster, J. M. (2010, Apr 27). Accent modification cited as "Best-Kept Secret." *The ASHA Leader.* Retrieved from www.asha.org/Publications/leader/2010/100427

Lippi-Green, R. (2012). *English with an accent: Language, ideology, and discrimination in the United State* (2nd ed.). London: Routledge.

Morley, J. (1991). The pronunciation component of teaching English to speakers of other languages. *TESOL Quarterly, 25*, 481–520.

Müller, N., Ball, M. J., & Guendouzi, J. (2000). Accent reduction programs: Not a role for speech-language pathologists? *Advances in Speech-Language Pathology, 2*, 119–129.

Munro, M. J. (2003). A primer on accent discrimination in the Canadian context. *TESL Canada Journal, 20*(2), 38–51.

Munro, M. J., & Derwing, T. M. (1995). Foreign accent, comprehensibility and intelligibility in the speech of second language learners. *Language Learning, 45*, 73–97.

Murphy, J. (1997). Phonology courses offered by MATESOL programs in the U.S. *TESOL Quarterly, 31*, 741–764.

Nemko, M. (2008, Dec 11). Best-kept-secret career: Accent-reduction specialist. *U.S. News & World Report*, Retrieved from http://money.

usnews.com/money/careers/articles/2008/12/11/best-kept-secret-career-accent-reduction-specialist

Piske, T., MacKay, I. R. A., & Flege, J. E. (2001). Factors affecting degree of foreign accent in an L2: A review. *Journal of Phonetics, 29*, 191–215.

Richards, J. C., & Rodgers, T. S. (2001). *Approaches and methods in language teaching* (2nd ed.). Cambridge, U.K.: Cambridge University Press.

Schmidt, A. M., & Sullivan, S. (2003). Clinical training in foreign accent modification: A national survey. *Contemporary Issues in Communication Science and Disorders, 30*, 127–135.

Sikorski, L. D. (2005). Regional accents: A rationale for intervening and competencies required. *Seminars in Speech and Language, 26*, 118–125.

Thomson, R. I. (2011). Computer-assisted pronunciation training: Targeting second language vowel perception improves pronunciation. *CALICO Journal, 28*, 744–765.

Thomson, R. I. (2012a). Accent reduction. In C. A. Chapelle (Ed.), *The encyclopedia of applied linguistics.* Oxford, U.K.: Wiley Blackwell.

Thomson, R. I. (2012b). *English accent coach* [Computer program]. Version 2.1. Retrieved from www.englishaccentcoach.com

Thomson, R. I. (2012c). Improving L2 listeners' perception of English vowels: A computer-mediated approach. *Language Learning, 62*, 1231–1258.

Thomson, R. I. (2012d) Demystifying pronunciation research to inform practice. In H.M. McGarrell & R. Courchêne (Eds.), *Special Research Symposium Issue of CONTACT, 38*(2), 63–75.

Timmis, I. (2002). Native-speaker norms and international English: A classroom view. *ELT Journal, 56*, 240–249.

Teacher training programs provide adequate preparation in how to teach pronunciation.

John Murphy
Georgia State University

In the Real World . . .

Soon after completing a master's degree in TESOL (MATESOL) at Teachers College, Columbia University, I was fortunate to secure a full-time position teaching ESL at a four-year college in New York City. At the job interview, which took place during a regularly scheduled department meeting, twelve members of the ESL faculty plus two members of the college's Speech Department were present. Among the many questions they asked, five they kept returning to were: Have you completed a course in phonetics/phonology? Can you teach the International Phonetic Alphabet? How would you work with learners of mixed proficiency levels? What are some ways of teaching English pronunciation communicatively? Do you have any experience teaching public speaking?

As background related to their first two questions, the MATESOL program I had recently completed featured a full three-credit course called Phonetics/Phonemics and Teaching the Pronunciation of ESL, as well as a practicum course component focused on teaching the spoken language. One of the reasons I had been invited for the job interview was that a classmate from the Phonetics/Phonemics course, Sally Mettler, had recommended me for the position. Though earlier she had been offered the very same job, Sally decided not to accept it because she already had a secure teaching position elsewhere. After she declined the position, the chair of the search committee asked her if she knew of anyone else who might be a good fit for their program. To my great fortune she replied, "Well, yes, I collaborated on a successful course project in the Phonetics/Phonemics course with a classmate named John Murphy. He has quite a bit of ESL teaching experience, he's really good at phonetics and phonology, and has many creative ideas about pronunciation teaching." Later that evening, Sally phoned me to share what she could about the position. Her impression was that the committee was looking for someone who not only had a strong background in ESL teaching, including the teaching of pronunciation, but who would also know how to incorporate phonemic symbols (e.g., the International Phonetic Alphabet) as a normal part of the instructional routine. Coincidently, one of my contributions to the course project Sally and I had worked on together featured procedures for introducing and using a color-coded phonemic chart in ESL classrooms (see Murphy, 2003, and Murphy, 1994, for later elaborations of these procedures). Since Sally had advised that pronunciation teaching was the search committee's primary areas of interest, I arrived at the interview with plenty of copies of the phonemic chart and was well rehearsed in how to make productive use of such material in an ESL classroom. When the question actually came up, I was ready. The eyes of several of committee members widened in approval as I distributed a copy of the chart to everyone present and proceeded to explain how I would use it in class (e.g., through listening discrimination and student-centered information-gap procedures). The Department Chair phoned to offer me the position soon thereafter.

After working in this position for several months, I realized some of the motivations behind the other questions. First, the members of the ESL faculty had little background in pronunciation teaching. Most were teachers of ESL reading, composition, or grammar, and they were looking for someone who could focus on pronunciation. Second, the two members of the Speech Department were co-directors of what is commonly referred to as the Introductory Course in Speech Communication (ICSC). At the time, this was a *bread-and-butter* Speech Department course that all undergraduates, including ESL students, were required to complete at some point during years of college study. ESL learners, however, were having a lot of trouble passing the required ICSC. To address this problem, the search committee was looking for someone who would be able to design and teach an ESL oral communication course that would better prepare ESL learners to later succeed as ICSC participants. In short, upon accepting the position, I was stepping into a potential minefield of instructional challenges and interdepartmental expectations.

Prior to the first day of class, I was told to use a traditional pronunciation text (Prator & Robinette, 1985) with a pedagogical sequence building from sound segments to phonological processes (e.g., assimilation, linking, and intonation) and to supplement the text with public speaking activities (e.g., 5–8 minute student speeches from the front of the class). With three years of prior teaching experience in Latin America in addition to the more recent master's degree, I spent the subsequent nine years fine-tuning the course to bring it more in line with contemporary understanding of ESL teaching (see Murphy, 1992, 1993). An essential lesson I learned was that pronunciation teaching is best envisioned within a broader framework of spoken communication. As discussed in Murphy (1991), this framework involves a continual search to balance the teaching of speaking (general fluency), listening (for both social interactive and academic purposes), and pronunciation (including both suprasegmental and segmental dimensions). In contrast to the anxiety I often experienced during my first year in the position, it was a search I eventually found to be both professionally rewarding and great fun.

In my ninth year of this particular teaching position, I interviewed for a new opportunity to serve as an ESL teacher educator on the graduate faculty of Georgia State University (GSU) in Atlanta. As part of the exit interview with GSU faculty, the chair of the search committee cited two features of my background of particular interest. The first I had anticipated since it was mentioned in the position announcement. The doctoral program I completed while teaching in New York included a strong focus on the observation, supervision, and professional development of ESL classroom teachers. The second feature mentioned was more of a surprise. The search committee was pleased that I had sufficient background (i.e., teaching experience and formal study) to be able to offer a graduate level course in Teaching the Pronunciation of ESL. Further, their faculty encouraged me to prioritize this area of specialization in both my research and teaching agendas. On accepting the GSU position, I realized that my interest in pronunciation teaching was even more of a professional asset than I had realized.

So, what about you? If you were offered an opportunity to teach an ESL or EFL course that featured a strong pronunciation component, would you feel up to the challenge? Your answer might depend, at least in part, on your previous experiences as a teacher-in-training and as a practicing teacher. One way to take stock of your readiness is to reflect on the scope and focus of the teacher preparation program you attended. Did the program include a strong pronunciation teaching component? Also, beyond your professional training, have you taught or practice-taught pronunciation before? If so, were you comfortable with the quality of your teaching and satisfied with the results?

What the Research Says

For much of the history of L2 teaching, very little research has focused on L2 teachers' knowledge, beliefs, or readiness to teach pronunciation. Prior to the 1970s, most TESOL/Applied Linguistics specialists depended on more established parent disciplines such as Linguistics,

Communication Science, and Educational Psychology to inform research and teaching practices. During the 1970s and 1980s, second language acquisition (SLA) specialists began to document the impact of factors such as age, exposure to language input, and transfer from the first language on the acquisition of pronunciation by ESL learners (See Myth 5 for more on related topics). In the years immediately following, instructional recommendations of several specialists in ESL pronunciation teaching were becoming better known (e.g., Celce-Murcia, 1987; Gilbert, 1993/2012; Grant, 1993/2010; Morley, 1991; Murphy, 1991; Pica, 1984).

It was not until the mid-1990s that specialists in second language teacher education (SLTE) began to pursue a different research direction. The direction to which SLTE specialists turned was the field of general teacher education. What they found were researchers who were attempting to define and explore the knowledge base of classroom teaching from the ground up (e.g., Peterson & Clark, 1978; Shulman, 1987), including the theme of instructor readiness to teach. A pivotal lesson SLTE specialists discerned from general education literature was the importance of turning to teachers by focusing research efforts on teachers' understandings of their own work in classrooms (National Institute of Education, 1975).

Eventually, this area of investigation came to be known as "teacher cognition" research (Borg, 2003, p. 81). By the late 1990s, proponents of this new perspective within the field of TESOL/Applied Linguistics (e.g., Freeman & Johnson, 1998; Richards, 1996) were signaling that research into the perceptions, beliefs, and understandings of L2 teachers was sorely underdeveloped. While continuing to embrace the field's longstanding premise that information about SLA, knowledge about language, and the recommendations of instructional specialists are important contributors to the formation of L2 teachers, SLTE specialists proposed that L2 teachers' cognitions are even more foundational to understanding what constitutes the knowledge base of language teaching. Some example findings from the several research traditions are listed.

- **Knowledge about Language:** Since some phonemes carry a heavier functional load than others, not all phonemes are equally important to teach (Catford, 1987; Munro and Derwing, 2006).
- **Knowledge about SLA:** Pronunciation success is correlated with the professional motivation of the learner (Moyer, 1999).
- **Specialist Recommendations about Pronunciation Teaching:** Thought groups serve as a requisite phonological context for teaching both prominence and intonation in English (Brazil, 1997).
- **L2 Teacher Cognition:** Many ESL and EFL teachers do not know how to assess students' pronunciation abilities (Macdonald, 2002).

Although knowledge about language, knowledge about SLA, and specialists' recommendations certainly are important and will continue to inform L2 teachers' professional efforts (Tarone & Allwright, 2005), Freeman and Johnson (1998) explain that, at its core, the knowledge base of L2 teaching "must focus on the activity of teaching itself; it should center on the teacher who does it, the contexts in which it is done, and the pedagogy by which it is done" (p. 397). The premise that L2 teachers are primary contributors to the knowledge base of L2 pronunciation teaching underpins the remainder of this chapter. As important as other knowledge sources may be, to truly be ready to teach pronunciation, we need to better understand the cognitions (e.g., perceptions, beliefs, understandings) of pronunciation teachers.

Overview

To report on what pronunciation teachers know and believe, I examined the available research literature on ESL and EFL teachers' perceptions, beliefs, and understandings of pronunciation teaching. The review features 13 studies with survey components, five studies with interview components, one study that includes in-depth classroom observation of five pronunciation teachers, and two other studies that include less extensive classroom observation components. Of these various sources of information, the 13 survey studies include nine surveys of language teachers, three surveys of teachers and students, and a survey of teacher preparation programs across the United States (Murphy, 1997). All of the studies fall under the category of teacher cognition research with the exception of the teacher preparation program survey. I decided to include Murphy's program survey to help set the stage for and to contextualize the remaining teacher cognition sources of information. Viewed together, the survey and interview studies gathered responses from 1,634 teachers, 68 teacher preparation programs, and more than 67 ESL programs in over ten countries. This might be perceived as an impressive range of data. However, it is worth noting that the studies were of different types, conducted in a wide range of settings, and spanned more than three decades. To these sources, I also include a recent review of available literature on L2 pronunciation teaching (Deng et al., 2009).

Table 7.1 lists the 18 research reports examined. Note that it features the year of publication, the research type, the number and type of participants, and the location of each study. The teacher surveys and interviews of teachers tend to focus on the teachers' values and beliefs about pronunciation teaching. Before summarizing findings gleaned from the sources included in Table 7.1, it is important to acknowledge the relatively small amount of classroom observation data featured in the research studies reviewed. Of the three observation-inclusive studies, one (Baker, 2011a) is notably more comprehensive than the other two (Cathcart & Olsen, 1976; Cohen & Fass, 2001) and will be discussed in greater detail. What makes Baker's 2011a study unique is that she complemented teacher-reported data (e.g., interviews with teachers) with both classroom observations and simulated recall procedures. (Stimulated recall is a research procedure that uses video recordings of teachers in action in order to provide opportunities for the video-recorded teachers to comment on what they were thinking while teaching as they are viewing recordings of their own acts of teaching.)

TABLE 7.1: Studies of Pronunciation Teachers about Pronunciation Teaching

Authors	Year	Research Type	# of Participants	Location
Akram	2010	Survey	25 EFL teachers, government schools	Pakistan
Baker	2011a	Interviews, observations, stimulated recalls	5 IEP/ESL teachers	USA
Bradford & Kenworthy	1991	Survey	33 ESL teachers, representative institutions	Great Britain
Breitkreutz, Derwing, & Rossiter	2001	Survey	67 ESL teachers & program coordinators	Canada
Burgess & Spencer	2000	Survey	32 ESL teachers	Great Britain
Burns	2006	Survey	148 ESL teachers from 6 regions	Australia
Cathcart & Olsen	1976	Survey & observation	38 ESL teachers	USA
Cohen & Fass	2001	Survey, interviews, & observation	40 EFL teachers in Adult English programs	Colombia
Deng et al.	2009	Literature review	Articles published in 14 academic journals (1999–2008)	International
Foote, Holtby, & Derwing	2011	Survey	159 ESL teachers	Canada
Hismanoglu & Hismanoglu	2010	Survey	103 EFL teachers, English prep schools of 5 universities	Cyprus
Jenkins	2005	Interviews	8 NNES EFL teachers from 8 different countries	International
Jenkins	2007	Interviews	17 NNES EFL teachers from 9 different countries	International
Macdonald	2002	Interviews	8 ESL teachers	Australia
Murphy	1997	Survey	68 MATESOL Programs	USA
Sifakis & Sougari	2005	Survey	421 EFL teachers	Greece
Timmis	2002	Surveys	180 ESL & EFL teachers from 45 countries	Great Britain
Walker	1999	Survey	350 EFL teachers	Spain

Research on Teacher Readiness and Teacher Cognition

Synopses of research findings from six studies that speak most directly to ESL/EFL teachers' cognitions, including factors impacting their readiness to teach pronunciation, are discussed. Murphy (1997) collected 68 completed surveys, two partially completed surveys, and 58 course syllabi for phonology-related courses offered by MATESOL programs across the United States. The study revealed that 57 percent of the programs offered at least one course focused on topics in phonology, and 43 percent of the programs offered a more broadly focused course, or courses, that included some attention to topics in phonology. These teacher preparation courses emphasized these six topics: sound segments, mastery of a transcription system, suprasegmentals, L1 English phonological processes, contrastive analysis, and common pronunciation problems of ESL speakers. Murphy found that the MATESOL courses gave only limited attention to pedagogical considerations and instructional techniques. Because the teacher preparation courses focused more on how phonological systems operate and less on how to teach pronunciation, the study serves as a useful prelude to the review of teacher cognition studies. Murphy concluded that pre-service ESL teachers across the United States need considerably more support in how to teach pronunciation. With the exception of Murphy (1997), we have no other national-level research examinations of how MATESOL programs introduce pre-service teachers to topics in pronunciation teaching. In fact, beyond a few discussions of the curriculum offered by individual programs, there is very little evidence concerning even the more general topics and experiential activities featured through coursework in MATESOL and TESOL Certificate programs. This seems to be one of the more glaring gaps in the research literatures tied to the professional development of ESL/EFL classroom teachers.

Burgess and Spencer (2000) gathered 32 ESL teacher questionnaires that had been distributed across several different types of adult ESL programs in Great Britain. In their responses, the teacher participants were requesting more and higher quality training in how to teach pronunciation. In terms of teacher cognition, the teachers considered suprasegmentals to be important to teach but difficult to teach. Also, most of the teachers preferred integrating pronunciation teaching into other ESL courses rather than offering a stand-alone pronunciation course. Like Murphy (1997), Burgess and Spencer (2000) called for a more direct emphasis on ways to teach pronunciation in teacher training programs rather than limiting teacher preparation to the study of topics in phonology. In Burgess and Spencer's view, when topics in phonology are contextualized under the overarching frame of "how to teach pronunciation," they are more accessible to teachers-in-training and more likely to have a substantive impact on teachers' cognitions and actual classroom practices.

Hismanoglu and Hismanoglu (2010) surveyed 103 teachers from English preparatory schools of five different universities in Cyprus. Seventy-three of the teacher-participants were non-native English speakers, and 30 were native English speakers. The study's focus was to identify the most common techniques the teachers use when they teach pronunciation. The top three techniques were: (1) reading aloud, (2) using dictionaries to look up the pronunciation of words, and (3) using dialogues. The researchers classified all three of these as "traditional techniques" (p. 988). In a discussion with implications for teacher cognition, Hismanoglu and Hismanoglu explained that EFL teachers in Cyprus prefer traditional classroom techniques to more contemporary alternatives because the participating teachers tend to teach in ways that are similar to ways they themselves were taught as language learners.

Breitkreutz, Derwing, and Rossiter (2001) surveyed teachers from 67 Canadian ESL programs. Their findings suggest several teacher cognition themes. For example, only 30 percent of the respondents reported any training in how to teach pronunciation, a condition that may limit the quality of teacher cognition in this area, particularly for the other 70 percent. In an open-ended section of the survey, a quarter of the teachers added that they "lack sufficient training and training opportunities" in pronunciation teaching. The authors quoted one representative teacher as saying: ". . . generally, ESL teachers in this area *are not well trained in teaching pronunciation, and usually avoid dealing with this subject"* [emphasis added] (p. 58). The majority of the respondents in this study considered pronunciation instruction to be important at all levels of proficiency and to have long-term positive effects. The surveyed teachers were also aware of the need for more communicative ways of teaching pronunciation but were uncertain as far as how to accomplish this goal. Furthermore, despite the fact that nearly all the teachers emphasized the need to integrate prosodic features (e.g., stress, rhythm, intonation) with individual sound segments, many of the teachers' responses revealed a tendency to focus on teaching sound segments. Likewise, the instructional materials teachers reported using in classrooms were primarily segment-based. Two of the study's broader findings were the need for better instructional materials and more teacher support through professional development opportunities. In addition, most teachers realized that speech intelligibility is a more appropriate goal for pronunciation teaching than accent reduction. The authors concluded with three major points: (1) almost half of the 67 ESL programs surveyed offer stand-alone pronunciation classes, (2) a majority of the teacher-participants recognize the value of pronunciation teaching, and (3) the teachers wanted more in-service teacher training opportunities.

Ten years later, Foote, Holtby, and Derwing (2011) extended Breitkreutz, Derwing, and Rossiter's (2001) investigation with a second examination of the state-of-the-art of ESL pronunciation teaching across Canada.[1] The researchers' efforts were more inclusive this time because they surveyed 159 ESL teachers and program administrators. They found few changes during the 10 years separating the two Canadian studies. What follows is a summary of some of the findings related to teacher cognition.

Although the respondents seemed to appreciate both the importance and potential benefits of pronunciation instruction, many teachers expressed a lack of confidence in their abilities to teach

---

[1] It is worth noting that one researcher participated on both of the Canadian research teams.

pronunciation. More than half of the teachers felt confident teaching either segmentals (58 percent) or suprasegmentals (56 percent). Most did not find pronunciation teaching to be boring (73 percent), and most believed that it has lasting impact on learners' pronunciation abilities (62 percent). This latter figure, however, signaled a 12 percent drop in the number of respondents who believed that pronunciation instruction leads to permanent change when compared with findings from the earlier Canadian study. Foote, Holtby, & Derwing (2011) found that a large percentage of educator-respondents (92 percent) believed "that some learners in their institutions would benefit from a stand-alone pronunciation class" (p. 15) and, as in the earlier study, that pronunciation instruction is important for learners at all levels.

A continuing concern reported by Foote, Holtby, & Derwing (2011) was the lack of sufficient support for teachers in terms of both pre-service and ongoing training in how to teach pronunciation: 75 percent of the 2011 respondents reported they wanted more training. Many teachers commented that there are few training opportunities offered through their local institutions. In fact, compared to Breitkreutz, Derwing, & Rossiter (2001), Foote, Holtby, & Derwing (2011) documented that 31 percent fewer teachers have access to such in-house support. Both of the studies, however, indicate that teachers are aware of professional training opportunities available at conferences. With respect to prior training, more than 50 percent of the teachers in the 2011 study had completed a general TESL or linguistics course that included some attention to topics in phonology, but only 20 percent had taken a credit-bearing university course centered specifically on how to teach pronunciation. According to Foote, Holtby, & Derwing (2011), only six Master's degree programs in Canada offer a full course on how to teach pronunciation.

Another change from the 2001 Canadian study is that, ten years later, "instructors may not be integrating pronunciation instruction into their classes as much as they did in the past" (Foote, Holtby, & Derwing, 2011, p. 15). There was a 27 percent drop in the number of respondents who said that most of the teachers in their programs regularly incorporated pronunciation teaching in their courses. Even though a large number of teachers (86 percent) reported addressing pronunciation in class, the researchers estimated that, for most teachers, only a small fraction of their weekly class time (e.g., an average of 6 percent while the most frequent response was 2 percent) is dedicated to teaching pronunciation.

Finally, Foote, Holtby, & Derwing (2011) provided a set of recommendations relevant to teachers' cognitions and pronunciation teaching practices across Canada, based on their own data and data gathered from the earlier 2001 study. The priorities among the recommendations related to issues of readiness to teach are:

- ESL programs should offer more in-house training opportunities.
- Since teachers recognize that intelligibility is a requisite instructional focus (and not accent reduction), teachers should be supported in learning how to apply this recognition to classroom teaching practices.
- In light of the prioritization of intelligibility, both pre- and in-service teacher training should focus even more closely on how to:
    —assess students' pronunciation
    —explore ways to integrate pronunciation teaching within general ESL classes
    —provide explicit feedback on both segmental and suprasegmental elements of pronunciation
    —give more attention to elements that have the greatest impact on intelligibility (e.g., sentence-level stress)
    —transition away from activities focused on individual sounds (since this is an inefficient teaching strategy that siphons away precious classroom time)
    —use modern technologies to design innovative ways of teaching.

In the final study to be summarized in depth, Baker (2011a) sheds additional light on the cognitions of L2 pronunciation teachers and illustrates a future direction for research into teachers' perceptions and understandings (Baker 2011b, 2011c) (see also Baker, 2013). She gathered data on five ESL instructors' perceptions and understandings of their work as pronunciation teachers within an English for Academic Purposes program in the United States. As noted earlier, Baker's data included teacher interviews, classroom observations, and video recordings of the five participants as they taught pronunciation lessons. In addition, the data also featured stimulated recalls with the participating teachers as they were viewing and commenting on their own video recorded lessons. Baker's purpose was to explore relationships that exist between L2 teachers' cognitions and their actual pedagogical practices, ways that these cognitions have developed over time, and connections that exist between students' and teachers' perceptions (Baker 2011a, abstract). Of direct relevance to this review, one of her core findings was that training programs (e.g., MATESOL) that feature at least one course dedicated to the teaching of pronunciation is the single factor most likely to have an impact on teachers' knowledge of and confidence in teaching pronunciation.

In addition to the need for such a teacher training course, other factors that impact teachers' perceptions and understandings of pronunciation teaching are their collaborations with colleagues who teach pronunciation, the textbooks teachers use in class, and reflections on their accumulating teaching experiences. Baker found ESL teachers' own L2 pronunciation learning experiences to be more limited than their first-hand experiences in learning L2 grammar and L2 literacy. Her study documented that both knowledge about phonology and experiential knowledge about how to teach pronunciation contribute in important ways to the development of pronunciation teachers. Also, teachers' prior experiences as learners of second or foreign languages, and the styles of pronunciation teaching to which they were exposed (however constructive or problematic they might have been), have considerable impact on instructors' ways of teaching pronunciation. As a general theme, Baker found that many ESL teachers possess insufficient knowledge about (a) how the sound system of English operates and (b) how to teach pronunciation. Baker closed her discussion with a well-reasoned observation: If one of the goals of the TESOL/Applied Linguistics field is to improve the quality of pronunciation teaching, then teacher preparation programs need to give more attention to ways of teaching it.

Having summarized the findings and implications of the six studies featured, Table 7.2 rank orders major themes emerging from the full literature review that pertain to teacher readiness to teach pronunciation. The five most common themes across all eighteen of the studies included are: (1) ESL/EFL teachers feel underprepared to teach pronunciation, (2) they believe that more training in this area is needed, (3) too few teacher development programs offer a full course dedicated to pronunciation teaching, (4) more fully developed ESL program curricula are needed for teachers to feel adequately supported by the programs in which they teach, and (5) teacher preparation programs are faulted for lacking a pedagogical focus in whatever might be the phonology-related courses they offer.

Related Teacher Cognition Research

Research conducted by contemporary L2 teacher cognition specialists, such as Bartels (2005) and Borg (2003), reflects many of the themes in the research studies reviewed. Borg (2009) posits eight "generally accepted" (p. 3) findings supported by more than three decades of general education teacher cognition research that seem consistent with the literature on ESL pronunciation teachers' cognitions reviewed thus far. According to Borg's synopsis, teachers' cognitions: (1) tend to be powerfully influenced by their own experiences as learners; (2) influence what and how they learn while participating in teacher preparation programs; (3) filter how they assimilate and interpret new information and experience; (4) may outweigh the effects of teacher education in influencing

TABLE 7.2: Themes from the Research Literature Pertaining to Teacher Readiness to Teach Pronunciation, Rank Ordered by Frequency of Mention

Theme	Studies Reporting the Theme
1. Teachers feel underprepared to teach pronunciation.	Akram (2010); Baker (2011a); Bradford & Kenworthy (1991); Breitkreutz, Derwing, & Rossiter (2001); Burgess & Spencer (2000); Burns (2006); Deng et al. (2009); Foote, Holtby, & Derwing (2011); Macdonald (2002); Walker (1999)
2. Teachers believe more training in teaching pronunciation is needed.	Akram (2010); Baker (2011a); Bradford and Kenworthy (1991); Breitkreutz, Derwing, & Rossiter (2001); Burns (2006); Foote, Holtby, & Derwing (2011); Macdonald (2002); Murphy (1997)
3. Few teacher training programs offer a full course dedicated to how to teach pronunciation.	Baker (2011a); Breitkreutz, Derwing, & Rossiter (2001); Burgess & Spencer (2000); Deng et al. (2009); Foote, Holtby, & Derwing (2011); Murphy (1997)
4. Stronger ESL pronunciation curricula are needed.	Akram (2010); Breitkreutz, Derwing, & Rossiter (2001); Burns (2006); Foote, Holtby, & Derwing (2011); Macdonald (2002)
5. Teacher preparation programs are faulted for lacking a pedagogical focus in the phonology-related courses they offer.	Breitkreutz, Derwing, & Rossiter (2001); Bradford & Kenworthy (1991); Foote, Holtby, & Derwing (2011); Murphy (1997)
6. Professional training usually consists of a phonology component within a more general linguistics course.	Bradford & Kenworthy (1991); Burgess & Spencer (2000); Foote, Holtby, & Derwing (2011); Murphy (1997)
7. Teachers do not like (or are reluctant) to teach pronunciation.	Breitkreutz et al. (2001); Macdonald (2002); Walker (1999)
8. Teachers lack confidence in teaching suprasegmentals.	Burgess & Spencer (2000); Burns (2006); Foote, Holtby, & Derwing (2011)
9. Teachers tend to teach in the ways they themselves were taught.	Baker (2011a); Hismanoglu and Hismanoglu (2010)
10. High-quality teacher preparation can have a positive impact on how teachers teach.	Baker (2011a); Burgess & Spencer (2000)
11. Both declarative knowledge about phonology and experiential knowledge about how to teach pronunciation play important roles in the development of pronunciation teachers.	Baker (2011a)
12. Other potentially positive impacts are collaborations with colleagues, textbooks, and teaching experience.	Baker (2011a)

how they actually teach in classrooms; (5) can be deep-rooted and resist-ant to change; (6) can exert a persistent long-term influence on teaching practices; (7) both influence and are influenced by experience; and, par-adoxically, (8) are not always reflected in how teachers teach.

Due to the consequential nature of prospective and current teach-ers' cognitions, teacher preparation courses and programs are more likely to foster changes in teachers' understandings and teaching prac-tices if they foreground sustained, focused attention to instructional implications and practice-teaching opportunities. Some of the more promising training opportunities move beyond declarative forms of knowledge (i.e., knowledge about phonology) by engaging learners-of-teaching in micro-teaching, one-on-one tutoring, practice-teaching, and other opportunities to apply what they are learning about phonol-ogy and pronunciation teaching through interactions with ESL learn-ers, other teachers, and peers. Without such opportunities, Gregory (2005) documented how uncommon it is for language teachers to be able to apply declarative knowledge they possess about phonetics and phonology in classroom settings. As Bartels (2009) explains:

> Given the complexity of teaching, such explicit reasoning would require far too much working memory capacity to be practical. Instead, research indicates that practitioners need implicit, practice-specific knowledge. (p. 127)

The research in this section explored the topic of ESL teacher readi-ness to teach pronunciation from a teacher cognition perspective. We have seen that over the last few decades most training and degree pro-grams have been doing a less-than-adequate job of preparing ESL and EFL teachers in this area. A comprehensive review of available literature on ESL teachers' perceptions, beliefs, and understandings of pronunci-ation teaching illuminated the considerable needs in this area. One recurring theme was that many teachers are hesitant when it comes to teaching pronunciation due to inexperience, lack of specialized training, lack of resources, and/or lack of institutional support. If such feelings of hesitation resonate with your own experience, you are not alone.

Teachers Who Are Non-Native English Speakers

A final consideration worth mentioning is the very large number of non-native English speakers (NNESs) who serve as English language teachers worldwide. By recent estimates, their numbers are already larger than the number of native English speakers (NESs) in our profession (Foote, Holtby, & Derwing, 2011). Unfortunately, many NNESs are reluctant to teach pronunciation. The underlying cause of such reluctance is not necessarily due to disinterest or lack of training in the area. Rather, many NNES teachers feel insecure about the quality of their own pronunciation even when such feelings are unwarranted. Such conditions seem especially problematic if they lead NNESs to avoid training or more advanced specialization in this area. When NNESs feel reluctant to teach pronunciation, the field as a whole suffers.

The truth is, NNESs have several advantages over NESs when it comes to pronunciation teaching. First, they know the experience of learning the pronunciation of English firsthand. Just as first-hand ESL learning experiences are perceived favorably when it comes to teaching English grammar, vocabulary, and reading, they are also an asset when teaching pronunciation. As long as NNESs have benefited from relevant training in pronunciation teaching, they are more likely to understand the process of acquiring English pronunciation from a learner's perspective. Since they have experienced the process firsthand, NNES teachers have stories and insights to share about elements that both impede and help to facilitate the development of intelligible ESL pronunciation. Further, one could build a convincing case that an NNES who is both intelligible and comprehensible (even if accented) constitutes a more relevant model of ESL pronunciation for most leaners of English. Some reasons for championing an expanded role for professionally trained NNESs (along with NESs) as teachers of pronunciation are listed.

1. The number of NNES teachers of English is large and continuing to expand worldwide (Foote, Holtby, & Derwing, 2011).

2. Most entry-level English language courses across the world are
   offered by NNESs.

3. Many intermediate and advanced-level courses are offered by
   NNESs.

4. NNESs teach English not only in EFL settings but also in ESL
   contexts.

5. An intelligible, comprehensible NNES's pronunciation is more
   likely to be perceived as attainable by EFL and ESL students (in
   contrast to the pronunciation of a native speaker, which learners often perceive as practically impossible to attain).

6. The pronunciation learning experiences of an intelligible, comprehensible NNES are more likely to resonate with students'
   own learning experiences.

7. Everyone speaks English with some sort of accent.

8. The "accented" quality of non-native speech should be welcomed
   in the speech of an NNES teacher of English pronunciation, as
   long as the teacher is (a) intelligible, (b) comprehensible, and
   (c) aware of what some of the more prominent accented characteristics of his or her speech might be.

While research documents that most L2 students of English who initi-
ate their study of English as teenagers or adults will never attain a quality of pronunciation equivalent to NESs (i.e., most NNESs remain
accented in English to varying degrees), the pronunciation model of an
intelligible, comprehensible NNES teacher is eminently relevant to
learners' actual pronunciation needs. Something practical we can do
that will go far toward enhancing the quality of pronunciation teaching in the 21st century is to welcome NNESs as teachers of pronunciation while encouraging them to pursue relevant training and
specialization. Avenues for gaining access to such training have been

featured in this chapter and in this book overall. By encouraging their participation, we will be expanding the tent of English pronunciation teaching while welcoming the contributions of both NNESs and NESs worldwide. The next section addresses what ESL and EFL teachers, NESs and NNESs alike, can do to better prepare themselves to teach pronunciation.

What We Can Do . . .

Several of the more prominent themes depicted in Table 7.2 suggest that if you feel underprepared to teach pronunciation, you are in good company because the research documents that many ESL and EFL teachers feel this way. The question is, what can we do to become better prepared? Lambacher (2001) discusses a range of activities and resources available to teachers to enhance their knowledge and skills of pronunciation teaching. These include: (1) continued academic training (i.e., TEFL certificate, BA, MA, and PhD programs); (2) distance training programs (correspondence and online courses); (3) self-study of the professional literature (e.g., linguistics books, teacher reference books, activity recipe collections, classroom textbooks, journal articles); (4) membership in professional organizations (networking, organization resources); (5) conference participation (e.g., networking, attending papers, poster sessions, workshops, pre- and post-conference institutes); (6) electronic resources (e.g., internet resources, CALL software, electronic visual feedback technology); and (7) knowledge to be gained from practice-teaching, teaching, and research (e.g., reflections on teaching, feedback on teaching from peers and mentors, action research). Although many of these supports are potentially useful, the remainder of this chapter focuses on ways to capitalize on professional development opportunities, lobby for opportunities to learn more about pronunciation teaching, and work with published resources for self-study.

1. Advocate for university-level credit-bearing courses that combine phonology with pronunciation teaching.

In Myth 6, Thomson makes a similar recommendation. Some of the more efficient means for learners-of-teaching to develop the forms of implicit, practice-specific knowledge needed for effective pronunciation teaching include: (1) coursework focused on how to teach pronunciation; (2) guided observations of more experienced teachers; (3) guided practice teaching; and (4) reflective teaching combined with supportive assistance from mentors, experienced colleagues, and peers. Evidently, as useful as declarative knowledge about phonology may be, it is not enough. To be effective in the classroom, learners-of-pronunciation-teaching must begin to participate within relevant classroom settings as part of the process of weaving together declarative knowledge and their own understandings of classroom possibilities. When applying for admission to a degree or certificate program, applicants might ask (e.g., in an application letter, through correspondence with the program director, when meeting faculty and other students) if a course centered on pronunciation teaching is offered. If it is not, a follow-up query is to ask what alternative forms of support for pronunciation teaching can be arranged. Perhaps there is a member of the faculty who conducts research, teaches a course, or is interested in an area related to pronunciation teaching or phonology. In some programs, arrangements can be made for degree candidates to work alongside faculty or senior ESL classroom teachers as research assistants, teaching assistants, or interns. Upon entering a program, pre-service teachers should let it be known that they are interested in working with possible mentors, experienced teachers, and peers to further develop their knowledge and skills related to pronunciation teaching. Appendix 7.1 (see pages 217–221) provides suggested syllabus topics and tasks for a course that combines phonology and pronunciation teaching.

2. Take advantage of practice-focused workshops on pronunciation teaching at local, regional, and national forums.

In most parts of the world, there are professional associations as well as less formal communities of language teachers which organize conferences, invited talks, and workshops. For the past two decades, for example, the TESOL International Association has consistently offered a full-day pre-convention institute (PCI) dedicated to the essentials of teaching of pronunciation. Similarly, many language programs sponsor in-service workshops, brown bag gatherings, and other professional development opportunities. As you become involved with such associations, communities of language teachers, and programs, take the initiative to propose and to help organize workshops centered on pronunciation teaching. You may be surprised to learn that publishing houses are not only ready but even anxious to help support such invited talks and local workshops by arranging for the participation of one of their authors. In fact, language programs and school districts (including TESOL affiliates) can inquire about having pronunciation specialists provide in-service workshops. One strategy for being proactive is to stay current with related literatures and network with colleagues so you are aware of which specialists might be available to lead high-quality workshops. The authors of the chapters included in this book, as well as many of the other specialists whose contributions are cited throughout this volume, constitute potentially useful professional contacts. One thing you can do is to create a list of possible workshop leaders and topics to share and discuss with colleagues.

3. Take advantage of available pronunciation resources.

For most teachers, published resources are even more readily accessible than intensive courses or workshops on pronunciation teaching. In fact, you have made a great start toward becoming a more effective pronunciation teacher by reading this book. In the sections that follow, some of the more interesting published resources are divided into three primary genres: (a) teacher preparation texts, (b) activity recipe collections, and (c) ESL classroom textbooks (including teacher manuals that accompany the textbooks). Something practical you can to do is to acquire and work with at least one reliable text from each of the three genres and continue to acquire and work with additional items from each genre over time. You might also encourage the program in which you work (or study) to place some of these books in an accessible teacher resource area.

TEACHER PREPARATION TEXTS AND RESOURCES

Contemporary teacher preparation texts introduce the sound system of English and illustrate how to teach it. Some excellent examples of the first genre that merit your consideration are: Avery and Ehrlich (1992); Celce-Murcia, Brinton, & Goodwin (2010); Dalton and Seidlhofer (1994); Fraser (2001); Gilbert (2009); Kelly (2000); Kenworthy (1989); Lane (2010); Rogerson-Revell (2011); Underhill (1994); and Walker (2010). In my estimation, Celce-Murcia, Brinton, & Goodwin (2010) is the most comprehensive first genre text currently available. It is a must-read for anyone serious about developing expertise in ESL pronunciation teaching. The co-authors' discussions of core topics in phonology are matched with many practical illustrations of how to teach them. Although several of the other texts are comparably comprehensive, Celce-Murcia, Brinton, & Goodwin (2010) is the standard against which other similar resources may be compared.

Gilbert (2009) is another strong resource, available in booklet format and as a free online resource. Through sustained attention to the image of a "prosody pyramid" (p. 1), Gilbert offers a broad context, clear rationale, and numerous instructional options for positioning thought groups, word-stress, prominence, rhythm, and intonation as teaching priorities. (See Myth 4 for a description of Gilbert's approach.) Two other options are Goodwin's (2013) sixteen-page book chapter (designed to serve as a course reading within an MATESOL methods course) and Murphy's (2013) teacher development booklet (which prioritizes the teaching of thought groups and prominence). Like Gilbert (2009), these may also serve as reliable gateways for further reading in the area of pronunciation teaching. Another option is Walker (2010), which addresses teaching the pronunciation of English as a lingua franca (ELF). Since Walker's is a more specialized discussion, his text serves as a complement, rather than as an alternative, to the other first genre resources listed above. Part A of Appendix 7.2 (see pages 221–222) provides an alphabetical listing of the teacher preparation texts and book chapters mentioned in this section.

ACTIVITY RECIPE COLLECTION RESOURCES

Activity Recipe Collections (ARCs) represent a very different sort of teacher resource material. Two early precursors to this genre were Pica (1984), the first journal article to feature a series of classroom activities illustrating how to teach pronunciation communicatively, and Celce-Murcia's (1987) comparable book chapter. Since the time of their publication more than a quarter century ago, the number of activity recipe collections has expanded to include several books wholly comprised of hundreds of classroom activities through which experienced pronunciation teachers make their work available to others. Perhaps the best examples of this second genre are: Bowen and Marks (1992), Brown (2012), Hancock (1996), Hewings (2004), and Laroy (1995). To these five, we can add two more broadly focused collections that feature useful sections dedicated to pronunciation teaching: Bailey and Savage (1994, pp. 199–262) and Nunan and Miller (1995, pp. 120–150).

As helpful as ARCs can be, for the most part they lack discussion of underlying theory. For theory discussions, we need to turn to first genre teacher development texts and other synopses of research literature such as those featured in the chapters of this book. The obvious strength of second genre resources is that ARCs lessen the need of having to reinvent the wheel when designing pronunciation activities. I recommend ARCs highly but with the following caveat: any specific activity description found in an ARC is no more than a springboard for further development and fine-tuning. Because they are produced by specialists who are unfamiliar with the particulars of our local instructional settings, our mantra should always be that even the best activity recipe description is never enough. ARCs' potentialities are enriched when we adapt the specifics of activity recipe descriptions to better fit local needs and personal teaching styles. Part B of Appendix 7.2 (see page 222) provides an alphabetical listing of some classroom activity recipe collections worth learning more about.

CONTEMPORARY ESL CLASSROOM TEXTBOOKS

Classroom textbooks focused on the teaching and learning of ESL pronunciation represent the final genre of teacher resource materials. Most teachers recognize how useful it is to be familiar with an assortment of texts that can be used in the classroom. Teachers can work with such textbooks for at least three related purposes. First, if you locate one that matches students' needs, most ESL and EFL students appreciate having a reliable text as an anchor for both in-class use and private study. Second, several of the best known pronunciation texts are accompanied by teachers' manuals written expressly to support teachers who have little or no background in teaching pronunciation (e.g., Gilbert, 2012a, 2012b; Grant, 2007, 2010). Third, pronunciation textbooks offer teachers a wide range of helpful ideas for teaching pronunciation even if students never see them. Teachers who own their own copies of different classroom texts are able to peruse them for ideas and inspiration. If nothing else, seeing pronunciation features and concepts presented from different perspectives by different textbook authors serves to enhance understanding of the concepts covered and may engender awareness of new instructional possibilities. Of course, when pronunciation textbooks are used for this third purpose, it is not only ethically unacceptable but illegal to merely photocopy or in other ways display a textbook author's work in a classroom without securing the publisher's formal written permission in advance.

A workable strategy when planning a course is to settle on one pronunciation text for students to purchase and use in class. Then, anytime you are supplementing the selected course text with additional ideas, classroom activities, and/or materials inspired by other sources, take care in protecting the intellectual property rights of publishers and authors. In this way, ancillary pronunciation textbooks may be used in ways comparable to the earlier discussion of how to work with activity recipe collections. Part C of Appendix 7.2 (see pages 223–224) provides an alphabetical listing of 16 contemporary ESL pronunciation textbooks that merit consideration.

References

Akram, M. (2010). Teaching pronunciation: Views and approaches of secondary teachers in Punjab. *Kashmir Journal of Language Research, 2*, 59–69.

Baker, A. (2013). Exploring teachers' knowledge of second language pronunciation techniques: Teacher cognitions, observed classroom practices, and student perceptions. *TESOL Quarterly, 47*. doi: 10.1002/tesq.99.

Baker, A. A. (2011a). *Pronunciation pedagogy: Second language teacher cognition and practice.* Unpublished doctoral dissertation, Georgia State University, Atlanta.

Baker, A. A. (2011b). ESL teachers and pronunciation pedagogy: Exploring the development of teachers' cognitions and classroom practices. In. J. Levis & K. LeVelle (Eds.), *Proceedings of the 2nd pronunciation in second language learning and teaching conference* (pp. 82–94). Ames: Iowa State University.

Baker, A. A. (2011c). Discourse prosody and teachers' stated beliefs and practices. *TESOL Journal, 2*, 263–292. doi: 10.5054/tj.2011.259955

Bartels, N. (2005). *Applied linguistics and language teacher education.* Dordrecht, the Netherlands: Kluwer.

Bartels, N. (2009). Knowledge about language. In A. Burns & J. C. Richards (Eds.), *The Cambridge guide to second language teacher education* (pp. 125–134). New York: Cambridge University Press.

Borg, S. (2003). Teacher cognition in language teaching: A review of research on what language teachers think, know, believe and do. *Language Teaching, 36*, 81–109.

Borg, S. (2009). Introducing language teacher cognition. Retrieved from www.education.leeds.ac.uk/assets/files/staff/borg/Introducing-language-teacher-cognition.pdf

Bradford, B., & Kenworthy, J. (1991). Phonology on teacher training courses. *Speak Out, 9*, 12–14.

Brazil, D. (1997). *The communicative value of intonation in English.* Cambridge, U.K.: Cambridge University Press.

Breitkreutz, J., A., Derwing, T. M., & Rossiter, M. J. (2001). Pronunciation teaching practices in Canada. *TESL Canada Journal, 19*, 51–61.

Brown, J. D. (2012). *New ways in teaching connected speech.* Alexandria, VA: TESOL International Association.

Burgess, J., & Spencer, S. (2000). Phonology and pronunciation in integrated language teaching and teacher education. *System, 28*, 191–215.

Burns, A. (2006). Integrating research and professional development on pronunciation teaching in a national adult ESL program. *TESL Reporter, 39*(2), 34–41.

Catford, J.C. (1987). Phonetics and the teaching of pronunciation: A systemic description of English phonology. In J. Morley (Ed.), *Current perspectives on pronunciation: Practices anchored in theory* (pp. 87–100). Alexandria, VA: TESOL.

Cathcart, R., & Olsen, J. (1976). Teachers' and students' preferences for the correction of classroom conversation errors. In J. Fanselow & R. H. Crymes (Eds.), *On TESOL '76* (pp. 41–53). Alexandria, VA: TESOL.

Celce-Murcia, M. (1987). Teaching pronunciation as communication. In J. Morley (Ed.) *Current perspectives on pronunciation: Practices anchored in theory* (pp. 5–12). Alexandria, VA: TESOL.

Cohen, A., & Fass, L. (2001). Oral language instruction: Teacher and learner beliefs and the reality in EFL classes at a Colombian university. *Íkala: Revista de lenguaje y cultura, 6*, 43–62.

Deng, J., Holtby, A., Howden-Weaver, L., Nessim, L., Nicholas, B., Nickle, K., Pannekoek, C., Stephan, S., & Sun, M. (2009). *English pronunciation research: The neglected orphan of second language acquisition studies? (WP 05-09).* Edmonton, AB: Prairie Metropolis Centre.

Derwing, T. M., & Rossiter, M. J. (2002). ESL learners' perceptions of their pronunciation needs and strategies. *System, 30*, 155–166.

Dickerson, W. (2010). Walking the walk: Integrating the story of English phonology. In J. M. Levis & K. LeVelle (Eds.), *Proceedings of the 1st pronunciation in second language learning and teaching conference* (pp. 10–23). Ames: Iowa State University.

Foote, J. A., Holtby, A. K., & Derwing, T. M. (2011). 2010 survey of pronunciation teaching in adult ESL programs in Canada. *TESL Canada Journal, 29*, 1–22.

Freeman, D., & Johnson, K. E. (1998). Reconceptualizing the knowledge-base of language teacher education. *TESOL Quarterly, 32*, 397–417.

Gilbert, J. B. (1993/2012). *Clear speech: Pronunciation and listening comprehension in North American English* (1st edition 1993; 4th edition 2012). New York: Cambridge University Press.

Grant, L. (1993/2010). *Well said: Pronunciation for clear communication* (1st edition 1993; 3rd edition 2010). Boston: Heinle & Heinle.

Gregory, A. (2005). What's phonetics got to do with language teaching? Investigating future teachers' use of knowledge about phonetics and phonology. In N. Bartels (Ed.), *Applied linguistics and language teacher education* (pp. 201–220). Dordrecht, the Netherlands: Klower.

Hismanoglu, M., & Hismanoglu, S. (2010). Language teachers' preferences of pronunciation teaching techniques: Traditional or modern? *Procedia: Social and Behavioural Sciences, 2*, 983–989.

Jenkins, J. (2005). Implementing an international approach to English pronunciation: The role of teacher attitudes and identity. *TESOL Quarterly, 39*, 535–543.

Jenkins, J. (2007). *English as a lingua franca: Attitude and identity.* Oxford, U.K.: Oxford University Press.

Lambacher, S. (2001). A brief guide to resources for developing expertise in the teaching of pronunciation. *Prospect, 16*, 63–70.

Macdonald, S. (2002). Pronunciation views and practices of reluctant teachers. *Prospect, 17*, 3–18.

Morley, J. (1991). The pronunciation component in teaching English to speakers of other languages. *TESOL Quarterly, 25*, 481–520.

Moyer, A. (1999). Ultimate attainment in L2 phonology: The critical factors of age, motivation, and instruction. *Studies in Second Language Acquisition, 21*, 81–108.

Munro, M. J., & Derwing, T. M. (2006). The functional load principle in ESL pronunciation instruction: An exploratory study. *System, 34*, 520–531.

Murphy, J. M. (1991). Oral communication in TESOL: Integrating speaking, listening & pronunciation. *TESOL Quarterly, 25*, 51–75.

Murphy, J. M. (1992). Preparing ESL students for the basic speech course: Approach, design & procedure. *English for Specific Purposes, 11*, 51–70.

Murphy, J. M. (1993). An ESL oral communication lesson: One teacher's techniques and principles. *Basic Communication Course Annual, 5*, 157–181.

Murphy, J. M. (1997). Phonology courses offered by MATESOL programs in the U.S. *TESOL Quarterly, 31*, 741–764.

National Institute of Education. (1975). *Teaching as clinical information processing.* (No. Panel 6, National Conference on Studies in Teaching.). Washington, DC: NIE.

Peterson, P. L., & Clark, C. M. (1978). Teachers' reports of their cognitive processes during teaching. *American Educational Research Journal, 15*, 555–565.

Pica, T. (1984). Pronunciation activities with an accent on communication. *English Teaching Forum, 22*, 2–6.

Prator, C. H., & Robinette, B. J. (1985). *Manual of American English pronunciation* (4th ed.). New York: Holt, Rinehart, & Winston.

Richards, J. (1996). Teachers' maxims in language teaching. *TESOL Quarterly 30*, 281–296.

Shulman, L. (1987). Knowledge and teaching: Foundations of the new reform. *Harvard Educational Review, 57*(1), 1–22.

Sifakis, N. C., & Sougari, A.-M. (2005). Pronunciation issues and EIL pedagogy in the periphery: A survey of Greek state school teachers' beliefs. *TESOL Quarterly, 39*, 467–488.

Tarone, E., & Allwright, D. (2005). Second language teacher learning and student language learning: Shaping the knowledge base. In D.

Tedick (Ed.), *Second language teacher education: International perspectives* (pp. 5–23). Mahwah, NJ: Lawrence Erlbaum.

Timmis, I. (2002). Native-speaker norms and international English: A classroom view. *ELT Journal, 56,* 240–249.

Walker, R. (1999). Proclaimed and perceived wants and needs among Spanish teachers of English, *Speak Out, 24,* 25–32.

Appendix 7.1: Sample Syllabus Topics and Tasks for a Graduate Course: Teaching the Pronunciation of English as a Second Language

Sequencing of Topics in Phonology: Thought grouping, phrase rhythm, primary word stress, consonant phonemes, vowel phonemes, International Phonetic Alphabet (IPA), orthography, dialect variability, consonant and vowel phonetics, phonological adjustments within connected speech (e.g., linking, palatalization), primary and secondary word-level stress, prominence (thought group, phrase, sentence, and discourse levels); discourse intonation; phonologies of English as an International Language.

Sequencing of Topics in Pronunciation Pedagogy: Models and goals for pronunciation teaching; needs analysis; historical perspectives; intelligibility, comprehensibility, and accentedness; stages of teaching (listening discrimination, controlled, guided, and extemporaneous practice); communicative pronunciation teaching; technology; teaching the pronunciation of ESL, EFL, and EIL; the segmental-suprasegmental debate; curriculum development; testing/assessment; research into phonological acquisition, future directions.

Sample Course Objectives: Upon successful completion of this course, students will:

- Have a fuller understanding of the sound system of English.
- Have gained guided experience in pronunciation teaching.
- Feel comfortable working within contemporary methods of pronunciation teaching.

- Appreciate the priority of teaching for intelligibility.
- Recognize the relative degrees of importance of thought grouping, stress, rhythm, intonation, and individual sound segments depending on the context of the teaching.
- Understand and be able to use specialist terminology for the classification of phonemes and other features of English language phonology.
- Be able to incorporate the teaching of pronunciation within general skills courses, pronunciation-inclusive courses, and pronunciation-centered courses.

SAMPLE TASK 1

This task weaves topics in phonology (consonant and vowel sounds, IPA) with topics in pronunciation pedagogy (intelligibility, needs analysis, assessment).

Segmental Problems of Selected Language Groups

Purpose:
1. To identify segmental variations in non–native speaker speech
2. To practice using the IPA in a real-world context

Materials:
1. Chapter "Problems of Selected Language Groups" from Avery and Ehrlich (1992)
2. "Accent Archive" maintained by Steven Weinberger at George Mason University: http://classweb.gmu.edu/accent

Scenario: You have been assigned to teach an oral communication course with a pronunciation component to adults whose predominant L1 is Spanish, Chinese, or Korean. You decide to listen carefully to a speech sample from two or three of your students in order to determine segmental features that might be especially problematic for that language group.

1. Click on the "Accent Archive" front page. Choose your language.

Spanish	Cantonese	Korean
(Speakers 1,2,4)	(Speakers 9,21,26)	(Speakers 1,2,6)

2. Listen to the three speakers numbered from the language group you have chosen. Write the variations that you think interfere with intelligibility for each speaker. Transcribe examples of the variations as follows:

   Example: Speaker 1: s/θ, *thing* = [sɪŋ]

Speaker 1:	Speaker 2:	Speaker 3:

3. Did you find any variations in common among the speakers? If so, what? _____

4. Were most of the segmentals you identified included in these sources: (a) phonological generalizations for the speakers listed on the GMU site (look for the yellow "i" in the red dot) or (b) Avery and Ehrlich, "Problems of Selected Language Groups"?

5. Identify two segmental features you would emphasize in your instruction with this group. Justify your answer.

NOTE: Next week you will compare findings with others in your same language group.

SAMPLE TASK 2

This task weaves topics in phonology (stress, rhythm, and prominence) with topics in pronunciation pedagogy (technology, curriculum development, and stages in pronunciation teaching).

Designing Activities for Suprasegmental Practice

Purpose: Prompt your thinking about the potential of the internet in pronunciation instruction.

Scenario 1: Your students have minimal interaction in English outside of class. Explore the sites listed and use either site to create an activity that would encourage your students to practice rhythm. Be specific.

Favorite Poetry Project – individuals read a poem and discuss its significance (transcripts of poems provided)
www.favoritepoem.org/videos.html

Repeat After Us
http://www.repeatafterus.com/

Scenario 2: You have just presented focus (a.k.a.: prominence, nuclear stress, primary sentence stress) to your ESL students. You want your learners to observe or pay attention to how focus operates in semi-authentic speech. How might you use this site? What would your specific assignment be?

Movie Trailers (with transcripts)
http://english-trailers.com/index.php

Scenario 3: You have several students who are struggling with stress in words. Specifically, their vowels are not long enough in stressed syllables and in stressed words. What is the advantage of this site for these students? What would your assignment be?
Praat Language Lab at the University of Minnesota
http://praatlanguagelab.com/

In the next class, share your best activity with your small group. Then select a representative from your group to demonstrate the most effective activity from the entire group. Note whether this activity represents listening discrimination/guided listening, controlled practice, guided practice, or extemporaneous practice.

Appendix 7.2: Teacher Resources by Genre

Part A: Teacher Preparation Texts and Resources

Avery, P., & Ehrlich, S. (1992). *Teaching American English pronunciation.* New York: Oxford University Press.

Celce-Murcia, M., Brinton, D., & Goodwin, J. (2010). *Teaching pronunciation: A course book and reference guide* (2nd ed.). New York: Cambridge University Press.

Dalton, C., & Seidlhofer, B. (1994). *Pronunciation.* New York: Oxford University Press.

Fraser, H. (2001). *Teaching pronunciation: A handbook for teachers and trainers.* Sydney: AMES NSW. Available at http://helenfraser.com.au/downloads/HF%20Handbook.pdf

Gilbert, J. (2009). *Teaching pronunciation using the prosody pyramid.* New York: Cambridge University Press. Available at www.cambridge.org/elt/resources/teachersupportplus/

Goodwin, J. (2013). Teaching pronunciation. In M. Celce-Murcia, D. M. Brinton, & M. A. Snow (Eds.), *Teaching English as a second or foreign language* (4th ed). (pp. 138–154). Boston: National Geographic Learning Cengage Learning.

Kelly, G. (2000). *How to teach pronunciation.* Essex, U.K.: Pearson Education.

Kenworthy, J. (1989). *Teaching English pronunciation.* London: Longman.

Lane, L. (2010). *Tips for teaching pronunciation: A practical approach.* White Plains, NY: Pearson/Longman.

Murphy, J. (2013). *Teaching pronunciation.* Alexandria, VA: TESOL International Association.

Rogerson-Revell, P. (2011). *English phonology and pronunciation teaching.* New York/London: Continuum.

Underhill, A. (1994). *Sound foundations: Learning and teaching pronunciation.* London: Macmillan.

Walker, R. (2010). *Teaching the pronunciation of English as a lingua franca.* Oxford, U.K.: Oxford University Press.

Part B: Activity Recipe Collection Resources

Bailey, K. M., & Savage, L. (1994). *New ways in teaching speaking.* Alexandria, VA: TESOL. See pp. 199–262.

Bowen, T., & Marks, J. (1992). *The Pronunciation book: Student-centered activities for pronunciation work.* New York: Longman.

Brown, J. D. (2012). *New ways in teaching connected speech.* Alexandria, VA: TESOL International Association.

Hancock, M. (1996). *Pronunciation games.* Cambridge, U.K.: Cambridge University Press.

Hewings, M. (2004). *Pronunciation practice activities: A resource book for teaching English pronunciation.* Cambridge, U.K.: Cambridge University Press.

Laroy, C. (1995). *Pronunciation.* New York: Oxford University Press.

Nunan, D., & Miller, L. (1995). *New ways in teaching listening.* Alexandria, VA: TESOL. See pp. 120–150.

Part C: Contemporary ESL Classroom Textbooks

Beisbier, B. (1994). *Sounds great: Low-intermediate pronunciation for speakers of English.* Boston: Heinle and Heinle.

Beisbier, B. (1995). *Sounds great: Intermediate pronunciation for speakers of English.* Boston: Heinle and Heinle.

Brazil, D. (1994). *Pronunciation for advanced learners of English.* New York: Cambridge University Press.

Cauldwell, R. (2012). *Cool speech: Hot listening, cool pronunciation.* [iPad application]. Birmingham, U.K.: Speech In Action.

Dauer, R. (1993). *Accurate English: A complete course in pronunciation.* Englewood Cliffs, NJ: Regents Prentice-Hall.

Gilbert, J. B. (2012a). *Clear speech from the start: Basic pronunciation and listening comprehension in North American English* (2nd ed.). New York: Cambridge University Press.

Gilbert, J. B. (2012b). *Clear speech: Pronunciation and listening comprehension in North American English* (4th edition). New York: Cambridge University Press. (1st edition 1993).

Gorsuch, G., Meyers, C., Pickering, L., & Griffee, D. (2012). *English communication for international teaching assistants* (2nd ed.). Long Grove, IL: Waveland Press, Inc.

Grant, L. (2007). *Well said intro: Pronunciation for clear communication.* Boston: Thomson/Heinle & Heinle.

Grant, L. (2010). *Well said: Pronunciation for clear communication* (3rd ed.). Boston: Thomson/Heinle & Heinle. (1st ed. 1993).

Hahn, L., & Dickerson, W. (1999). *Speechcraft: Discourse pronunciation for advanced learners.* Ann Arbor: University of Michigan Press.

Hancock, M. (2003). *English pronunciation in use (intermediate).* Cambridge, U.K.: Cambridge University Press.

Hewings, M. (2007). *English pronunciation in use (advanced).* Cambridge, U.K.: Cambridge University Press.

Marks, J. (2007). *English pronunciation in use (elementary).* Cambridge, U.K.: Cambridge University Press.

Miller, S. F. (2006). *Targeting pronunciation: Communicating clearly in English (2nd ed.)*. New York: Houghton Mifflin.

Reed, M., & Michaud, C. (2005). *Sound concepts: An integrated pronunciation course*. New York: McGraw-Hill.

Epilogue to the Myths:
Best Practices for Teachers

Donna M. Brinton
Educational Consultant

As a young teen, due to a research fellowship that my father had received, I spent a year living abroad in Germany—a country that happens to be part of my ancestral background (my mother was second generation German American). Prior to living in Germany, I had spent one year in my local junior high school in California studying French, but had no knowledge of German. One of my first recollections of my time in Germany was playing with neighboring children in our backyard in Stuttgart. Among the many phrases they uttered was one that sounded like French *oui* (*yes*) followed by the German word *bitte* (*please*)—one of the few German words I had learned and was able to recognize. I recall being confused at the time as to why my German playmates were using this curious combination of French and German. Only later did I learn that the phrase they kept uttering was the German phrase *Wie, bitte?* (literally "what, please"), indicating that they didn't understand what I was saying.

This incident may have a somewhat tenuous relation to the teaching of pronunciation, but I see it as evidence of the claim that learners interpret the incoming stream of speech based on their knowledge of both their L1 and any additional languages that they have learned (in my case French). It is also evidence, as Field in Myth 3 points out, that learners tend to process lexical "chunks" at the syllable, word, or phrase level rather than at the level of the phoneme. Note that in my mishearing of *oui*, I did not process the initial phoneme /v/ of *wie* but instead processed the incoming speech at the phrasal level, hearing two words (*oui* and *bitte*) that were already part of my linguistic repertoire. I spent the rest of that year attending German-medium school (as one of only two native English-speaking students in the school, the other one being my younger sister). And surrounded by German-speaking schoolmates in a highly supportive environment, I am pleased to report that my acquisition of German, in particular its sound system, was quite successful—so much so that I could typically (as a result of my near-native pronunciation and my German looks) pass myself off as a native speaker.

In part because of my own experiences of successfully mastering the sound system of German and in part because of my own professional interest in practical phonetics and the teaching of pronunciation, I was thrilled when Linda Grant asked me to write the epilogue for this volume. As she notes in her preface, myths about the teaching of pronunciation abound. Witness my acquisition of German: We might arrive at the conclusion (based on the belief that young children are adept at learning languages and pronunciation) that I was so easily able to master the sound system because I was young. But any of us who have taught English to immigrant students know that the picture is a much more complex one, with many young immigrants never fully mastering the sound system (or other aspects of the target language for that matter). For successful phonological acquisition, there is the need for input at an accessible level and for a supportive learning environment. There's also the need for the learner to be highly motivated and to receive targeted, constructive feedback. I had all of these. My schoolmates, who had already spent one year learning English, spent hours coaching and encouraging me to learn German. I was eleven years old at the time, an age where one is very susceptible to peer pressures and painfully aware of being different than others. As a result, I desperately wanted to look and, more to the point, sound like my German youngteen counterparts. I no longer recall if I communicated this to my schoolmates, but I do recall them having me practice aspects of German pronunciation—for example, making me repeat hard-to-pronounce phrases such as *Morgens in der Frühe* (*early in the morning*), and, via demonstration and repetition, coaching me to produce the high front umlauted vowel in *Frühe*. (They also teased me mercilessly about my American "rrrrr," a practice which was perhaps not quite so supportive but nonetheless effective in my case.)

Recently, an electronic discussion list of pronunciation experts to which I belong had a quite informative discussion about the core knowledge and skills needed for L2 teachers to address pronunciation in the classroom. In an effort to share this with our local community of L2 teachers, two of my colleagues and I refined the list and presented it at a recent CATESOL State Conference (Chan, Brinton, & Gilbert, 2013). The list that we generated appears in Figure 8.1.

Our purpose in presenting this framework was twofold. First, we wanted to convince teachers that, armed with this information about practical phonetics, they could begin to more effectively address this essential skill in their classrooms. And second, we wanted to underscore (as does Murphy in Myth 7) that teachers without this requisite knowledge will be hard pressed to help their learners become more intelligible. Murphy notes that even trained teachers of ES/FL are often hesitant to address pronunciation in their classrooms due to a conspicuous lack in their training programs of a comprehensive course on teaching pronunciation. He also notes that non-native speaking English teachers, having themselves wrestled with the sound system of English while learning the language, may well be better equipped than untrained native speakers to teach pronunciation.

Sadly, the myth that the native speaker is the best teacher of English (and by extension, of pronunciation) persists in many areas of the world. We see this belief perpetuated in the many international job postings specifying the need for a native English speaking teacher—this despite the strong position taken by the international TESOL organization and other affiliates that oppose such preferential hiring practices (California Teachers of English to Speakers of Other Languages, 2013; Teachers of English to Speakers of Other Languages 1991, 2006). Ironically, institutions advertising for native speakers often prioritize native-speaker status over prior teaching experience and/or TESOL training in TESOL. Figure 8.2 contains sample verbatim listings from some recent job postings on one of the most popular internet job sites, Dave's ESL Café (Sperling, 2013).

So what wisdom can we take away from this volume? I believe that first and foremost, we should recognize that the volume itself debunks

FIGURE 8.1: What L2 Teachers of Pronunciation Need to Know

Conceptual knowledge: A basic philosophy of pronunciation
1. Spoken language differs from written language.
2. Pronunciation is a physical act.
3. Awareness of vowel duration is essential.
4. Listeners of English perceive the relative importance of information based on stress, intonation, and pausing.
5. Learning how to "listen mindfully" is essential to any kind of pronunciation improvement.
6. Pronunciation can be integrated in classes for all language skills.
7. Some aspects of pronunciation are more important than others.
8. Pronunciation work does not disrespect a learner's L1, home culture, or identity.

Descriptive knowledge: The basic facts of pronunciation
1. The smallest building block of pronunciation is the *phoneme* (unit of sound) and its *allophones* (variations).
2. Pronunciation consists of *segmentals* (the individual phonemes) and *suprasegmentals* (stress, intonation, rhythm, and connected speech features).
3. Syllables and stress are the building blocks of rhythm and intonation.
4. Thought groups/tone units are the basis of all *prosody*/suprasegmental work.
5. Pitch change occurs on the most important word (the stressed syllable of the key word/focus word).

Procedural knowledge: The basic skills needed to teach pronunciation
It is important for teachers to:
1. have a working familiarity with both segmental and suprasegmental features of speech.
2. perceive intonation patterns/pitch changes.
3. perceive variable vowel duration that produces rhythm in English.
4. teach pronunciation in connection with listening discrimination skills.
5. use movement in teaching pronunciation.
6. prioritize pronunciation issues for communicative purposes.
7. provide useful feedback through demonstration and explanation.
8. integrate pronunciation into language teaching.
9. help learners develop automaticity.
10. teach compensatory strategies.

Source: Chan, Brinton, & Gilbert (2013).

FIGURE 8.2: Sample Listings on the International Job Board of Dave's ESL Café (retrieved October 29, 2013)

- [Name of Company] in Mokpo is looking to hire a female native English teacher who is dedicated to teaching elementary students in a small-class setting... Applicants who have teaching experience in Korea and the necessary documents for an E-2 visa (notarized degree and criminal background check) will be at an advantage.

- [Name of Company] is seeking a native English–speaking high school ESL teacher for China. Experience is preferred but we will consider recent graduates.

- Native speaker is wanted to teach in Various cities: Beijing, Guangdong, Kunming, Hefei, Xi'an, Nanjing. NO degree necessary!

- [Name of Company] is one of the biggest language training schools in China. It has been in operation for 14 years. Schools all located in Shandong province, which is only a few hundred kms away from Beijing. We would like to help you make a difference for your future! We require:

  1. Native English speakers from America, Canada, Britain, Australia, and New Zealand.
  2. Must enjoy teaching! Be responsible and motivated!
  3. College degree in any subject!
  4. Between the age of 21 and 50 and in good health.
  5. Be able to commit to one-year contract.
  6. Have no criminal record of any kind.

- [Name of Company] is looking for native speakers of English to join our friendly teams. If you like teaching English and want to discover Russia, this vacancy is for you.

a highly pervasive (yet often unvoiced) myth lurking beneath the surface of academia—namely that research and practice are unrelated entities that fail to inform each other. The contributors to this volume successfully address this myth and demonstrate the direct connection between research and practice by (1) synthesizing research findings (in the What the Research Says section of the chapter) and (2) making direct connections between these findings and research-informed best practices (in the What We Can Do section).

The following synthesis of research insights and best practices as recounted in this volume is colored by my own thoughts on the subject. I highlight (in no particular order) what I believe to be the most important ideas and practices that readers of this volume can apply to their own teaching of pronunciation.

1. Research Finding: *Accent* and *intelligibility* are two separate but related constructs.

Best Practice: Accent refers to the degree to which a speaker sounds "foreign" while intelligibility refers to the extent to which that speaker's utterances are understood by the interlocutor. A close corollary of intelligibility is *comprehensibility*, the degree of effort required on the part of the listener to comprehend the speaker. Research shows that aspects of L2 speech contributing to a lack of intelligibility include incorrect word stress, misplacement of or missing prominence in a thought group, rate of speech (either too slow or too fast), overabundance of or overly-lengthy pauses in the stream of speech, unarticulated consonants in syllable final position and in stressed syllables, and lack of differentiation in pitch or vowel duration (Goodwin, 2014). In the past, pronunciation classes focused on eliminating learners' foreign accents, a goal that was seldom realized. Today, we recognize that a more realistic goal of pronunciation instruction is increased learner intelligibility. This includes bringing to learners' attention, where relevant, the above-noted barriers to intelligibility and including plentiful and focused practice in these areas. Sadly, as Thomson documents in Myth 6, many pronunciation programs reinforce our learners' misperception that they can (and, more importantly, should) achieve a native-like accent through accent reduction or modification programs. As teachers we need to be up front about what is and is *not* achievable in our pronunciation courses—informing learners that while we can assist them to become aware of those patterns of speech that impede their intelligibility and to achieve the goal of more intelligible speech, we are not in the business of accent eradication. These two goals are all the more important given the fact that the vast majority of those learning

English today will use the language to communicate with other non-native speakers of English (i.e., as a lingua franca) rather than to communicate with native speakers (Walker, 2010). In this endeavor, intelligibility is indeed the new "gold standard."

2. Research Finding: Not all aspects of pronunciation are equally important.

Best Practice: Derwing and Munro note in Myth 1 that one of the most important uses of our time in the pronunciation classroom is awareness raising—that is, drawing learners' attention to the differences between their own production and more intelligible forms. This means that we need to help learners prioritize those aspects of their accent that interfere with intelligibility. While there is no complete consensus as to which aspects of English pronunciation are most critical for intelligibility, most pronunciation practitioners would agree that on the suprasegmental level, a primary focus on word stress, prominence (e.g., new vs. old information), the stress-timed rhythm of English, thought groups and pausing, along with pitch change on the focus word in a thought group are all areas of priority. As for segmentals, work on functional load (Catford, 1987) indicates that problematic or frequently confused consonant contrasts such as /p/ vs. /b/ and vowel contrasts such as /iy/ vs. /ɪ/ should receive priority over those contrasts with a lower functional load. Further, recent research on English as a lingual franca (Deterding, 2013; Walker, 2010) indicates, for example, that the often-taught dental fricatives /θ/ and /ð/ are not critical for overall intelligibility and should therefore not receive priority. However, he stresses that initial consonant clusters are important, as are the distinctions between /n/ vs. /l/ and /r/ vs. /l/.

3. Research Finding: Segmentals, long considered the staples of pronunciation instruction, are critical building blocks of the sound system.

Best Practice: In traditional pronunciation instruction—especially during the heyday of contrastive analysis in the 1950s and 1960s (Eckman, 1977; Tarone, 2012)—pronunciation instruction tended to focus on those L2 consonant and vowel contrasts that were predicted to be problematic for learners of a specific L1. Thus the /p/ vs. /b/ contrast might figure prominently in lessons for L1 speakers of Arabic while the vowel contrast /ɑ/ vs. /ow/ might appear in activities designed for L1 speakers of Greek. Practice often took the form of minimal-pair listening discrimination and production exercises such as *The teacher collected/corrected the homework* or *Don't sleep/slip on the floor*. In today's pronunciation classroom, such practice may still take place during the listening discrimination and controlled practice phases of the lesson. However, research (see Field, Myth 3) underscores the fact that phoneme discrimination may not play a significant role in the listening process, such that learners recognize and access language via larger chunks (at the syllable, word, or phrase level) and that therefore putting undue emphasis on phoneme production in our classes may not serve our learners well. Additionally, many pronunciation practitioners argue for putting equal or greater emphasis on the suprasegmental aspects of language, claiming that teaching students about English rhythm, stress, and intonation contributes more to increased intelligibility than focusing on segmentals. Does all this imply that the teaching of segmentals constitutes wasted time in the classroom? I'd suggest not. Teaching segmentals is still important and for many learners, difficulties producing the vowels and consonants of English may be a significant part of their foreign accent as well as a barrier to their intelligibility. However, we should teach segmentals selectively, with a view toward those phonemic contrasts that (1) most impede our learners' intelligibility and (2) carry the greatest functional load. And most importantly, the teaching of segmentals should be integrated into an overall pronunciation curriculum that also recognizes the importance of the suprasegmental aspects of language.

4. Research Finding: The majority of adult L2 learners will not learn to speak without an accent.

Best Practice: This finding is closely related to Research Finding 1 above. It clearly reinforces the need to make intelligibility rather than target-like pronunciation the goal of classroom instruction. Along with this finding goes the recognition that our goal is not to eradicate a learner's foreign accent, but rather assist learners to modify their accents in ways that do not disrespect their L1, home culture, or identity. Grant in Myth 5 notes that we must work in partnership with our learners to identify pronunciation goals (e.g., through the use of learner logs), all the while assuring them that having an accent is not equated with being unintelligible (see also Derwing and Munro, Myth 1). Our goal, rather, is to raise our learners' consciousness about pronunciation features that may interfere with intelligibility and provide them with the means to alter these features or, in cases where this is not possible, employ compensation strategies (Cohen & Macaro, 2008). We must also, as Thomson reminds us in Myth 6, practice ethical pronunciation instruction by being up front and honest with our learners about what *is* and is *not* attainable in our pronunciation courses.

5. Research Finding: Learning to pronounce a second language is different from learning grammar or vocabulary in that it involves more than just cognitive skills.

Best Practice: Teaching pronunciation should involve the use of multimodal activities. True, like other skills, learning to pronounce does involve the teaching and learning of rules (e.g., when to pronounce past tense or plural endings syllabically, when aspiration occurs with the stop consonants /p/, /t/, and /k/, and how pitch change in a tone unit corresponds with the focus word). But teaching pronunciation is fundamentally different from teaching other skills in that it also involves auditory, visual, and kinesthetic modalities and is therefore best approached through a multi-modal approach. The authors in this volume suggest numerous ways to integrate multi-modal activities: clapping or tapping out word and/or phrase stress; using "gadgets" (Gilbert, 1991) such as rubber bands to emphasize vowel length and kazoos to illustrate intonation contours; and having students do a "walkabout" to recognize the importance of stress-timed rhythm in English. For additional creative suggestions on using visuals, rhythm, movement, and touch, see Acton (2012) and Chan (n.d.).

6. Research Finding: There is a relationship between perception and production.

Best Practice: Conventional wisdom in the pronunciation classroom dictates that we introduce a phonemic or prosodic feature by first providing learners with an explanation of the feature and then following this with copious listening discrimination practice. This conventional wisdom is underscored by several studies indicating that work on perception leads not only to better listening comprehension but also to more target-like production (Goodwin, 2014). Celce-Murcia, Brinton, & Goodwin (2010) suggest that a useful progression when introducing new material in the pronunciation class is to begin with awareness-building and perception activities before proceeding with controlled, guided, and communicative practice (see also Zielinski & Yates, Myth 2). In Myth 1, Derwing and Munro support the critical role played by perception, noting that many learners (especially fossilized ones) have established their own perceptual categories, colored by their L1, which impede their ability to perceive and produce more target-like or intelligible forms. These researchers propose exposing learners to a wide variety of target forms (e.g., via computer software programs) along with feedback on the learners' ability to correctly perceive these targets.

7. Research Finding: Learners benefit from targeted, explicit feedback.

Best Practice: Many of the authors in this volume emphasize the need for systematic, explicit, and targeted feedback on learners' output. As Derwing and Munro point out in Myth 1, such feedback is especially important for the many fossilized learners in our classrooms since practice alone (without feedback) cannot help them to break the fossilization barrier. This finding is in keeping with evidence from research into instructed L2 learning (Ellis, 2014), which emphasizes the importance of focus on form. Such feedback needs to be integrated into all phases of pronunciation instruction, beginning with work on perception and continuing into the various stages of practice (see Research Finding 6). As Zielinski and Yates remind us in Myth 2, feedback also needs to be judicious, so as not to overwhelm learners and undermine their confidence. Celce-Murcia, Brinton, and Goodwin (2010) suggest that when teaching segmental features, for example, teachers should provide explicit feedback on aspects of the articulatory system—demonstrating via diagrams and kinesthetic activities how the articulatory organs function to produce the various sounds of the language. They further suggest that the role and extent of feedback may vary depending on the stage of practice (controlled, guided, or communicative). Feedback is most direct and immediate during controlled practice, where the goal of practice is accuracy. In guided or communicative practice, the focus shifts gradually to meaning; in this case feedback may be delayed until after the activity so as not to interrupt the flow of communication. A further aspect of best practice relates to the delivery of feedback, which should not be restricted to the teacher alone. In fact, during pair and group work, one or more participants can be assigned the role of providing feedback to their peers.

8. Research Finding: The success of a learner's acquisition of pronunciation is strongly colored by factors such as L1, age, identity, motivation, target language exposure, and use of the target language outside the classroom.

Best Practice: As Grant points out in Myth 5, certain of these factors such as the students' L1 and age are ones over which we as teachers have no control. However, as she reminds us, we *can* address the remainder of these factors via our classroom practice. As for the inter-woven factors of identity and motivation, it is well documented (Goodwin, 2014) that second language learners often resist acquiring certain features of the target language that they perceive to threaten their identity. As a remedy, Dörnyei (2014) suggests that students be encouraged to create an image of the "possible self" (which includes both the second language self they envision for themselves and the second language self that that they fear). This possible self represents the learner's long-term goal—one that can be reinforced and nurtured by the teacher—for example, via journal entries, motivation surveys, and learner contracts (Acton, 1984). Finally, regarding target language exposure and use of the target language outside of class, as classroom teachers we have the opportunity to exert a powerful influence. This can be achieved through the variety and types of tasks that we assign we give our students (e.g., posting links to authentic listening sources on the course management system, having them conduct outside-of-class sur-veys that require them to interview native speakers, and the like).

9. Research Finding: Learners' L1 exerts a strong influence on their acquisition of English pronunciation.

Best Practice: This statement holds true for the acquisition of segmen-tals as well as for that of suprasegmentals. During the era of contrastive analysis (Tarone, 2012), the L1 was largely seen as "interfering" with a learner's acquisition of the target language. However, today we recog-nize that transfer from the L1 can be both positive and negative and that transfer alone cannot account for all aspects of L2 phonological acquisition (Abrahamsson, 2012; Major, 2012). Nonetheless, it is useful for pronunciation teachers to be aware of the differences between the learners' L1 and the target language, and also, as Gilbert reminds us in Myth 4, it helps to raise learner consciousness about the differences between their L1 and the L2. In classes where the learners share the same L1, this is facilitated by the fact that the teacher (herself perhaps a native speaker of the same L1) is usually quite familiar with the challenges that learners face when learning to pronounce English. The task is slightly more difficult, however, when learners do not share an L1 as this requires the teacher to be familiar with the challenges faced by students from multiple language backgrounds. Here, resources such as Swan and Smith (2001), which helps the teacher predict the pronunciation difficulties that may be encountered by learners from a variety of L1 backgrounds, can be of great use.

10. Research Finding: Learners need to be exposed to authentic language.

Best Practice: As language learners, we probably all remember our first encounter with a native speaker of a language we learned in a classroom context and the experience of being overwhelmed at the difficulty of understanding his or her "authentic" speech. Today's listening materials are much more authentic than those of bygone eras (where every syllable tended to be clearly enunciated and the features of authentic speech such as conversational overlap or false starts were absent). However, with today's wealth of web-based resources, we are no longer totally reliant on our textbooks and the accompanying listening materials. Instead, as Field suggests in Myth 3, we can easily expose our learners to a variety of voices and accents as well as to varied contexts in which to practice their listening. Derwing and Munro remind us in Myth 1 that streaming video, easily accessible on the web, is a rich source of authentic listening and can help focus learners' attention on key aspects of native-speaker pronunciation such as connected speech, intonation patterns, or prominence.

One additional myth that I would have liked to see treated in this volume involves the perception (by teachers as well as by laypeople) that pronunciations such as *didja* (*did you*) and *sinshoo* (*since you*) in native speaker speech represent "slang" or incorrect English. As a teacher educator, I often encounter this attitude (along with the related insistence of certain audience members that they themselves never talk like this) when presenting on the topic of connected speech features. Certainly, the presence of connected speech features such as those mentioned by Grant in the Prologue (linking, assimilation, reduction) may vary slightly from native speaker to native speaker and may also be colored by the speed of speech and by issues of register or formality. However, it is safe to say that they are a normal part of native speaker speech and as such deserve emphasis in the classroom.

When my co-authors and I first contracted to write *Teaching Pronunciation* (Celce-Murcia, Brinton, & Goodwin, 1996), we had prolonged discussions with our publisher about whether it was possible to write a volume dealing with (1) a detailed description of the sound system of English, (2) a synthesis of the research, and (3) practical aspects of how to teach pronunciation to second language learners. As authors we believed that not only was this feasible but that a combined focus on these three areas was what was missing in the market and in teacher education programs both in North America and elsewhere (see Myths 6 and 7 for further discussion of this issue). The publisher was of the opinion that the resulting volume would be both too difficult to write and too unwieldy for users. In the end, we prevailed as authors and the resulting volume and its second edition (Celce-Murcia, Brinton, & Goodwin, 2010) have provided a comprehensive treatment of both the English sound system and practical classroom applications.

In its initial pre-publication version, *Teaching Pronunciation* was divided into two separate sections, the first summarizing the research at hand and describing all relevant aspects of the sound system and the second providing practical advice to teachers as to how to teach these various aspects. However, the folly of this organizational plan soon became evident to us as authors as it was difficult to cross-reference the necessary knowledge base with concrete suggestions for classroom

FIGURE 8.3. Sample Chapter Organization: Connected Speech, Stress, and Rhythm

---

   I. Introduction to Connected Speech, Stress, and Rhythm
  II. Connected Speech: What the Teacher Needs to Know
 III. Teaching Connected Speech to Students
 IV. Word Stress: What the Teacher Needs to Know
  V. Teaching Word Stress to Students
 VI. Sentence Stress and Rhythm: What the Teacher Needs to Know
VII. Teaching Sentence Stress and Rhythm to Students
VIII. Conclusion

From *Teaching Pronunciation* by Celce-Murcia, Brinton, & Goodwin (1996; 2010).

practice, especially in cases where several hundred pages intervened between the two related discussions. Given how research, theory, and practice are inextricably intertwined, we therefore arrived at an organizational plan that described in detail the knowledge base needed by the teacher in any given area of the sound system followed immediately by suggested pedagogical applications. An example of the resulting chapter template for the chapter on connected speech, stress, and rhythm is shown in Figure 8.3.

Murphy emphasizes in Myth 7 the need for the L2 teacher's knowledge base to include not only knowledge about language, the acquisition process, and recommendations from research, but as well the activity of teaching itself. As described above, this was the intent of *Teaching Pronunciation*. In much the same vein, I believe that *Pronunciation Myths* succeeds because of this combined focus on these requisite elements of the teachers' knowledge base.

I am indebted to Linda Grant for her ideas on structuring this epilogue, to my *Teaching Pronunciation* co-authors Marianne Celce-Murcia and Janet Goodwin for shaping my thinking on teaching pronunciation in general, and to Marsha Chan and Judy Gilbert for helping to generate ideas on the essentials that teachers need to know to teach pronunciation. And perhaps most of all, I am indebted to Kelly Sippell of the

University of Michigan Press for her tireless efforts to produce volumes such as this one to inform teachers of English as a second or foreign language.

References

Abrahamsson, N. (2012). Phonological acquisition. *The encyclopedia of applied linguistics.* doi: 10.1002/9781405198431.wbeal0907

Acton, W. (1984). Changing fossilized pronunciation. *TESOL Quarterly,* *18,* 71–85.

Acton, W. (2012, October 23). Explaining the EHIEP 'haptic' system to students and colleagues. [Web log post]. Retrieved from http://hipoeces.blogspot.ca/2012/10/explaining-ehiep-to-students-and.html

California Teachers of English to Speakers of Other Languages. (2013). *CATESOL position paper opposing discrimination against non-native English speaking teachers (NNESTs) and teachers with "non-standard" varieties of English.* Retrieved from http://www.catesol.org/ppa-pers.html

Catford, J. C. (1987). Phonetics and the teaching of pronunciation. In J. Morley (Ed.), *Current perspectives on pronunciation: Practices anchored in theory* (pp. 87–100). Alexandria, VA: TESOL.

Celce-Murcia, M., Brinton, D., & Goodwin, J. (1996). *Teaching pronunciation: A reference for teachers of English to speakers of other languages.* New York: Cambridge University Press.

Celce-Murcia, M., Brinton, D., & Goodwin, J. (with Griner, B.) (2010). *Teaching pronunciation: A course book and reference guide* (2nd ed.). New York: Cambridge University Press.

Chan, M. (n.d.). The pronunciation doctor. [Video file]. Retrieved from http://www.youtube.com/PronunciationDoctor

Chan, M., Brinton, D., & Gilbert, J. (2013). What language teachers must know to teach pronunciation. Paper presented at the 44th Annual CATESOL Conference, San Diego. Available at http://www.slideshare.net/purplecast/presentations

Cohen, A. D., & Macaro, E. (Eds.). (2008). *Language learner strategies: 30 years of research and practice.* New York: Oxford University Press.

Deterding, D. (2013). *Misunderstandings in English as a lingua franca: An analysis of ELF interactions in South-East Asia.* Boston: Walter de Gruyter.

Dörnyei, Z. (2014). Motivation in second language learning. In M. Celce-Murcia, D. M. Brinton, & M. A. Snow (Eds.), *Teaching English as a second or foreign language* (4th ed.) (pp. 518–531). Boston: Cengage/National Geographic Learning.

Eckman, F. R. (1977). Markedness and the contrastive analysis hypothesis. *Language Learning, 27,* 315-330.

Ellis, R. (2014). Principles of instructed second language learning. In M. Celce-Murcia, D. M. Brinton, & M. A. Snow (Eds.), *Teaching English as a second or foreign language* (4th ed.) (pp. 31–45). Boston: Cengage/National Geographic Learning.

Gilbert, J. B. (1991). Gadgets: non-verbal tools for teaching pronunciation. In A. Brown (Ed.), *Teaching English pronunciation: A book of readings* (pp. 308-322). London: Routledge.

Goodwin, J. (2014). Teaching pronunciation. In M. Celce-Murcia, D. M. Brinton, & M. A. Snow (Eds.), *Teaching English as a second or foreign language* (4th ed.) (pp. 136–152). Boston: Cengage/National Geographic Learning.

Major, R. C. (2012). Foreign accents. *The encyclopedia of applied linguistics.* doi: 10.1002/9781405198431.wbeal0420

Sperling, D. (2013). *Dave's ESL Café international job board.* Retrieved from http://www.eslcafe.com/joblist/

Swan, M., & Smith, B. (Eds.). (2001). *Learner English: A teacher's guide to interference and other problems* (2nd ed.). Cambridge, U.K.: Cambridge University Press.

Tarone, E. (2012). Interlanguage. *The encyclopedia of applied linguistics.* doi: 10.1002/9781405198431.wbeal0561

Teachers of English to Speakers of Other Languages. (1991). *A TESOL statement on non-native speakers of English and hiring practices.* Retrieved from http://nnest.asu.edu/articles/TESOL_Statement%5B1%5D.pdf

Teachers of English to Speakers of Other Languages. (2006). *Position statement against discrimination of nonnative speakers of English in the field of TESOL.* Retrieved from http://www.tesol.org/about-tesol/press-room/position-statements/social-issues-and-diversity-position-statements

Walker, R. (2010). *Teaching the pronunciation of English as a lingua franca.* Oxford, U.K.: Oxford University Press.

Index

Accentedness: defined, 10; maintaining as expression of L1 identity, 148

Accent modification programs, 164, 174

Accent reduction, vi, 165; defined, 163–164; educational background of program owners/providers and, 170–171; ethical pronunciation instruction in, 178–180; giving attention to pronunciation instruction as part of English language classes in, 180–181; giving students tips on how best to avoid charlatans in, 183–185; growth of industry, 9; mode of delivery and program content in, 167–170; program cost in, 171–172; program marketing claims in, 172–178; pronunciation instruction in, 9, 160–185; research on, 163–167; urging your language program to give more explicit attention to, 181–183

Accents: defined, 9, 230; exposing learners to variety of, 101–102; intelligibility versus, 1, 8–9; in pronunciation materials, 183; relationship among intelligibility and comprehensibility and, 9–10; as separate but related constructs, 230–231

Activity Recipe Collections (ARCs), 211–212

Acton, W., 39, 131, 234, 236

Adult learners. *See* Beginning-level adult learners

Adult Migrant English Program (AMEP), 58–59

Adult Migrant English Program (AMEP) Research Centre, 75

Affricates, 22, 83

Age: at onset of learning English, 140; research on pronunciation related to, 139–141

Allophones, 24–25

American Speech-Language-Hearing Association (ASHA), 164, 177; Code of Ethics of, 176

Applied linguistics field, 20, 183. See also MATESOL programs.

Articulatory phonetics, 13

Articulatory setting, 15; as global dimension, 15–16

Aspiration, vii, 231

Attitudes, subjective rules based on intuition about, 117–119

Audiolingual method (ALM), 2

Auditory training, 7

Authentic language: learners exposing to, 237–240; sources of, 50–51; using, 50–51

Baker, A. A., 4, 60, 68, 194, 195, 201, 202, 203

Ball, M. J., 163, 176, 177, 179